# CONVERSATIONS THROUGH MY SOUL OF PRESENCE

David Router

BALBOA.
PRESS
A DIVISION OF HAY HOUSE

Balboa Press books may be ordered through booksellers or by contacting:

Balboa Press
A Division of Hay House
1663 Liberty Drive
Bloomington, IN 47403
www.balboapress.com.au
1-(877) 407-4847

ISBN: 978-1-4525-0360-8 (sc)
ISBN: 978-1-4525-0361-5 (e)

Because of the dynamic nature of the Internet, any web addresses or links contained in this book may have changed since publication and may no longer be valid. The views expressed in this work are solely those of the author and do not necessarily reflect the views of the publisher, and the publisher hereby disclaims any responsibility for them.

The author of this book does not dispense medical advice or prescribe the use of any technique as a form of treatment for physical, emotional, or medical problems without the advice of a physician, either directly or indirectly. The intent of the author is only to offer information of a general nature to help you in your quest for emotional and spiritual well-being. In the event you use any of the information in this book for yourself, which is your constitutional right, the author and the publisher assume no responsibility for your actions.

Any people depicted in stock imagery provided by Thinkstock are models, and such images are being used for illustrative purposes only.
Certain stock imagery © Thinkstock.

Printed in the United States of America

Balboa Press rev. date: 02/03/2012

# A QUICK CONNECTION TO THE
# SECRET KEYS AND CODES

# THIS IS DESIGNED TO HELP YOU UNLOCK
# POTENTIAL AWARENESS AND ABILITIES
# WHICH AT PRESENT ARE SITTING DORMENT

## Are You Ready For New Secrets That Have Never Been Revealed?

Over the millennia our personal self-capacity has eroded without us being aware. Within this capacity exists every self-purpose, also every personal self ability which has simply not reconnected.

Is this sparking your interest, or a contemplative view that we are not living up to all which is possible – our full potential?

This I have not only found to be absolutely correct but I have been astounded where and why all this self limitation has taken place and to be quite frank, gone on totally un-noticed, or in a space of unawareness.

To redeem this state of affairs, guides have shared many new intuitive natures that are like a whole body mass and ready to use immediately.

Why?

Put simply, it is so that no missing parts, which are presently in a state of separation, are left out when reconnecting.

How?

This is one of the greatest sharing gifts of the new millennia; and yes this is to be shared with you freely in the form of keys and codes, not perhaps in the way you might be envisaging, with hieroglyphs, but with 'light' keys and codes.

It is imperative that these codes are not judged on how they look when seeing them for the first time.

Why?

As all whom have connected to these will testify, the strength of what you are to unlock is in how you interpret the vibrations and frequencies with the senses within your hands, not on how they look.

These keys and codes, while they may not look exciting, familiar or may even resemble a child's drawing or 'scribble on a page', are in essence, a most powerful healing activation tool. Whether one understands the content of the book or how this came about or not, the significance of the automatic healing that occurs in simply holding your hand up to the keys and codes, cannot be overstated.

The healing will occur, the energy will flow and the consciousness shall be transferred automatically.

How you actually manage this opening of new senses is in the **Instruction Manual** on the web site.

You can access this free

**Keys and Codes Download**

and find the **Instruction Manual** of how to use them

as well as sense the light activations response @

www.ConversationsThrough

MySoulOfPurpose.com

www.ConversationsThroughMySoulOfPresence.com

# DEDICATIONS

This book is dedicated to the person who has helped keep me sane, while pushing every spiritual and physical boundary that is explored in this book: my sister and confidant, Julie.

This book is also dedicated to the many guides who have contributed in breaking new ground in so many areas. I only pray that I have done them all justice.

Of course, nothing is achieved without the love and support of family and great friends. Every contribution has been appreciated in so many ways.

# CONTENTS

# INTRODUCTION

## ARE YOU LOOKING FOR LIFE CHANGE?

This book fits into a niche that really hasn't been explored until now. Instead of diagnosing emotions or rehashing the same old genera of material, we take a totally new look into why things don't add up.

Energy is what creates the emotions, feelings, and motivations to get things done each day, so doesn't it make sense to look into it?

All old-time faith is based on messages received through channelling, so doesn't it make sense to do the same in our time and not rehash the mistakes of the past?

If you are looking for secrets to the new millennium, they are scattered throughout this book.

If you are looking for energy exercises that are integrated with new-time consciousness in order to sense what energy does, then this book is for you.

If you are looking for new reasons for energetic responses that stem from us being separate from the conscious energy that shifts us to release the interferences of unconscious energy, then this book is for you.

If you are looking for a new spiritual journey linked to new energy aspects that haven't been used in millennia, then this book is for you. It explores new possibilities as you connect to these aspects in a conscious and physical manner.

Have you ever considered that there are many self-resources right under our noses, doing nothing, just wanting to contribute to our lives?

Isn't it time to take a new look at the limited perspectives of examining just our emotions and feelings? Don't we need to explore all possibilities that link to our energy—in a new manner that we have never entertained before?

Many of the questions about what will happen in the new millennium are linking new consciousness to new energy activations. Therefore, if you think about it, we also move in a new way or manner.

Do you desire to experience quantum energy exercises with a new-millennium outcome?

If you were unaware of a whole load of subconscious abilities and potentials that can create a wealth of life, wouldn't you what to know about them? Now you can.

As a species, we have a limited sensory system. This book unplugs many of the evolved sensory abilities that are ready to be explored and are opening daily, unfolding new life.

Each chapter we unfold means releasing the limits that we have accepted, knowing that our evolved potentials are just waiting to be unearthed.

Each and every sensory perception is an insight to all that is possible. Although we have limited our past focus to what we perceived as full, it is now possible to explore many extrasensory perceptions that have been sitting dormant for millennia—a real reason to open a new millennium.

Every sense needs a new current to connect to this evolved energy. We need to consciously move self-matter that has limited our self-focus and our self-potential. All that is now a possibility.

This new sensory perception needs a whole new language, as we will be communicating as multisensory individuals. This also means we must see the world in a totally new light, another reason for the emergence of the new millennium.

To encapsulate all purposes that are within all new sensory abilities, we will be examining all new responses, not simply emotions, because soon our old emotions will express only our limited intentions.

This might sound a little contradictory, but it is a fact, as our emotions simply haven't been telling us the whole story—only a much-abbreviated one, at best.

Remember, when we begin to use all of our sensory perception, we need to also think with a new cognizance. We need to initiate real sensory-conscious thought that produces a real sensory-conscious reaction that results in sensory-conscious reasoning. Then we are definitely on the correct path to our consciously sensed desire, intention, ability, and potential for creating our utmost conclusion.

All that has just been outlined is to formulate a new-time foundation to create a sensory-conscious love or a real emotion toward all that is complete, rather than focusing on the separated incompleteness of unconscious or subconscious reactions.

So, you may ascertain that we are delving deeper than you might expect in order to dislodge these incapacitated senses.

# 1

## OPENING CONVERSATIONS
## THROUGH MY SOUL PRESENCE

If you are game enough to challenge some conflicting emotions in your life, then sure as hell, you are going to unlock many self-beliefs—the things you're used to or don't even question as truth. I guess we all sort of fall easily into this category, don't we?

Have you thought that by following your own intuition you were, in fact, questioning a lot of your past beliefs, as though, somewhere in the depths of your innermost self, not everything added up?

Well, why else would you be reading this, unless whatever religious belief you hold or follow is missing something? Perhaps you don't feel complete, or life feels challenging, to say the least.

In my case, I just felt that I didn't quite fit in or, to be honest, even belong here. A lot of people I have talked to feel the same way, but that isn't why I wrote this book. I must now say that I am quite happy, as I have found out why so many of us feel this way.

I also need to be quite frank and open about what is to be introduced to you. Why? I have pushed the envelope until it has exploded with a whole lot of new knowledge. Essentially, many old responses don't add up now, since the discovery of many intuitions that had been buried for millennia.

How did this all come about? Well, I was shown how to think outside the square and, thus, how to connect to suppressed consciousness. Or perhaps you could think of this as consciousness that left us, and therefore we have not been able to access many self-abilities.

I was then shown that if you take away these self-abilities, a whole lot of self-purpose just flies out the window. This is why we are so unaware of the many missing parts that we haven't been able to use or have been unable to respond to.

This is a bit like having a supercomputer but having no software to make it work. I have found this to be a fair representation of our selves at present.

To unlock this potential, I had to not only challenge myself but open many beliefs of self-faith that I didn't know existed.

I was then guided to a self-resource of self-will that I had no idea existed in me. Remember, if you are going to confront areas that are outside the spectrum of normal thought channels, it is a somewhat lonely journey.

Thank god for family and friends—and of course, new friends who popped up when synchronicity was needed.

Before I sound like too much of a tripper, I do need to clarify that I have channelled naturally since I was a child, so accessing new or different information is more of a possibility for me; I have no aversion to new knowledge. Apparently, however, this knowledge is not new; we simply stopped using our many efficient abilities over many lifetimes.

This is where my journey has taken me, but for many different reasons.

Have you considered how this changing time we live in affects those of us who are so sensitive? It is impossible for us not to be affected. If you think about it, this is why you are reading many new spiritual books now. You want to understand why you are so affected, and many of the sources of information that exist just don't cut it or add up or really bring in the self-freedom we are seeking.

Fortunately, I have learned that past information indicates that we are simply rehashing old information or putting on a new coat of paint to make it seem relevant.

This insight extends to the fact that we need material of the same vibrational frequency as the place we are heading toward. So, once again, we see that some of the past is very relevant, but much needs discarding as well.

Now, armed with more relevant understanding that equates to all-new frequencies, we are able to raise our self-vibrations to fit in and be cohesive, to easily integrate with this evolving energy.

This implies a paragon of relevant information as to why our vibrational energy was able to devolve and where, when, and how it was able to happen.

When this journey started, I was totally oblivious to this devolution. I just wanted some answers to what I saw as irrelevance and untruth.

This seemingly innocuous question opened up a plethora of questions and answers, and I was unable to put the lid back on my own personal Pandora's Box.

The first problem I encountered was that not all the questions and answers lined up. This might seem a strange revelation, but soon I hope you will understand how this affects each and every one of us.

Another point in which this book differs from many others is that we really aren't looking at emotions. What, no emotions? How are we going to tell what is going on or where we have become stuffed up?

From the outset, I have said that our vibrations don't equate to the new rising frequency about us, so how would past emotions relate to this new energy? What a conundrum! Are you thinking about this dilemma?

The next and most vital conundrum is that so many of us are working at different levels of frequency and different vibrations, so we aren't coexisting in a harmonious manner. The raising of vibrations is having a couple of different effects on us.

One of the many controlling influences, where a few go and the rest just follow, is the financial crisis of late. This shows us that a power struggle exists around us and—without our awareness—within us.

Now we move to the crux of this new equation. This unawareness involves the emotions that we experience each and every day, the pushing and pulling of energies and emotional responses. It is impossible to determine where these responses start from or why they start at all, when a resolution will occur, whether this outcome will prevail, or how this energy was undetected at the start.

All this can be explained in the energy systems. This is not to say that the emotions aren't vital; they most certainly are. But you have already read a mountain of emotion-related books that answer many of the questions.

In a way, my guides desire to fill a niche market, an area of our self that isn't being catered to at the moment. Believe me; there is a huge gap in this market, something I was totally unaware of previously.

You might be wondering why I'm almost talking in financial terms, but this only reflects the wealth of our self, the wholeness of our self.

In the plainest of terms, this means that we are able to use our full resources without depleting our reserves. This, of course, will need a lot more explaining.

To enable this to happen, and to facilitate constant energy, we need to reconnect to our conscious tools, which also means finding where in the past we haven't been able to figure out what was happening to our resources, as our abilities simply didn't stretch to this level of energy or comprehension.

In short, this is the direction this book is heading, with quite a few surprises to be unfolded along the way. This book is predominantly concerned with how energy is used. Our guides also desire to open our understanding in a totally new way.

This means introducing you to activations of energy—how, why, and where—when it pertains to you. It also involves embracing energy sequences from the whole source, the collective consciousness of all that exists, in a language that we can interpret at this moment and pass on.

This means opening you to the senses of energy or asking you to feel energy in a conscious manner. This is sensing, from the source, through exercises that help us to feel the different vibrations.

To make this a little easier, any affirmation that is received is then broken down into our language, to ensure no misunderstanding. It is then taken on as belief.

This is the status quo of every translation: not only is information unravelled or put forth in different manners, it is then related to energy movements that are open and available for you to sense in a physical manner. However, the choice is always yours.

So that you are also able to tell for yourself what is correct or true, the source introduces you to some exercises that check your own self-truth. In fact, this whole book is full of exercises to introduce you to many conscious activations.

These activations describe, in a way, how our energy and consciousness have moved in the past and will move in the future—but most importantly, how our consciousness was suppressed, was unable to move, and was never even connected.

Remember, if our energy is unable to move, it is therefore stagnant, meaning that no energy is traveling through this part of our self. This would also become a reaction of emotion. Perhaps now you can understand my guide's insistence to follow this train of thought.

Before following this train of thought, perhaps you can excuse my insistence on not following immediately, as I want to ascertain that I am in fact receiving a true question and answer. I never thought it would turn into such a long journey.

Finding truth through a new perspective was challenging in the early days, but it is now matter of fact. I must admit that I am constantly surprised and always grateful to be able to appreciate conscious energy, which brings compassion to myself—or what you might interpret as grace, ease, and synchronicity.

Perhaps we might move on to how this conversation started in the following chapter.

# 2

## CONVERSATIONS THOUGH MY SOUL PRESENCE

Years ago, after seeing that I could in fact pass on quite an amount of relevant information to help people, it was difficult to find a title that reflected this.

I did, however, write a book, *Secrets of the New Millennium*. After it was finished, I found that it might help people who had been looking for different solutions to many mainstream afflictions. The only problem was that most people would have trouble comprehending this channelled information.

In my spare time, I managed to write three other books in a totally different format, which were easy for everyone to read.

The only problem was that none of those sequels could be released, as the foundational information only existed in the first book. So I was back to square one.

On starting this new undertaking, the information flowed quickly, but it wasn't just one book; it was many books that I had outlined.

To digress somewhat, I will mention that I needed to outline in my own mind why the books were so different from each other. You see, in each book there was one very strong theme that never varied, a foundation that helped to determine whether we are on the correct path.

My reflection, I guess, was due to the fact that, while I had always channelled on and off, I was a little different and I knew this intuitively, so I could suppress this part of my life somewhat, knowing that no one around me was open to the information. Nonetheless, the foundations always stayed, no matter where or when I was receiving.

Mind you, shutting off or revealing what is going on in your life are totally different from each other. I always explored certain possibilities alone, and not being able to share my gift repressed my own intuitions.

When I did restart, however, I had forgotten many natural abilities and had to relearn them—relearning, most importantly, what was true and what was crap.

With this out in the open, and after finding that I had been listening to crap, I did remember that I needed to channel through my soul. Later I found out what people where connecting to in a wrong manner.

This wrong manner was also what a lot of people were using as intuition, off and on. No wonder so many people were getting angry, anxious, and distorted. When I saw that this was then going to be reflected in every form of self-information that we relied upon, I was stunned.

I knew instinctively that I needed to stop channelling in this manner and just listen to my own intuition that came through my soul—and *only* through my soul.

I had quite an epiphany, awakening, or just an intuitional awareness that hit me like a brick—not just through one window but through a multitude.

After this, I was quite excited, to say the least, especially as this also affected people in many different physical ways.

My largest problem was that I might be able to fix myself, but fixing somebody else was a totally different kettle of fish.

I was then open to many different possibilities, many of which I guess I wasn't really prepared for. But seeing that I couldn't find too many others following the same direction—as some were close in a few areas but distant in most—I knew that it was going to be a lonely search.

The reason this search is sometimes lonely is that sometimes you just can't share what you have found, as it affects others.

Thankfully, I was blessed with many guides to point me in the right direction to be released or restored.

This changed the entire demographics, in that I was able to receive the questions I needed to answer and to understand how one area of energy related to another, which, quite frankly, I would never have expected to be relevant.

In the simplest of ways, I was able to comprehend how our previous self-focus was limited. I needed to be able to recognise many different perspective potentials that so many of us are totally unaware of.

These different perspective potentials then opened many new foundations that were, for the time being, in a state of either unconsciousness or subconsciousness. We simply were not using these aspects or elements of potential in our daily lives.

The largest misrepresentation we could possibly have of this is that we don't utilise our brains enough.

While we reason that this may be correct, it is also correct that there is not enough connected to the brain to allow it to open up many new possibilities of reasoning.

This reasoning perspective led me to be guided though to a new starting point. All of a sudden, I had guides in every direction around me—not in a confusing manner but in a helpful one.

With this collective guide-consciousness, I was easily able to ascertain that many parts of my self-consciousness were simply not connected; or if they were, they were only connected in a limited way.

Reflecting on these missing pieces soon gave me the answer to many questions, but they didn't equate or correspond to any certain energy.

This total lack of correspondence meant that many foundational points of consciousness were in fact totally missing, so whole bodies of our self were in a state of unawareness. We didn't have a damn clue what was really going on.

I found this quite disconcerting to say the least. Then I had to ask, "Is this just in me, or does it relate to everybody else as well?"

Finding that it reflected where *all* human consciousness sits at present, this was sort of a relief. Then it hit home: I was definitely not alone in this quest to make my self whole; I was just using a different method to show the apparent disconnection between consciousness and energy.

Using an energy-related approach meant that I wasn't just using emotions to find where we were separate; I was following whole energy activations, which pin-pointed where we were separate—or correct.

These whole definitions meant that we now had a point for sending and for receiving—where, how, when, and why to receive—in a new and conscious manner.

We had a starting point with a full-energy circuit, and if the circuit was correct, then the message sent was correct, and the message received must therefore also be correct or true.

Then this scenario hit me like a truck. If we were unable to determine whether or not a full circuit was completed, then how would we be able to respond to the correct reasoning? This is where the emotions come in.

I would like you to think about this next bit for just a moment longer.

If you receive many messages through your subconsciousness, doesn't it make sense to change this so that you are aware of receiving these messages and whatever they connect to on a full-time basis?

This full-time basis means being in the presence of every aspect, ability, or potential of your whole self. This then equates to being able to send a message or to respond to one.

Unfortunately, the ability to respond is missing at the moment, as the consciousness is sitting in constant unawareness.

You see, the guides have shown me that much of our conscious circuitry isn't able to communicate within itself. It's as simple as that.

Does this make sense then, that when our guides ask us to be more aware, this is what they are actually saying?

Have you thought about how many books you have read in which this point of awareness was discussed? Think about it. Have any of those books given you a new awareness in forming your personal equation of how things add up?

Another point of reflection I would like you to think about is this: if you have a starting point where the self-message starts and where it ends, doesn't it also stand to reason that you can't get lost, as you are open to receiving with awareness?

The not-getting-lost factor, or direction, prompts us to examine what is a true direction—or a misdirection.

My guides explained this to me, and it follows the line of thinking from the previous chapter. Perhaps this analogy may help you.

If all consciousness is at a denser level, then the self doesn't react to or question higher vibrations and frequencies about you, nor does it create upheaval in your emotions.

However, with the heightening of all frequencies about you, your old belief will sense a disharmony with your self-faith, which may be interpreted as an interruption. Extra or higher vibrations create more currency to move stagnant energy, and this means that you instantly become aware of where a full current of energy is or is not flowing. This means that you are instantly aware of where you are unable to contact a certain conscious aspect of your self.

Just because something is of a subconscious or unconscious nature doesn't mean that we don't care to use it the way it was meant to be used.

All that we have just discussed adds up to separated matter that is unable to communicate, and this is the basis for all the emotions we can't figure out. It's why we feel as we do. We simply are unable to communicate in a conscious way.

This just shows how damn important consciousness is. Without it, we are unable to communicate efficiently, and this is just for starters. It also means that the spirit aspect of our self has been undervalued when compared to our physical make up. Yes, our spirit does physical stuff, even if we just concede that it helps in communication.

Once again, we need to consider that, while we have been evolving, parts of us have devolved due to this lack of communication.

Now, if we are to consider how this condition came about, we need to start at the beginning, at the original point where our soul was not able to communicate with our heart in an efficient manner.

Once we know where this equation started, then we will find a simple equation opening.

If this is correct, then every self-equation may be lacking this efficient manner of communication throughout the whole body. If the foundation isn't correct, no other aspect of our self can be correct. You see the can of worms we are opening here.

You see, when our selves were vibrating at a denser level, all was hunky-dory, as my mum would say—not challenging, at peace. But this changed somewhat as our vibrations increased.

If our vibrations increase, we need to get rid of some excess stuff that is weighing us down. But really, if we get what seems like excess working, there *is* no dead weight. This is what the sources are talking about.

Consider this. If we reconnect all these areas of our self that aren't doing much or remain in a dense state, then we need loads of current to connect them.

Also, we need to know where this dense self-matter is sitting and why it is disconnected, so that if we connect it up again, this new energy won't disrupt all the other correct energy. It's a lot of fuss just to vibrate at a higher frequency and receive self-truth, to know how truth equates to our own energy and to be true to our selves energetically.

Now, I guess, is as good a time as any to consider what is connected and what is sitting outside our regular conscious zones, to consider how this energy affects every aspect of our lives, often without our awareness.

Our unawareness of energy provides answers in a way that emotions can never explain. This is the equation in life that my guides have pushed me to bring to light. This, in a way, was one of my reasons for writing this book.

Our self-reasoning was raising vibrational energy, responding as if it was in disharmony with all surrounding energies, making us question our relationship with our surrounding environment. This meant that we had to find new, conscious questions that related to this disharmony, as past questions never gave us rational answers for this new-time millennium.

This gives a pretty clear picture of the direction this book will be taking, but don't forget that quite a few surprises can be expected along the way.

# 3

## THIS ISN'T JUST A DREAM

I essentially started this book to help people—not just to bring in different information, but also to look at quite a few situations that so many people seem unaware of.

Our most blatant unawareness seems to involve our ignorance of the many special abilities we have.

In the past, I found this to be a little confusing, until I used some of these abilities to form different questions and different answers.

I used to think that many of the answers lay in what could be called our personal ability—a vast, unused ability that everybody has, no exceptions. Most of us are aware of the idea that we use only a fraction of our brain capacity, but have you ever thought that perhaps we have interpreted this incorrectly? Instead of calling it our *brain capacity*, what if we were to refer to it as our *consciousness*? You see, if we actually break this down a little, we find that we are simply unaware or unconscious of what we are really capable of.

I was guided to look at myself in a very different light some time ago, as a very different scenario was presented to me. You see we all think of our brain as the conscious point of our existence, don't we? I'll give you an idea of how a conversation changed my awareness.

It started with the question of how I was made.

My answer was, "I was made from conscious matter, and I am simply a collective consciousness."

I was then asked, "Is your head all that matters? Nothing else?"

The whole point of this conversation was that every part of us is conscious—not just our heads—but we act as if the head is the only real part of us that matters.

I then said that I didn't think this was correct.

I was then asked where all my consciousness was stored. I was about to say, "In my head"—until I remembered that my whole body is conscious.

"Then why does your whole body react as if your head, rather than your whole self, is the centre of your universe?"

I was then told that mine was an instantaneous reaction, not one of reason, and I had to admit that this was true.

I was then asked, "Why did you answered the way you did?" My response was that all consciousness had to go through my brain in order for me to be conscious.

Once again, I knew I was wrong. I intuitively knew that the brain was more about reasoning, understanding, comprehending, and cognisance.

Then I sort of understood the direction of our conversation, that people only want to understand what is in their heads, so to speak—not what exists in the whole body.

I was then asked if this conclusion was in a spirit sense or a physical one.

My response this time was, "I guess we have been doing this in our spirits *and* our physical bodies, not realizing it that we are responding this way."

I was then asked what implication this would have on me. I had to ponder on this for a few moments before answering. I said that most of our consciousness was in the whole of both spirit and physical bodies, which we were only using in a minimally conscious manner.

I had to sit back and wonder about this implication for quite some time before realising that perhaps there is a lot in my life that I am unaware of.

After this conversation, I needed to comprehend the situation more clearly. While contemplating the scenario, I was interrupted with a new conversation asking why there are so many different forms of conflict and interference that stop us from reaching our potential.

After a rather long and animated conversation, I was directed to put pen to paper.

The part I forgot about was that I had already written many such understandings daily, but I had not used all of them when I came to write my first book.

The main reason for this is that I had been shown to think way outside the square. Understanding this myself was one thing, but sharing such uncommon lines of thought, I wondered how other people would respond to them.

The mitigating factor was that those whom I had healed had responded to the energy connected to my newly activated consciousness.

I then knew that I was following a different formula of reasoning. Instead of just following my reaction to emotion, I was following the direction of my conscious energy rather than old, limited patterns.

The next scenario was to explore why conscious energy was unable to connect to so many vital points of spirit or physical consciousness.

As you have probably ascertained, I am receiving a load of help. How else would I know these things. I'm not having a conversation with the Tooth Fairy.

Yes, I do channel, and I make no secret of this fact. I'm not about to pretend that this information suddenly appeared to me or that I'm all that gifted, as I definitely am not.

There is only one thing I do a little differently: I remember how to access some of this conscious matter in a different way.

You see, you can do it too. We all can. And we only need to take responsibility for actually connecting to the base foundations where our real consciousness exists.

So this was my desire, my intent, and my direction—with the help of some very patient guides and friends: to make sure that this works.

Right from the outset, I would like you to recognise the largest foundation that needs to be recreated in a conscious manner. Even after ages of questions and answers, I wasn't able to identify this vital, foremost foundation for a long time.

As a channeler, I can ask loads of questions—and this I will expand on later,—but I needed to understand why I couldn't readily connect to the correct answer.

I was asked what it was that my heart and soul did, and then I remembered how I had used them.

The answer unlocked everything: *I use my soul and heart together*, don't I? I had better repeat this, as it is so relevant. I had intuitively used my soul and heart together as one; I had asked questions through my combined soul and heart.

The ramifications of this are vast and vital to what we do and how we do it.

Have you ever considered this? I know I had not. I had never seen this information written or heard it mentioned before.

Why is this so relevant?

Consider that if our soul and heart work as one united body, then this desire and intention will be reflected in the rest of our self. It also means we desire a relevant outcome.

This actually unlocked something else. It unlocked the reason my guides often didn't respond when I wanted them to: I wasn't communicating through my soul and heart as one energy. Consequently, without interference or conflict or confusion, the body desires to follow when we integrate our spirit and physical matters.

Please remember, though, that the joining of the soul and heart is a vital step. Learning how to use this as a conscious energy in all that we do means relearning many of our old senses.

Essentially, this is just to give you an indication of some of the different thought patterns or lines of reasoning that our guides have desired us to follow.

There are, of course, many other applications of this first and vital foundation, which will pop up from time to time.

One application that you may want to consider right away is that this really adds up to more than the old, misinterpreted thought patterns. I guess you could say that I was shown the outcomes of using only the soul or only the heart.

We will discuss all of this in the following chapters, but the goal here is to knock us out of the old dream-state of just following what everybody else is focusing on, or just following what others do without questioning whether it is relevant to us or not.

This isn't meant to be confrontational; it is meant to release what is being rehashed as self-confrontation each and every day.

Why?

If we don't question what we are connecting to in order to know how this energy affects our own self-conscious matter or conscious parts, we are living in the dark.

The connotations of this have reverberated all the way back to our very self-foundations. As our guides have indicated, we are simply unaware of how many conscious foundations we really have. We have all these secrets to unlock, but all we need to do is reconnect to these foundations. In a way, this book is about where to find them, how to make sense of them and find out what they actually do.

I don't know if this excites you, but I was beside myself when I realised that we often communicate with our soul and heart separately—never together.

You see, my intuition was going ballistic at how this affected us in so many ways that I had never contemplated.

I did comprehend one massive point: Use your heart alone, and it doesn't have the strength to access all the foundations of self that the source is talking about. Join your soul and heart together and they do have the necessary strength. Together they are able to access all that has never been possible before.

This was one of those lightbulb moments, my own little epiphany, when I just *got* it. However, I was missing the bit about *how* to do it.

I now felt like an excited kid with a massive jigsaw puzzle. Then the enormity of the task set in, and I realised that it wasn't something I was doing each and every day. Anyhow, I was just a bit more consciously aware, so self-awareness was always going to be a vital key.

The lesson I am passing on need not be overwhelming. Just do a bit at a time; then all the pieces will soon fit together like a jigsaw.

Figuring out how this unfolds and what is really relevant has meant reflecting on absolutely everything.

This also has meant scrutinizing every aspect of myself. I needed to find out where I was actually connecting with my combined soul and heart. You see, I had tried to figure out what was going on in others. Why try to understand somebody else, when you don't comprehend every aspect of yourself?

This attitude worked up to a point, but I also needed to understand how this same energy would effect others.

Thank god for sisters, especially one who is seeks what is going on, channels, and works as a healer. Add to this equation that much of our DNA is shared, so we wonder why our energy works so differently yet so much the same.

There was so much to unlock that it looked like I was going to need loads of help, which meant that I needed new sources.

How these new sources came to be integral to me is also part of the story, but it is how their input changed old thought patterns that I have found intriguing.

How appreciative I am for all that has been shared with me to simply cast new light on things. All is not what it seems to be; this I have found to be true, time and time again.

I hope this brief outline indicates that whatever has been passed on to me—those things I find relevant—I am passing on freely. If this helps to relieve conflicts or intrusions that interfere with self-stability, then thank my guides for persevering.

Please consider how this has unlocked so many new-time senses that have helped me and others to recognise that there is a brighter future for all humanity.

A new, multi-sensory self is unfolding, and with this body we soon recognise that we are automatically reflecting on unlimited new-time intuition at our fingertips. Therefore, I see no reason to be gloomy. Just be aware that perhaps quite a bit is going to change.

Embracing change is difficult sometimes, but it's easier when we are helped to see, to become aware of how and why the changes in our self are going to unfold.

This connects us to the grace, ease, and synchronicity needed in our future. This synchronicity, which is held within the sacred self-spirit, is then integrated into the physical self-nature.

This can only be appreciated through an integrated soul and heart, our aware, natural self.

This whole chapter is a brief preparation for all that that is to be unlocked using the soul and heart as one whole energy. But of course there are to be many surprises.

One of the largest surprises is that we are able to facilitate this energy to connect to many consciousness-opening exercises that we were never aware of. Each of these exercises opens up a new conscious sense or enables us to contact many other sensory-aware bodies that haven't been used for millennia.

So, this is quite a discovery journey. It is also a way to reconnect to what we have been unaware of, which means that in many ways we have both devolved and evolved, all at the same time. This is another point that my source clarified on many occasions.

How this unawareness developed, I have found to be mind-boggling. That we have all this potential and have been so unaware that it exists, untapped and unused, is beyond comprehension.

The fact that this energy is able to be used all day, every day, without exception, has led me to ask why we haven't seen it? The frustrating part is that the questions and answers have been right under our noses all the time. We just couldn't see them.

Well, how could we? We didn't have the sensory perception to remind us that this awareness existed. This is just one of many reasons for writing this book.

This really is a foundational point as well: without the sense that we are living a limited potential, we focus on what we do not have instead of what we do have—not all the time, but often enough to disrupt our focus on creating with the resources we have. Then we would probably create in a devolving manner, using others' creativity.

Others' creativity breaks down to simply purchasing every conceivable element that we distinguish as bringing us joy or happiness. The full breakdown of this we will be able to sense as we advance, but there is one underlying phenomenon that this statement relates to. If we don't become a multi-sensory body, how will we ever be able to relate to becoming a multi-dimensional, interactive being with an awareness of our abilities and potentials?

Once again, this whole scenario comes down to the fact that without correct awareness, it is not possible to focus on what we have rather than on what we don't have.

Perhaps it is time to remember what the source is continually projecting: Don't consume processed material or dwell on we don't have, as all that you desire is attainable using self-resources.

Using this philosophy, I have been able to connect to many self-resources that I could not sense but were ready when I desired to connect to them. While I enjoy pursuing self-potential, the choice to connect is always yours.

To help with this connecting, sensing, unlocking, or redefining where potential exists, there are keys and codes to help.

At the moment, they may look like kids' playtime adventures, but each is a representation of light consciousness—not hieroglyphics of past times.

So how do you use them? Hold your hand up to the screen, but not too close, please. Sense the vibrations being connected through each hand.

This exercise will change as you read on and become more aware, or as you become more sensitive to what is being shared with you, so perhaps it is worth repeating a little later on.

For those who have already done years of work at this, it might be worth closing your eyes as you experience each code; each is an unfolding instrument that is only accessed when you are ready.

Perhaps it is time to move on now to where your guides desire to connect in a more intimate manner.

You see, as your guides share the many intuitive and intimate self-resources you are not communicating with, you can explore all these capacities. They do exist, and we desire for you to find this out intimately.

Perhaps it is time to move on to how this actually comes about.

# 4

## A NEW-TIME ESSENTIAL SELF

I am about to broach an immense subject for just a moment, and then we will return to it later so as not to get sidelined here.

The subject is telepathy, and it is an underrated sense. The amount of influence telepathy has in our everyday life is nothing short of astounding. The many facets of everyday energy that use telepathy in some form is huge. So why bring it up now?

Julie had done many courses on essences and their physical healing abilities; I had different uses for them in healing the spiritual aspect rather than the physical. Because Julie and I were healing together, a lot of her knowledge opened up to me what I already knew in this field, although I had never done the courses or read her literature.

This meant that by opening ourselves to new-time senses with source understanding, we often automatically passed information between us in a telepathic manner. Why?

I will be covering this more in depth later, but for now I will mention that I stumbled onto one huge fact—that by using my soul and heart together as one energy, I had created an immense strength of conscious purpose.

This meant that my consciousness had regained some abilities automatically, or that my consciousness was aware of what it needed to connect or respond to. Another way to interpret this is to conclude that the senses of the sensory self never forget real conscious life experience, so after this awareness, I did reconnect.

After a few months of using bought essences and using them intuitively, I had to go and find ones that weren't readily available.

This is where we were lucky in our location, surrounded by national parks and reserves, not to mention state forests.

So, all of a sudden, I couldn't come home until I found a certain plant that was flowering.

Walking in the bush was great fun but rather time-consuming, so other things like mowing had to wait. Spring was a busy time.

I was more than amazed at the different vibrations each flower gave off, and where I could sense it, this energy sort of hit me in either my spirit or my physical body.

I was also aware that the energies I connected to through the flower essence also connected to much energy that I had seen but had not really used.

I have got to tell you, this was just great fun, and the other great aspect was that it was unlocking stuff I already knew instinctively.

After a while, things began to change, and I was easily able to see the energy around certain plants. For some plants, the energy circle was huge, but often it was just a small plant.

At other times the plant almost ungrounded me until I connected. What the heck was going on? Plants had never effected me this way before.

So I had to ask for help. I was told, "You are just being opened to different properties that usually goes unnoticed."

I asked what they might be but was told that I would remember soon enough.

We had a lot of rain one week, with everybody grumbling that no work could be done, but I was ecstatic because the rain had brought out the wildflowers.

I was just ambling along when I saw some bluebells. I had already made tinctures, so I wasn't too excited, but I suddenly remembered and knew what I needed to find out.

I knew that if this or that plant was giving off a more universal, galactic, or cosmic energy, these were to be combined to become a celestial essence.

I was then able to see how this energy stabilizes our bodies, and then I saw how this energy activated many dormant areas within our bodies.

Open one door, and then many others doors open for you, meaning: open up one huge sense, and all of a sudden many new senses are opening

21

with new awareness, automatic knowing, and limited comprehension of how they all tie in together.

Wow! This was something new, but how the heck did it all tie in together? I was going to have to ask a lot of questions now.

The parameters went back to quantum thoughts. So much for thinking that just a drop of essence would balance one thing or clear another.

This concept was looking rather huge, and all of a sudden my exuberance for finding certain flowers died. Why?

After sitting down and contemplating how everything had unfolded, I soon saw a vision of lots of bodies in front of me. Yes, I was being guided to unlock a different understanding.

I was able to sense certain energy bands that went way outside any aura field or meridian field. Also, this was where my guides directed me to unconscious awareness, and they opened a conversation to explain.

"This is where the keys and codes that you understand fit in. Dave, you understand how the quintessence and *quintrex* energies integrate and work."

So I asked volumes of questions to endeavour to piece this all together— like how plants reflect certain essences, seemingly from every existing solar system. This sounded a bit out-there, until I stopped to observe what was being shown to me.

From my observation, it was easy to see that I just needed to use a quantum term for the essence; but this seemed a little *too* easy.

You see, I was quite aware that many essence energies were flowing through me. I didn't need any additional essences, as the ones I had were now connecting. Why? Because there was a collective, unlimited consciousness relating to essence.

If parts of my consciousness are separated, I can't comprehend all that I want to understand about essences. This is why certain bodies appeared outlined to me; they contained this consciousness.

I understood that these bodies contributed to our wealth of health, and I needed to understand how to use them in a more efficient manner.

I reconnected to this consciousness to make sure that everything was working, to discover what was the first step to take, to ensure automatic understanding, and to connect to the correct sensory responses.

These responses indicate why something is relevant or not. They also direct you to the next conscious response, showing how everything fits together logically.

How does this all pan out in the grand scheme of things? When you think essence, you think fluids or physical fluids. I needed to take into account how the vibrational essence as a flow of energy related to the physical essence in fluids or chemical make-up.

Now I had another quandary to explain. I had already rediscovered element grids, lay lines, matrixes, nets, webs. If these existed in essence, they must also exist in the same way in elements.

You see, this was way before I was shown the inception of my soul and heart. Later, I would have much more clarity as to why everything works as it does.

Using one group of essences at a time, I was able to see the harmonizing effects that an essence has on our bodies—first in spirit, then in the physical.

*Wow! This is great,* I thought. Then a new reality set in. Did I need to travel around the world, gathering essences to stabilize everything? I had just returned from a little adventure a thousand kilometres away, finding all sorts of great new essences. The thrill of finding something myself told me that something great was out there, but I didn't have the resources to keep up the search.

You see, I had been driving along near some open-cut coal fields near where I had worked years earlier. Suddenly my head felt like it was lifting off, and my whole body was swaying.

I quickly pulled over, wondering what had happened, and then I just laughed to myself in realization. I had been following grids and lay lines. The essence energy was undisturbed, but the energy in the coal pit hit the essence lines, disturbing the energy that I was following, even though I knew where I was going.

This was just one introduction to the interference of energy lines.

Later, I hit on the revelation that it was possible to connect every plant in the whole of Australia without going out to collect them. I will explain this later when you are able to understand.

The source could have shown me this a little earlier, but then I would have missed out on so many vital experiences that make up understanding something.

I was told that I still needed the essences I had collected and would be using them in the future—just in a different way.

This left me with the question of how to connect all the essences at one time and then pass on the ones needed by myself or others.

23

Well, the clues soon came together when I remembered that the essence was a collective consciousness of energy. All I needed to do was integrate the energy.

I was able to achieve this in a limited way, starting with my angel collective consciousness, in order to stabilize and help all the energies in myself flow in a more efficient manner. The essence opened essential knowledge of where the different self-energies weren't flowing.

The number of different spirit essences I had never encountered was unexpected, and they opened me up to many physical elements when I joined them together.

After doing this, the self-balance changed remarkably, and the activations of energy became vast.

This also opened different opportunities to sense where my own automatic, sensory understanding was opening.

The difference I detected in my awareness of the many energy grids around me correlated to many aspects within me, which are now alive, moving, or activating.

This involved months of work, as there was just so much to explore. I also determined that if I could connect to all the essences in Australia, then I need to get cracking and see if it was possible to connect to whatever the world was offering.

I did, however, start using the principles of connecting essences to elements. I needed a bit of help here, to say the least.

After linking the essences and elements together through the divine life matrix, all was really taking shape—even with my limited understanding.

I was surprised at how this energy related to the physical to unlock stagnant areas. And then came another breakthrough.

I have touched briefly on androgenous energy. Well, apply this to the unfolding landscape of integration between spirit and physical, essence and elements, and many muscle constrictions begin to loosen—not one hundred percent, but the results are encouraging.

Not long after this episode, I was in need of a lemon bath. My muscles were aching, and I hadn't done anything physical, but I knew I had a few toxins building up.

One minute I was in the bath, and then—*whoosh*—I was in a maelstrom and off.

"You were asking why, David," said my guide. I was looking down at many large pyramids in the bay and in the lakes near my home. Next, were like the tops of pyramids, all shining but just out of the water, connecting to the larger pyramids.

I felt instant recognition. Aha! This was how consciousness was transferred. The higher the pyramids, the higher the connection where consciousness sat in the area.

"So the oceans act as a like satellite dish?" I asked.

"David, look at the level of consciousness near cities." Of course, the levels were quite low. In fact, some were almost invisible.

Next we ventured inland to see how this was replicated in land.

"David, I would like you to consider the national consciousness of a few countries. Also, consider how the makeup of identity and past conflicts affect what you sense."

So then I was taken on a little tour, if briefly, to sense how certain national consciousnesses were affected and how certain countries identified with a certain image.

"David, this is more of a preparation for the future, to help raise all consciousness. Yes, humanity is able to connect, when they are ready. You are also able to sense how old beliefs and faiths caused so much conflict."

So how do we change this? So many are just holding on to dense consciousness. "This is why it is essential for people to learn how to sense in a conscious way, not with unaware, unconscious feeling."

The understanding was automatic, but how do I get this message across? So many are comfortable, used to living in this dense environment. Everybody is happy to hold on to the resentment of the past. I could see it as my guides showed it to me.

I told my family and friends about this, and then I thought I'd do a little experiment.

This was a little bit out-there, but if I could see it, could others. I grabbed a few family members and friends to have a look from a hill, where we were able to see all the lakes and the bay. Sure enough, they were all able to see what I described.

So this is quantum consciousness. "David, by opening conscious senses, you are able to pass this on telepathically."

Now, I needed to get my head around this. Using the whole of my body to interpret quantum essences and elements in a conscious manner,

I could tell what other people's whole bodies were telling me in an aware way, whether or not conscious energy was connected.

"David, this is a foundation to forming a new, true, conscious, sensory awareness of energy, which so many desire but are not aware of."

"So," I said, "you are saying that by holding on to past resentments—and this is in energy terms—people remain bogged down, unable to sense all that they are missing out on, since they are unable to properly sense."

"Not only this, David. They are also unable to evolve energetically. Their energy is tied to the past, so most are unable to connect the evolving energy about them.

"David, look at the energy about them. It is light and desires to help them, but they are unaware that this enlightening energy exists. They are relying on old feelings, not senses.

"This is why, David, we desire to show all people their own self-environments. Then you are able to resist the resentments and cycles of past feelings. You do not need to live in a war-torn environment to understand this, do you?"

Now I was beginning to see how energy senses help unlock energy blocks. We had no understanding of how they were created; they were just cycles of the past. And here we were just following the cycles, totally unaware, except for an emotion that said we weren't able to receive a full circuit of energy.

Does this throw a bit of light on how and why we aren't aware of cycles of the past? Everybody is doing the same thing, holding on to them. Thus, we are unaware of them.

I asked a question then. "If we are separated from sensing, then this is why we are separated from consciousness?"

Now I get it. We could be following others' unconscious thoughts, and if everybody is following them, then we all just think the same, not independently, and we wouldn't have a clue because of our lack of conscious senses.

This little conversation ages ago gave me much to think about, until it dawned on me that senses are conscious foundations. So, how do I join all my senses together or find all these separated senses for automatic understanding, knowledge, and wisdom to create conscious comprehension?

I instantly had a new, true direction to follow, and I thought there must somebody else on this same path, since it is huge.

Wouldn't new, conscious senses make it so much easier to be aware of what we are missing out on? Or am I the only one who can see their potential?

After following this potential for ages, I admit that when some person comes to my place, it is easy to find many separated bits of consciousness in many different states, but I do not focus on this. Rather I focus on where they are complete or connected.

This is where our story or conversation is heading now, but before I get too far ahead of myself, I would like you to understand how this book first came about. There is a reason.

# 5

## HOW THIS BOOK CAME ABOUT

Frustration is a strange animal, but it is a great indicator of the direction to what seems relevant.

We all seem to read when we desire to find new material that corresponds to what we have tried or tested, hoping somebody else is on the same wavelength.

There is nothing new about channelling. Many of us connect daily, receiving some new, conscious understanding that is relevant for now or the future, and I'm no different.

The only difference is that with each knowing, I receive an array of activations to release, heal, rejuvenate, or regenerate. It is like a different way to receive a message—a sensed message.

To get these activations working, my guides have facilitated many new tools for me to use and pass on.

This book primarily shows how some old-time, unconscious memory has contributed to our not being able to connect to these activations.

So what is an activation? It is how, why, where, and when many different types of your energy moves. It must be connected to or through a conscious aspect of your self, or it just spirals about the place.

This spiralling means that your energy desires to fulfill its purpose but is simply unable to do so, because it is not connected to your own conscious aspect, which is its job.

Many new solutions need to be found. Separation over many years has led to the need for connection through many new-time guides, and the purpose of guidance is to strengthen places where not enough current exists.

I would like to share a couple of very relevant understandings and how they have made my life and many others' lives so much easier. I guess they are just part of a formula that not only makes sense but adds up to comprehension of the reason for the new millennium or new time.

In other words, we are going to have to get used to thinking just a little differently, with new conscious reasons and with a new sensitivity.

There are many thoughts that reoccur, book after book. The first is that we have all separated, or parts of us have separated. The vastness of this separation makes it clear why we are not more aware.

The exception is when a certain feeling, emotion, or illness tells our intuition that something just isn't complete. Why?

Each and every separation is connected to a sense. Now, the term *sense* must be comprehended a little differently and thought of differently. How so?

Real senses are only made of conscious matter—no *if*s, *but*s, or *maybe*s.

So as not to confuse any understanding, let us just concentrate on real senses, and then we can discuss illusional senses.

Real senses need one very large element to work, and this is the correct, conscious current that links everything together.

This current, of course, comes from your soul and heart—not your mind, not your brain, and not your memory.

Your soul and heart contain not just sacred knowledge, not just god-purpose or angel connections or any other spiritual purpose. They hold one of life's largest purposes.

This is a point so many overlook. What is this great life purpose that we have forgotten to employ throughout our day?

Truth, truth, truth, and nothing but real truth.

Now, don't take this as religious or as relating to any faith, belief, or great hope. This is simply about how to connect to self-truth, because, if you can't rely on everything being true, what's the point in living?

Real truth can only be reached by combining the soul and heart to create one immense presence of strength. Yes, I know we are repeating this, but there is a reason.

Please think long and hard about this, because, without creating a point of foundational truth, how on earth can we access knowledge, comprehend consciousness, align to wisdom, reaffirm any affirmation, or access information that we haven't accessed before?

Simply, we would be following blind faith, not true faith.

How is this done? Just integrate your soul and heart to create spirit strength and connect to your innermost self-knowing.

Without this strength of real spirit appreciation, little can ever be reached. These, of course, are not my words but ones I have simply interpreted.

Because we are free to connect in any way we please, I decided to follow my intuition and give this interpretation a go.

Since connecting to this basic foundational truth, I and many others have found that it works to gather our inner strength and all that flows through us into stable thought patterns.

These stable thought patterns also open up a new flow of synchronicity, so life itself becomes less tedious. How do I add to this synchronicity? With sequences of true foundations. The added bonus is that this also stops a lot of the why-did-I-do-this-again syndrome of old thought patterns.

There is also another train of thought to add to this formula. We have, over many lifetimes, created and received many different types of separations. Each separation is, of course, connected to a separate sense. This is easy to comprehend, isn't it? You see, my guides are ensuring that I don't miss some parts that are speaking to your consciousness. I may seem to be filling in little bits of tedious information, and then, out of the blue, you understand in a different way.

Now, imagine how much harder the mass of your consciousness would have to work as many separated parts that are not available to contribute.

This is a bit like losing your sight. As the sight sense fails, the other senses need to work overtime to compensate for this loss of sight. After a while, all the remaining senses become overworked.

Overworked senses can never make up for senses lost. The result is that the remaining senses become acute or overly sensitive.

When you become aware of this oversensitivity, there is of course a reaction, because there is a limit to what the senses are going to take.

We then interpret this awareness as fear that we are repeating issues, anxiety, loss, abandonment, or a host of other lost elements.

So, the scenario my guides desire you to comprehend is this: When you use an integrated soul and heart, you are more complete and you are able to identify the sense that is missing or the reason for a certain anxiety.

This brings up one underrated sense that I use every day—the sense that indicates where certain energies exist, as well as how, why, and when they influence our daily lives.

This applies not only to spirit but to the physical. It is a tool I have immense appreciation for, and I am grateful that my guides have explained the intricate equations until I was able to grasp every foundational understanding.

I am talking about activations, and they unlock so many secrets. Why?

The activation indicates where many consciousnesses are not connected. This means that you are not really working on a particular level. It doesn't sound too exciting, does it?

Now imagine an indicator that shows you how, why, where, and when separations occur. Can you imagine how much intuition would unfold?

This is way beyond immense. This is a real, quantum tool that keeps opening up questions that relate to new-time truth.

Understand the questions, and you unlock the real, conscious comprehension or cognizance.

There are, of course, many such tools that our guides have opened for us and continue to open daily. For this I am beyond grateful.

There is a reason, though, why these tools have been tithed: so we can comprehend where the new-time, conscious energy-direction is heading. Without the correct tools, we would simply dismiss so much that the source desires to tithe to us.

If you cannot appreciate something's worth, how can you have gratitude for how this tithing contributes and opens opportunities in spirit and in real life?

To give you an indication of an activation, a new-time guide named "Sordlion" will facilitate the opening of this interpretation.

Please understand that this small tithing is only to introduce you to a limited self that sits in separation. This is an understanding that perhaps you would like to introduce to yourself.

Please hold the flat of your left hand in front of your soul and heart.

For some of you who are quite in tune, this hand will begin to vibrate and connect to your senses of intent.

This intent is then linked to a desire to your own self source sense, a connection between your soul and heart.

The grounding sensation you are receiving is connected to all new-time guides. Thus we are connecting to your personal guide.

Don't be in a hurry here. Close your eyes and connect to all senses that are unfolding, please.

Next, my friend, please place your right hand in front of your left hand. Once again, you will sense a grounding, yes?

As you ground, both hands will feel like dropping, so please let them do so.

Now, bring both hands up and out as if to receive, which is what is going to happen. An orb will sit within the palm of your left hand. Please do not play with this, as you desire to sense this orb and all intuition that needs to be reacquainted with your self.

This orb sitting in your left hand will be spinning in clockwise motion, with the right-hand orb spinning anticlockwise.

You may now be aware of the mass and the weight of stagnant energy represented in your left hand, yes.

This is a reflection of a mass of matter or volume of matter that separates your soul and heart. Don't worry; you will not be sensing even briefly any unpleasant feeling this mass reflects. Remember, this was dense energy between your soul and heart. You understand this connotation, not to mention the relevant outcomes as this releases.

Straightaway, turn your left hand to your right hand; this would resemble an open prayer stance. At this moment, you are simply neutralising any separating energy.

Immediately you will sense the self rising, yes. You are moving from a point of separate conscious. Also, the vibrations and frequencies of yourself are rising.

Please bring your hands to clasp, poised. For those of you whose senses are quite active already, an integrating sense, or a coming-together feeling is now activating all currents within all that was once separated.

In our language, this is a preparation or opening of yourself to receive in a new way. It also enables you to lighten the density of your mass, and your energy gains strength.

Perhaps others' energy may not seem more important than your own; you will find out how vital it is to appreciate the wealth of energy that exists in you.

Simply put, this is to help you seek self-truth, not where others tell you happiness lies.

Perhaps it is time to appreciate all that is already in your life, to rethink every desire for whatever element could make my life so much happier.

Perhaps your desire is true and correct, but this could also be others' influence, telling you in a subconscious manner what you desire in your life. This is why advertising reflects a self-image. It is not being aware of what our consciousness is telling us. This is why advertising works so perfectly and why we become consumers.

Now that you have opened yourself to sensing a sense, perhaps it is time to reflect on some differences between feelings and sensing. With sensing, you become more aware of energy that exists, and you also sense how it moves or where it is coming from.

Is this terribly important? Consider this statement carefully and ponder it for a while, as I and many have found this to be correct.

Gabriel and I were having a conversation one day. I was a little disgruntled, to say the least, and this statement was presented to me.

"David, please consider that whatever exists in reality also exists in illusion."

"Yes, I have heard this said before," I replied.

"So then, David, which of the two forms presented to you is the real one?"

"Neither," I replied. One was pure illusion and the other was illusion plus truth.

"Now, David, you are beginning to comprehend one other point of understanding, yes."

The dilemma that unfolded for me was that in reality we are able to exist. On the other hand, in illusion, we are in an existence but not living up to our potential.

The other scenario is that if we don't become aware and use both at the same time, we are unable to decipher where we are heading.

"If you unknowingly take either the illusional or the mixed form as an answer, imagine the dilemma for your understanding. This is why you were given this tithing: to appreciate, David."

Only questions bring understanding, comprehension, and the cognizance to connect to a real, conscious conclusion.

So, from the outset of being shown how to integrate the soul and heart, you have an immense tool at your disposal, and learning how to use this tool efficiently is also a large lesson.

My new-time guides presented activation awareness for how to unlock an activation that guides you through many questions in order to understand a new-time direction.

What does this equate to? Simply, this means that you're not covering the same ground, time and time again.

This means that as you unlock many new understandings, then many of the pieces of life are able to fit together. Now you're able to see the larger picture. You're not blinded by the forest and unable to see the trees. Now each and every tree stands out, but I must admit I have found many types of trees.

You see, the precursor to this book, *Secrets of the New Millennium*, was written years ago, and I wanted to rewrite it, as we all move on and new energy in the world has been created.

While I had been directed to leave it in a raw state, it soon became apparent that I was in fact joining the understandings from four books into one understanding.

This simply meant that more could be shared quickly, without as many interrupting energies breaking down source tithing. No matter how long this book existed, it wouldn't *fall* into existence. This is so that what is written doesn't become effected by any change of energy, and our environmental vibrations and frequencies are balancing to new tones and harmonies.

This is also about using a new-time atmosphere and environment, which will become apparent as you look at the new awareness that is evident each day.

As you can probably ascertain, there are a couple of new tools to help with the understandings of a new time.

As we stated earlier in the previous chapter, there are many physical exercises along the way to help interpret the differences between old-time energy, and new-time sensing of energy.

Soon the reality and the vast differences between these energies will not only become apparent; they will also point to some vast changes that we might desire, not just for ourselves but for the environment or our self-environment.

Opening this environment means that soon you will become aware that it is something akin to a new-time phenomena. This is like a new-time self-aura, only with a more inclusive and vast presence of our reflection. Such is this vastness, that if you are able or used to seeing your old aura, then your new one may be unrecognisable to the old one that is being replaced.

Does this reflect the vast changes our guides desire to share with you in a tithing manner?

Please, take this statement quite seriously. There is a vast array of new knowledge, which implies that the source desires to pass it on. Connecting to this knowledge requires new senses. Why?

Each and every sense to be used is, at present, in a state of unconsciousness. If it is unable to be used for self-worth or to unfold a sense and make this sense fully conscious, then it becomes a vital component once again, doesn't it?

Take this a few steps further and, using this conscious sense, link it to the senses you have corrected to be present and conscious. This creates a collective consciousness.

The term *collective consciousness* is also defined as god-consciousness, so in a way, you are recreating senses to recreate your own self-god consciousness.

If we define all senses that you are recreating as a collective consciousness, then we can add the definition that you are also connecting to foundational or sensory senses to recreate your own self-collective conscious senses.

By recreating these foundational sensory senses, you are able to relate to all that is currently connected to yourself and to the whole collective consciousness that exists. Doesn't this make sense?

In our language, we are actually recreating our own self-collective consciousness and finding out how to use it in a more true way to ensure that we learn not to create with illusion and true consciousness at the same time.

The next issue is this. When we recreate a self-collective-consciousness, which is now present and absolutely active, the correct current is flowing through it. Then we are able to relate or actively communicate with our collective consciousness and to the whole collective consciousness that exists. Isn't this worth considering?

The tithing of self-presence that accompanies this affirmation holds many new time keys and codes. How they work will be revealed later, because at this moment, all is about receiving and opening your self to receive with grace, ease, and synchronicity.

"I now open, with all real intent and all real purpose, all that has resided in the intuition of this self.

"I open all that exists as a true reflection of real humanity in this new time, all that is of this self and is to be a new knowing of new-time presence, and an awareness of all opportunities that this presents.

"This evolved preparation is to only evolve the true potential of this new-time manner and to form all environments in this real-time manner.

"With all love, Sordlion and J'spirin

This may seem a small affirmation, but this has so many links to other affirmations through out this book. How this affirmation unlocks questions will be discussing in the following chapter.

This leads us to what our guides have interpreted as opening a secret time to the new millennia.

In essence, this also means getting rid of some barriers that are stopping us from examining the truth from a new perspective or eliminating all perceived secrets.

This means getting rid of the secrets. Everybody must be able to access the same base foundations that we perceive to be restricted, when in truth they are not.

This understanding took some time to get my head around. At first I was unable to see the clear limitations placed before me.

This might seem a strange analogy, but I hope in the end it is easy to comprehend. It is a little like looking through a window but being unable to ascertain whether a pane of glass exists between us and the real environment.

It ends up looking like window after window, as we are unaware of so many facets of our self that actually exist but are unused or unsensed—or we simply do not have the correct current to connect to this truly remarkable sense.

Remember, as we reconnect to so many base foundations of our self, we are able to ascertain what it is in this aspect of our self. Only then can we consider and conclude what it is that we have not been able to understand or comprehend.

This opens many dimensions of understanding to exist in our new time.

In the end, we have no self-dimensions, and in the end I hope you will find that these are in fact unresolved issues of past lives.

By resolving past-life issues—and this term may change somewhat—soon you will see that so much of our self is able to be whole. But perhaps I'm jumping ahead too much, as much that we are talking about is like a preparation for your conscious energy system and all that is to follow.

This means relearning how to interpret much of our past, which leads to our next chapter on how to interpret the self.

# 6

## REDEFINING HOW TO INTERPRET
## THE SELF PRESENCE

Perhaps, like the rest of us, you have been wondering about the implications of the new millennium or new time. In a way, it has already opened and is helping many to download new information that, in a way, had been prevented from being sourced to us.

The breakthrough for this new material has been flowing quite steadily for a couple of decades now—small tidbits to entice us, but not large amounts, as we usually take time to adjust to getting our heads around minor changes.

Another point is that if something is new, we wait for others to explore the new waters first and see if they survive, wondering if this new information is relevant or just some fad.

So, how are we going to access any new information? We have tried rehashing lots of old stuff, and occasionally a piece of new information is accepted and found to work, so we all give it a try. But where does this new information come from?

Well, there is one way that not everybody identifies as a relevant method. However, if somebody just plunks a whole load of new and profound information on us and shows us how wonderful it is, then it is generally accepted as good information—as long as he doesn't mention where this information came from, because generally this person is channeling in some form or another.

You see, it would be great if this information was already in some ancient scripture, but if some person was to tell you that they channelled it, you might tell them to go away. But have you considered where past information was dug up from? It didn't just appear on scrolls. Somebody had to sit down and write it; more to the point, somebody was guided to write it.

Perhaps you should redefine where conscious knowledge comes from and remember that this is a very conscious matter that we reflect on.

You see, right from the outset, I'm being up-front and identifying that all new information I have accessed is brought to me this way.

But while I channel naturally, I still had to learn what was correct and what had been tampered with.

This seemingly insignificant thought has led me onto one of the greatest journeys of my life, which is why I define channeling differently.

The last chapter shared that if we recreate our self-collective consciousness, we are then able to relate or communicate with our source collective consciousness of all which exists. Well, what do you think this communication is?

Yes, it's really a perspective of our intuition, first and foremost, but it is also using a resonance of our sensory senses—in other words, channeling.

If I were to say that I communicate through all sensory self-perceptions that resonate through my integrated soul and heart, you might think me a little egotistical.

On the other hand, if I were to say that I use my self-collective consciousness to communicate with the whole collective consciousness of all that exists, you might think I was reflecting that I was a god. Well, we all are a god-presence, aren't we? Every individual is. Whether or not we desire to communicate through our intuitive collective consciousness in a conscious manner, though, is something we are all free to choose.

Channeling is just a more refined version of intuition, where we all communicate in this more intuitive manner, using more of our real consciousness.

You see, it is one thing to channel but another to learn how, why, where, and when everything comes together. This takes many constant hours, every day, over years, to become crystal-clear.

So, in a way, interference in my self-truth has been my life work, but thankfully I had an amazing break that started me in the correct direction.

This new direction came about when I was trying to understand a meditation I had been guided to have. It seemed like a very complicated understanding, and I was a little perturbed about how I was going to figure it out.

The next morning while I was pondering this, one of my guides asked why I was bothering with the complicated tasks.

I replied that I was endeavouring to find the truth of what I was being shown.

I was asked where all my truth sat; of course, this was in my conscious soul and heart.

My guides asked if everybody accessed truth the same way. And now I had my direction.

This seemingly simple equation of how we use our soul and heart seems so simple, but it isn't. I'll share why now. It automatically opens an inner knowing in the intuition, which so many people seem to have overlooked from the outset. It is right under our noses.

Imagine we have a little problem that stops our world from going around; I'm talking about a personal love problem. We would instantly dig deep into the heart to find out why things were not working out as we desired, as this is the logical place to start, isn't it?

It is if you like an instinctive reaction, because we are reacting to an emotion that is blinding us from all else that is going on in our lives. It is the only thing in our life that we are able to focus on; everything else that we would normally do is pushed aside. One emotion stops all the other lateral thought processes, as nothing else can be concentrated on.

Yes, we might go to work, but we are spending all our thought on how to resolve the situation. But you see, we aren't thinking laterally or logically, so we can't resolve the situation.

Why aren't we thinking laterally or using our whole conscious mind? Because we are only asking a question from a smaller part of our consciousness, aren't we?

You are only asking the heart what is relevant at this time rather than using the whole of your capacity to find resolution.

Right from the outset, our question is floored. How, then, can we figure out a real solution that is the result of using all our intelligence, understanding, and knowledge?

This, of course, was not some thing I thought up. This explanation was shown to me, or I would never have comprehended the implications.

Every time we have an overly emotional issue, we could be just asking questions to a separate, unconnected part of our self. Separation results when we don't talk to our heart and soul together.

This is apparently one of the focuses of the new millennium or new-time consciousness to make us aware that we do in fact think and act quite often without using our integrated soul and heart.

This whole understanding came about when I was trying to get a true answer to a problem I couldn't figure out at the time. I asked for some help and was given this piece of understanding to figure out as the answer.

"David, answers don't bring comprehension; only questions do. You need to ask the right question."

"So I need the correct question?" I asked. I also asked how to find this question and was told that my guides and source would help. After many more questions, I reached an understanding of the initial question.

Once I comprehended this, an affirmation automatically opened in my inner knowing and just came out. Some affirmations were short, and some took around fifteen minutes to complete.

This was a natural part of my life, but I did wonder why. While I was able to resolve so many issues, it seemed strange that I was programmed with so many affirmations.

Eventually, I received the right question. "David, what do you use daily without thinking, naturally, now that you have the understanding?"

The understanding is something I had to remember from my childhood: harmonic keys and codes.

The unlocking of these keys and codes has proved to be a vast vehicle, and I must admit to being lost for the correct connotation. You see, they unlock many interesting questions, but above anything else, when finally unravelled, they provide new awareness and point to a vast future to be explained in further books.

After so many questions, my understandings led me back once again to my childhood, which I thought of as playing with energy—sensing it and seeing what it did, how it did it, where it went to, and when it did.

Don't forget that a young child does this innocently—and correctly.

This all adds up to one conscious use of energy in a correct manner— or activations, as the source calls them.

My next understanding—after countless questions and a considerable amount of time—involved figuring out which were the correct activations rather than just interfering energy.

Imagine opening a can of worms that you can't put the lid back on. Well, this is what I did, didn't I?

This then led to a barrage of questions, but the one underlying, foundational understanding was that real consciousness needed to be connected as a complete consciousness or a full circuit.

This might seem a simple enough task, but it also revealed how fragile this circuitry is in some parts of us. Why were we so fragile in so many parts of our consciousness?

My next quest was to find out how to make our consciousness and our whole spiritual and physical makeup strong, how to create harmonious current flowing in the correct manner. This also led to my being shown some rather amazing revelations that I had never considered, about how inharmonious current debilitates us in so many ways.

These debilitating malfunctions were a real challenge to get my head around. What was shown to me made sense, but if it was correct, then we were going to be very vulnerable in some areas of our energy.

This vulnerability meant that we could easily be feeling these interferences in our daily lives, either mentally or physically, without a clue that they were contributing to our everyday life—but definitely not to our welfare.

I was shown how the unconscious and subconscious were affecting us. Yes, I may have blabbed on and on about what might seem a trivial point of view, but each of these points has major repercussions that probably have never been evident.

Don't think I'm an alarmist; I'm only showing or sharing some new self-awareness that most of us are unaware of. Eliminate what we are unaware of, and we instantly become stronger. We are able to cope in this ever-changing world and to find huge self-potentials that we never had a clue about.

Once we connect to these potentials in an aware manner, then we are able to also connect to many aspects of life that we have been missing out on.

If there is something else you would rather be doing with your life, perhaps it might help if you to those conscious activations that will help create the life you are asking for. But is this what your *energy* is asking for?

One of the benefits of this awareness is that you are able to find happiness in being you. This means that you're not only at peace with who you are but with *why* you are you and what is in your makeup that you love so dearly. This is simply appreciation, isn't it? Do you appreciate your own personal abilities?

Perhaps you could also think about it this way as well. Once you know all that you're conscious of, you might find different aspects of yourself to appreciate; you might actually have some compassion for yourself.

This doesn't mean being selfish; it means living up to who you really are, opening huge potentials that you simply aren't aware of but your self desires to activate. Remember, this all started out with the desire to use the soul and heart together and not in a separate manner. Do you desire this strength for yourself?

I was directed to this as the foundation of my strength, the way to access all self-truth, not just for the past but for my future and my present life.

This is important, isn't it? We need all the help we can get with our future, don't we? This is just something my guides wanted you to understand from the outset, and I have never taken this message for granted.

Another awareness that my guides desire to share with you is a tithing, a way to learn how to sense these activations of real energy.

This is a physical exercise, not just a spiritual one, meant to open many receptors that aren't being used at present but are sitting within the self-collective consciousness.

To help with this understanding, we will need to initiate new-time key's and codes so that we aren't limited to just rehashing the past or old-time cycles again.

This helps us to be able to look into the deepest recesses of our self. It is a self that is only working at a fraction of its capacity and stops us from identifying where we could be focusing and maximizing our energy as self-potential. This corrupts our currents, so we don't really examine the environment that we are sitting in, and we don't receive all that could be gravitating to us.

This means that we don't notice certain interferences, such as our minds always being turned on to full speed and chewing up anything that's in our energy field.

You see, we seem to have forgotten that we are really a lot larger than just our chakra, aura, or meridians indicate at the moment, and that there are many different energies connected to many self-aspects.

This is a reason for writing this book, but it is far from being the whole reason, although it is where so many different activations of our self start from.

When we look a little more closely at this energy, we find many different reasons as to why we do certain things and, more importantly, why we connect to only a fraction of our potential. This may seem drawn out, but comprehending where our selves are coming up short is important.

My guides have pushed certain issues of unidentified self-confrontation. This unawareness basically blinds our reasoning and our ability to judge self-truth, and it affects our responses.

Finding what is true for our self is important, isn't it? The inability to correctly understand our own energy has often debilitated us. This debilitation means we can't find out what our energy is really doing, which is necessary to give us new a direction to connect us to so many self-potentials.

I would like to introduce you to how this interpretation came about.

# 7

## A NEW-TIME PERSONAL ACTIVATION

More than any other activation, this one is very personal and comes from an intimate understanding. It was the first activation that meant much to me, and it freed many aspects of my self way beyond intuition.

This activation is all about peace to the self, and though it might sound corny, you can't be at peace when you're unaware that you are sitting in an existence and living in pieces. How strange it is that so many parts of ourselves are in constant conflict, and we're unaware of it.

Awareness is a rare gift that we often underrate. Perhaps we don't take notice because it may tell us something we don't accept as truth. The alternative is that we are only able to know it exists if it hits us right in the face and says, *Hey, I'm here; remember me.*

Awareness is a sort of intuition with many connections, and everybody's is different.

If you are repeating a life lesson, how many times have already you gone through this cycle? Countless times, if you consider the many lives in which we have repeated the same mistake over and over again.

Awareness is linked to these cycles of repetition, and when we are on the correct path, self-focus is in tune, as are so many conscious aspects of our self.

Perhaps you can imagine a whole self that is unable to communicate with you, as your vibration is not high enough at the moment to integrate this self. These parts that aren't in tune sit in separation, and this out-of-tune self is unable to contribute.

Imagine a body that is somewhere between the self that needs a higher vibrational frequency and a body that is already at this higher vibrational frequency. This in-between body is a modulator or harmonizer for communicating in the correct time frame. Over many lifetimes, vital parts of our resources became unable to create harmony. How could they in their state of separation?

Let's move to the next image. Each time we desire to sense harmony or balance, we find that this is impossible due to missing parts. This also explains why you feel incomplete, in disarray, or unable to articulate how or what is missing in the self.

We can follow this line of perception and add that if some part of us seems missing, then we desire to fill the void. Seeing that a major part of our spirit is unable to communicate, we want to fill this gap with physical stuff. This can mean buying stuff, working on physical jobs, or surrounding yourself with people. All of these are forms of consumption meant to fill the void of what is separate in your life.

Would you like to respond to this interpretation?

You see, our self-spirit is a wonderful part of our self; it is the basis of our strength of purpose, our direction to find synchronicity. In fact, our spirit helps us connect to many self-aspects that aren't separate but are present and functioning right now.

*Presence* is simply a state of using all self-abilities to the best purpose possible, with the best resources possible, to create the best response or whatever needs to be created in a present sense rather than a past feeling.

Well, this simply means that many of your abilities are connected to your spirit. Use what you have to create enormous amounts of current, and begin to reconnect to the separated parts again. Stop whining about what you don't have, and use what you do.

Remember that you are unable to create with what you don't have, so use and enjoy what you do have, and then the rest can gravitate to you.

To help this along, though, remember this: by being still and thinking—rather than dreaming—where your next step is going to take you, a lot of automatic results happen.

By connecting to your self while in a still state, many questions are answered. Yes, this is when you are connecting to your own self-spirit, which is the highest-vibrating self-version of a self-collective consciousness.

When you connect this self-connective consciousness to the connective consciousness of all that exists, then you are asking if it is possible for this sequence to be created, fixed, or healed—or whatever term you want to apply. Remember, you do this unconsciously. How would you like to do this consciously?

This is just another conscious foundation to be connected to. When we still our self, we use self-consciousness more efficiently, and then we are negating all the cycles where you used your conscious inefficiently.

This is how we create self-faith and belief—by creating as strong a communication of consciousness as possible. This is another true foundation of our self-awareness.

Using the energy that communicates to our highest self facilitates a real connection to our whole body, which just keeps unlocking our self-potential, our abilities, and all that we desire to create for our self. This makes all miracles possible. Do you comprehend this statement?

By now you may have detected that there has been a fair presence of source help in explaining this concept. Were you aware of perhaps a few tones that where vibrating in your ears?

These tones may become more detectable when you relax or are stilling yourself. Please let me expand on that stilling, helping you relearn how to use your consciousness. With the many abilities that you have, this takes practice, but the benefits are huge.

Vibrations and frequencies can be transferred. This is what the tones are: a source harmonizer to share the rising frequency as you open your self body to communicates more easily with your higher-vibrating self. The body is able to talk to the higher frequencies that open so many self-abilities.

The benefit of this is twofold. First, it helps you connect to the self-harmony that enables you to still yourself more easily. Second, the tones raise your frequency to encourage separated aspects of your self to realign or reconnect.

Perhaps you could also perceive this as a foundational harmony, opening your self-perceptions to receive all higher-vibrational frequencies. These not only help you, but raise the frequency in your whole home.

Remember, as you raise the frequencies in your home, you attract like frequencies. There is a lot of room to explore this topic, but if you raise your vibrations, it makes sense that you would rather live in this kind of environment.

Yes, this effect will expand as your frequency does. We will discuss this later as well.

At this moment, though, there are a few new harmonies now presently ready to be shared with you. Some of you may sense that an energy in your back is pulling you backward. This only means that you are reconnecting to whole self-aspects that will help you. If you sense calmness soon, this is why. If this is not possible at the moment, it will happen when you are ready. Essentially, the knowledge of how to still yourself is reconnecting to your self.

To help this along, just imagine that you are lying down. Notice how your breathing wants to slow. Don't worry. You won't stop breathing, but you will sense how a greater mass of your self is coming together.

Now, when you desire to be more connected in a now presence, it will be much easier.

When you ground something, it stays with you. Ground an activation and it desires to stay current and moving and to be utilized in a conscious, contributing manner. Of course, this happens immediately.

Please clasp your hands physically to stabilise this tithing balance. Yes, you are responding a little differently. Now hold this clasping exercise until your consciousness raises all self-expectations.

Once again, as this initiates and is complete, your legs will sense a release behind the knees. Thus you are now presently current.

Let's approach something new about us, something that relates to how special we are. People often laugh when I tell them how important they are—and I do mean out-loud, falling-off-the-table laughter. At this point, I am talking to their soul and heart verbally and with my consciousness.

I then move to a point that they are afraid to look at. How strange it is that people really laugh uncontrollably about being of value. Yes, I am joking about it with them, but the release is always the same. Why?

I mentioned that the very first activation I connected to was very personal, which indicated that I wanted to change myself without knowing it.

I was having a meditation after dinner one night, rediscovering what I used to do naturally. I had remembered how to use my whole body to interpret, but I was aware that I had forgotten a vital piece of the jigsaw.

When you look through your body, do you concentrate on your chakra or aura? I used to do this. Then I thought, *Just go straight to the soul*—that rather beautiful, green energy on the left side of my body, which was at that time a small ball of energy near my navel.

Of course, I needed to include my heart, which was where I saw a beautiful blue energy on my right. (Hang on, I thought it was pink. "Not in your spirit body, David," I was told.)

I remembered how I used to sort of play with this energy as a child and could see what was connected. But I wasn't expecting the flurry of energy that happened next.

"David, your spirit energy is needing some attention." I then noticed how my soul and heart expanded. I was all green on one side and blue on the other, and a sense of love just enveloped me.

I did, however, notice that my eyes were all white. "That is correct, David. You are receiving new insight." I gave out a very long *ah* that went on for ages. I was connecting back to how I remembered myself, and it was like coming home.

Yes, I looked like my old self again, when my soul and heart had intertwined. I then saw another part of my spirit beneath that matched the top half, only the other way around. This automatically joined in as well.

"This is your androgynous energy, a vital balancing component that is needed when conceiving all real self-matter and how you came to be."

Back to my indigo self-colour, I was also aware that much of myself was now unfolding. "This is your true spirit, David, yes."

Automatically, I said one profound sentence that was to change so much. Yes, I channeled this. "Now I am present in the presence of my self-spirit."

This was to unlock so much confusion in my life, but at the time I didn't know it. I was just grateful to be how I remembered I had been as a child. If you have been seeking your inner child, perhaps this is the missing part you are seeking—real self-spirit. If I were a car, this would be the source of my super-charger.

From that night on, I was able to channel in a whole new light. So many answers to the questions that had been bugging me became clear, and as you clear a few, you're able to clear many. What I'm indicating here is that this is a vital foundation that I had been shown.

Put into a new context, vital foundations awaken us to be aware of all that exists in us. Therefore, we are not focusing on all that is in existence separate from us.

In the past, this has played out rather differently for a few obvious reasons. Whenever we are separated from something, what is our immediate reaction? I want it *now*, not later.

This has one rather large ramification on us. It reopens our instinct or goes back into the past to find the missing aspects that we know exist but are unconscious of.

Those of you who have become aware of this might have felt this sensation of sliding back to past instinct. Do you see how you were almost shocked that this actually happened?

Don't worry. You are back to the heightened vibration as before, only now you are stronger, as you are more aware in that present self-consciousness that you desire to follow.

There is another scenario to unfold, using our intuition instead of our instinct, as instinct is physical memory, not a conscious memory of our spirit.

Now that you have been able to share in how I reconnected to my spirit to become present in a continuous manner, perhaps we can discuss how this changes things in the greater scheme of things.

I was immediately aware that if this spirit was missing from my life, then a lot of my self-worth wouldn't be present, as the self-spirit had the strength to open new senses of self-worth that had not been present before.

I don't mean this in a selfish manner, but when you are able to recognise that there are many aspects of you to appreciate, then you are able to have a greater understanding of your own makeup, I guess.

Once you begin to understand your own makeup, you are able to rationalise what is really of worth to you. Thus you are able to create a strength of self that is now more conscious, as you are now more aware that it exists. Does this make sense?

Now I would like to visit the *now-presence* and show the difference between *now* and *now-presence*. Every time you ask for or demand something *now*, are you aware that this relates more to the past than the present?

Why? Well, we have had many *now* times in the past already. How many times have you said, "I want it right now"? I didn't comprehend this at the start either, so I'll let my guides do this bit.

"At this moment in time, there is a great misunderstanding that is, in truth, dividing how your spirit is able to be present now. I am Uriel, and throughout time, each and every one of you has debilitated yourselves by holding on to unresolved past-life issues. You desire to fix up your past mistakes and all that you have been unconsciously separate from.

"Each of you holds gratitude for all that is physical, as this is easily sensed, but gratitude for your spirit has been undetectable, due to the separations of spirit senses that align to all forms of self-worth.

"This simply means that the spirit that directs your physical nature is not moving in a *now* direction but in a direction toward the places of separation. This is why you concentrate on past resolutions and not on the present; you are unaware that you desire to be whole again in your spirit.

"Remember, if you are unresolved in spirit, then you are unable to connect to your true physical nature. This is why your life seems devoid of worth. Without senses, your life is becoming senseless, yes, so you are unable to connect to true, conscious matter, which matters."

"This is another reason for the new millennium to raise the vibrations and bring to awareness all that you are in fact separate from. This is why each and every one of you is experiencing undiagnosable responses to what seems like physical discomfort.

"Love, Uriel"

Every part of this translation has a different frequency to it. This is like receiving a healing that was needed to raise all self-expectations.

While this translation seemed clear, I guess I still need to outline a couple of points. If we were separate in each lifetime from a major part of our spirit, then we desire to reconnect to it.

The manner in which we interpret this is an indication that we desire to move physically back to where we assume this took place so we can reconnect. This is how a major part of our self can get stuck in the past.

These parts of us that are stuck in the past are the reason so many of us interpret multidimensional feelings, when really you are just reconnecting to past life experiences—or lots of *nows*.

Yes, multidimensional energy exists, but you need senses of a higher vibration and frequency to be able to interpret this, ensuring that you are not in fact just revisiting past life.

There is an immense reason for what I have just unveiled. So many people think, *Oh, isn't this fantastic? I just went through the third or fourth dimension.* But in reality, this is just past-life awareness of being unaware.

Does this explanation fly with you? Do you realize that you are connecting to resentments that hold on to past issues? This is what you are revisiting.

So, how do we *not* revisit them? There is nothing to be gained by continually revisiting past regrets or resentment, is there? It just eats away at you, so your spirit directs you away from hurting yourself or being disappointed again.

This is a preview of where you desire to go and where you have no need to go, as they are cycles of the past. There is no need to make them current.

Do you see how relevant your spirit is in the grand scheme of things. It is vital in self-direction.

We are going to revisit a formula shared before. You see, this means that you follow your own formula and not somebody else's.

Remember, the greater mass of people have loads of separated conscious. The greater mass is also not using their spirit. In a way, the greater mass is asking your own personal alignment to gravitate toward not using your spirit sense.

I'll give you a better idea of this. In your left hand is the mass of your spirit; in your right hand is the mass of others not desiring to use their self-spirit. The mass of others can influence your decisions and weight them down slowly.

This is a new awareness, isn't it? Don't freak out. We can change this quickly. Once again, the mass in your left hand is gaining strength. Check it and see that it is heavier but not denser. Also, it is rising.

This is where your mass desires to follow. Now, twist your hands so that they are facing each other and bring them together. As you do, they might want to come up like a prayer stance, so let them. Automatically you will be grounding this self-desire to gain strength in all self-faith and belief.

For those who meditate regularly or who are in touch with their intuition, this grounding will be more intense, as you are asking so many more aspects of your consciousness to participate.

Don't be surprised if you start seeing a metallic, indigo colour throughout your self. You will see this with your eyes open. A new environment is stabilising about you. This will open quite a few reconnecting senses, so watch for small changes of awareness.

This changing of awareness relates to everybody. Small changes soon become larger, as inner strength helps the greater mass of your body to work in sync with your energy.

To sum this up another way, imagine the mass of unconsciousness of humanity. Now imagine the mass of what we are aware and conscious of, which holds the greater mass.

Remember the unconscious mass in the left hand, how dense it was. Well, the gravity of this mass is enticing you magnetically to join it and raise your vibration. Then you are automatically less susceptible to denser interference.

Please remember that this life is not a level playing field like it is in a sporting competition. If you were to round up everything you did in the previous match before you played the next one, imagine how much you would change. But what is the sense of being wise *after* the match? The next match will not be an exact repeat or have exactly the same plays.

Next, add the dilemma of having different players. Some of these don't always follow the same rules you do, so of course ethics comes into play.

All of a sudden, we are noticing influences different from last time. Damn, there's another cycle mixed up in this one, which makes matters even more confusing.

Who would have thought that awareness could become so complicated? Believe me, this is a complicated affair at present, but there is a way to simplify it.

This is how to have real awareness. This is something the source has been getting you used to in every sentence thus far, preparing you.

Separation is the fundamental cause of every pain. We don't want to experience this, so we push the separation further away, or we become unconscious that we are in fact holding on to the pain.

You see, whatever the pain, we always pretend that it will go away. However, the issue doesn't go away when it's treated this way.

An issue that causes mental anguish is dense, not of a high vibration, and it is definitely not something you desire to hold on to. But when you do, there is a fair chance that you will repeat the scenario again. In a way, you are inadvertently holding this dense schedule as something you desire.

In the core of your soul, you have the ability change this. Are you aware of this?

Before you ask if this is correct, I had better give you an image of how it looks.

Imagine a corkscrew-type energy, which is what much of our selves are made of. Now, cut the current and see what happens. Remember, this is a sped-up version. The coil becomes straight and can hold no current. Being straight now, it holds little strength. Then it is severed.

Next, the coil receives too much of one current and none of another. It constricts or contracts, depending on the pulse.

These are all terms for what happens to *us*. I wonder why.

Gravity allows us to channel in a sensory consciousness each and every day, which is sometimes time-consuming, but it does allow us to uncover some good knowledge.

Consider the energy of this word *gravity* and the implications of not giving much appreciation to such a word. Gravity should also be implicated with awareness.

As with all current, you are able to create a magnetic polarity that either attracts or repels.

This is all dependent on your structural integrity. If your foundations of spirit are strong, you attract; if they are weak, you repel. It's not complicated.

Now we will venture back to the pain issue. If we use the power within the soul to create strength, the heart converts this to the correct magnetic polarity.

The integrated soul and heart are then able to perceive that this pain is not desired, so all self-consciousness is cut off from it.

We are made of consciousness, so if unconscious energy is causing pain, we check to see if the unconscious is coming from us. If not, we ensure that it is cut off, and the pain subsides.

Now for the complicated bit. What if we are holding on to this pain for many lifetimes, and it is an unresolved issue that we are holding on to in an unaware way? All the previous tithing affirmations are meant to release the unresolved past that you are unaware of, just as you are unaware of the immense strength that is held within the soul and heart when combined as one energy.

You see, if I had told you that many people mix past-life levels with real, multidimensional self-presence, do you think you would be as aware of why this actually happens?

Without real, conscious senses, it is impossible to create the foundational senses that enable the conscious multi-sensory perception to differentiate between past-life separation and real multidimensional energy.

Conscious and unconscious awareness and our real desires and intentions create a sense of self-integrity, ethics, and balanced self-worth.

To be a creation of conscious self-awareness, able to sense where you are consciously connected—this is a direction for this new millennium.

Awareness of reason creates a strength of purpose, and at the end of the day, we all desire purpose over blind faith, don't we?

This is a foundational presence that the source desires us to follow, to ensure that there is a conscious reason for all we connect to.

Open yourself to conscious awareness, and then you will never blindly connect to any energy without sensing all that is attached. This also opens your self to the basic understanding of how we become connected to attachments.

I simply desire to connect you to the source. Then you will understand how our energy is absolutely relevant to comprehending what is really going on in our lives from many perspectives. This helps to chop down the illogical mythology and to find relevant meaning in every aspect of our real self.

If you miss out on the interference that makes life more complicated, you also miss some of the most fantastic contributions. These fantastic essences and elements are the foundations to the real, absolute, true connections—the doors to real multidimensional presence.

The foundational desire of the source is to ensure that there are no secrets that can become self-barriers.

Imagine a barrier that keeps your real current away from where it needs to connect to. Energy just builds up, doesn't it? The same is happening on the other side as well—a growing mass of resentment over not being able to complete a desired circuitry. This creates a mass of energy on both sides of the barrier.

This mass of energy then short-circuits other circuits as it grows. If we understand that a barrier is there, we can often just ask to neutralize it, and it will disappear, which is probably something that in a past life stopped us from achieving a goal.

This is one of my pet dislikes: people who never desire to share fantastic knowledge. It is also something I prefer to laugh about these days, for so many reasons. Why would I not share in a tithing manner? I would basically be cutting my source off.

People desire to use knowledge as multiple sources of current or to use their power in an unethical way. Hence the worth of one's self is instantly split or limited.

But we are also free to learn by our mistakes.

This is something I learned many moons ago, which was something of an intuition, so the knowledge keeps flowing, not stagnating. As soon as I find something great, I desire to share it with others.

I am certainly not saying it is wrong to receive in a tithing manner all that you have learned. I am, however, implying that it is wise to use this knowledge, not as a controlling tool but as a tool to free.

As you probably surmised, this came as a hint from the source, not so much from me. However, it does come straight from my absolute soul and heart. If I am able to help someone connect in any manner, form, or function, no matter how small, then I have received much joy. Everything I desire to share makes me a very happy person.

To understand this happiness, you need to be able to comprehend real, multidimensional appreciation—gratitude and compassion—as there is no comprehensible way to describe this in a real sense.

I hope words are adequate to share some of this understanding with you. Then you can connect to an innermost comprehension so deep inside you that it awakens a beauty that can only be sensed and never explored with an emotion or feeling.

When this connection occurs, I will be more than just happy. I will really, really know that this world is going to be a much better place than any I was conceived in, and I have had a fortunate life.

Why do I consider this life of mine to be so fortunate? Simply, I am able comprehend in a real manner how many sources of worth are integrated to become a collective consciousness. I hope that you can one day appreciate this too.

This may sound a little bit out-there, so before you consider me too loopy, please let me elaborate.

We must venture back, and we are only able to do so now that you have so many different understandings into a more conscious self-presence. This opened your awareness, so you are ready to be a lot more aware of what actually exists in the you, without knowing it exists.

No more mucking about. Let's get right into this. I described earlier how I was able to comprehend how and what people around me were going through in their lives. I also described being set free and put into a state of peace. Well, by now you all are aware of how much you actually channel each and every day, since the source and I have opened it up to you in a few different ways.

Really, we have only scratched the surface, but now you have enough foundations to receive a little extra peace for yourselves. Not only does this open a sense of peace that perhaps you haven't felt before; it also opens you to a self-understanding that leads to inner peace as well.

All states of peace are created by inner strength—the desired piece in the foundational jigsaw—that we desire to put into place. By now you may have interpreted how much strength can be gained by making use of your spirit.

To enhance the strength of spirit, we engage the understanding that if you use many levels of consciousness at one time, a greater strength is created. The tricky part is to actually get this to happen, and this only happens with everything being in one place at one time in a continuous manner.

So we introduced synchronicity and affirmed the need for this to be always present in the self-presence.

Next, we discussed the need to be aware that we do not want to repeat past-life mistakes, and we definitely don't want to add to these mistakes with resentment or the inability to achieve.

Now, with this little round-up, I hope that we are all on the same page.

Many people seem to think that consciousness is something retained in the head. Why? Because we have so many sensitive or over-sensitive parts all in one area.

Consciousness is held in every particle of the body, not just the head. Remember, we are made of or from a collective consciousness, aren't we? Any part of the body not made of conscious matter would, in a way, cease to exist. I don't know about you, but I enjoy my body as it is.

Consider how we ground or treat our bodies in meditation. We desire to connect to many parts or energies represented as bursts of colour. In a way, we also desire to connect to the elements and essences represented in our bodies, and I am being very general here.

As we connect to this energy, we are often in a hurry to connect to our head. We want to feel how the energy spurts out through the portal at the top of our heads and watch a clean energy flow like a fountain. We are clearing everything in our auras, chakras, or meridians. Hopefully, we bring this energy back to where this started from and re-ground it.

What have we forgotten to do? This is so very important. Got any ideas? Well, we have left our self open to invasion, so to speak. Did you bother to put energy into that rather large portal at the top of your head, or is it gaping wide open? Sometimes it closes when we ground, and sometimes it doesn't. It depends on how expansively you have connected.

Actually, you may have inadvertently connected to something not consciously connected. You could have connected to one or many points of separated consciousness.

Imagine parts of your consciousness that you aren't communicating with. These are still an energetic part of yourself makeup, but they are sitting outside your body's energy field. This is a scary thought, isn't it? It is an affliction I see in so many people who walk through my door.

So, with a bit of luck, your portal would have closed, and not too much was able to invade you or add interfering thought patterns. For now, we will assume that not much was able to come in at all—a close call!

Let's look at one scenario. We all know that when we relax our physical bodies, we connect more to our spirit bodies as we sleep. What exactly do we connect to when we sleep?

This depends on a couple of thing. As children, we are more consciously aware of our spirit bodies. Consider that if you are more aware, you also tend to explore, don't you? If you have something, you tend to use it to see what it can do.

When a child is seen as a dreamer, it is sometimes because the spirit side is more attractive to him than the physical. The child may also be spiritually gifted, so to speak—an indigo who is very connected to the real aspects of themselves. In this case, there is every possibility that this will be a very strong child indeed.

The other side of the coin is the child I usually see—the one who has connected to a few of the separated parts. This child may become a little more withdrawn, but not always. He will be aware and annoyed by this energy but is usually unaffected because of the strength of his spirit.

When I see such children, it is more often the parents who need help than the child, and they are very aware of this. I'll expand on this later.

Another scenario applies to the bulk of us, even the gifted ones. When we relax, we connect more to our spirit bodies. Notice I said *relax*, not sleep. In this relaxed state, we connect to our intuition or the strength of this body. We can start doing the same thing when we sleep. Yes, I said *start*. At the start, we connect to our conscious strength. If we have some issue we are trying to resolve, we may go deeper into the subconscious.

You do appreciate how deep you are at present. While in this state, it is not possible to venture out through the portal at the top of your head; the spirit strength is just too strong.

The flip side of this scenario concerns us all. Imagine that we are having a beautiful sleep. There were a couple of things concerning us during the previous day, but nothing to get uptight about. The week before, though, was pure hell, and the stress levels were maxing us out. While in this sleep-state, we became restless, looking for answers. The people we were dealing with were quite uncooperative and hostile, and at times, very aggressive.

While looking for answers to this hypothetical problem while sleeping, we can make contact with another consciousness rather than the unconscious. This is an in-consciousness that isn't really attached, and it is sitting more in the energy about us. In-conscious energy is separated, and as such it sits right outside our body. I was surprised at this the first time I encountered it.

Separated consciousness is rather susceptible to the mass energy of others' separated energy.

You might be living clean, but imagine the density of people who consume loads of booze, prescription drugs, and illegal drugs, and they also contribute to the greater dense consciousness of humanity. This unconsciousness might be contributing to your own separated consciousness. Can you factor in this revelation, or is it a bit too way-out for you to factor in?

This means that a part of the real consciousness is asking why there isn't enough strength to solve this problem. Thus, connections are sent out in all directions to find extra strength.

Problems can occur when your real or connected consciousness is unaware of the consequences of reconnecting to separated consciousness or extra sources of unconscious energy.

Take into account that this consciousness is way outside your chakra or aura, though it is still partly connected by your meridians. This in-consciousness is vulnerable to interference, as there is little protection where it sits outside your self-energy field or environment, so you will be unaware and unable to sense the conflicting energy influencing your unconscious energy.

This isn't the prettiest of scenarios, but I believe in showing all that is happening. You can't do a damn thing about what you are unaware of, can you? Now, perhaps you see why you needed relevant preparations to strengthened you beforehand.

We are then able to ascertain that the contributions of the in-consciousness don't help—quite the opposite, in fact, when we factor in the interferences experienced by the in-consciousness. If this happens a few times, then quite an amount of interference is about to occur.

If this person also enjoys a drink—or many—everything is sped up and expanded. Now there is an immense amount of interference to contend with. Why?

Because a few of your energy defence mechanisms are sitting wide open, or your strength of consciousness has more of an unconscious aspect to it now. Your consciousness is taking on more of an unconscious aspect, and you just lost the damn strength in all that you worked so hard to retain.

This is where I want to be blunt and almost hit some people with a brick to wake them up. If having a couple of drinks separates your consciousness, what do you think drugs do?

If we take into account that we make up a collective consciousness, then losing our consciousness is like killing ourselves off. This is another reason for the new millennium: to wake people up.

If there is little strength of consciousness—not to mention a mass of confused matter interfering in all forms of communication—is it any wonder that so many people suffer irritability, anxiety, fear, isolation, or abandonment? Are you seeing how this correlates to a lack of self-strength of consciousness?

If we consider this *mental* excommunication, imagine when it becomes a *physical* matter.

There is a reason this energy is more than likely to leave certain elements of itself open.

Interference blocks communication or current so that no message gets through. This is because the self wants to find a peaceful solution, one that involves a disconnect wherever it experiences discomfort or influence from a past life.

Because the past-life element rehashes everything, any symptom is then magnified. All past *nows* combine. It's an interesting and complicated situation. Why? Lack of strength in the self-spirit that is relayed to the physical.

Once you explain to your real consciousness where it is stuffed up, this element of yourself comprehends where the problem is.

The "when" factor will kick in with the strength, which is totally able to free every aspect of interference.

With this understanding, perhaps we are moving in new territory, for the explanations you have received to prepare you will be linked to the activations you are about to receive.

The following tithing should be read in a quiet and comfortable place to facilitate ease of connection.

With absolute freedom of self-peace, I open all self-presence to receive all truth of tithings throughout this whole self.

I ask to connect all self-reality to a new time of security with all self-energy and to receive all true collective consciousness direction.

This truth is resonating with true self, reflecting with new purpose to a new time of connecting to each and every facet of real self-love.

All self-disintegration reflecting innermost self-peace has been replaced with new-time strength of purpose.

All natural, creative natures absorbed with each and every creative element are now rejuvenating and regenerating, with all collective appreciation freeing each and every aspect of real self-wealth.

All creative endeavours now only reflect real matter in a real manner of gratitude.

All strength of self comes only from within. This compassion of self is reflected in each and every aspect of real self-wealth.

Love always.

This affirmation—for those not familiar with or used to receiving them—opens up and frees the self-energy lines or grids. To explain this in the simplest of terms, this is the understanding Sordlion passed on to me.

Everything in life has energy; absolutely nothing is exempt—not rock, thought, tree, or air. All contain energy.

Now, relate this to how our energy is working at present. It will explain a lot if we dissect it so it's understandable. This, in a way, is what we have already been doing, but to appreciate the outcome of some simple resolutions, we need to take the complicated elements out to see real logic.

Multiply the amount of energy stored in this life or even a past life. This could add up to an enormous amount of energy. And what is this energy doing?

Now that we are on a roll, perhaps you can grasp the amount of stagnation, constriction, and restriction this would cause in your body at this moment—absolutely enormous amounts. Now you might just be able to unravel a clue given to us eons ago that was so plain and simple that we were totally unable to fathom it: Get rid of the baggage and release the clutter in your life. We need to be able to interpret clearly; we need to be able to translate what is really being said.

Amazing isn't it?

This is another familiarization exercise that I hope will help you to experiencing the sensation of moving energy.

Slowly, in your own time and your own way, you will relearn what your energy is telling you; this will be automatic. For many of you, this will be instantaneous. This, of course, depends on how you have stored your past-life energy.

Please hold your left hand out to receive the sense we are seeking: a spinning sensation in the palm of your hand.

This is a notification from your innermost spirit to sense energy in a different manner. Even if you are used to using energy, this is still intended to reactivate senses you are not used to interpreting. It's a different connective consciousness that is to connect to an automatic knowing within.

There is one immense challenge here, though. You are not to control the energy that sits in the palm of your hand. The controlling nature of your past will almost certainly want you to play with this energy. You must resist. This is like saying, "Don't touch; it's hot," while there is a part of you that is compelled to find out if it's true.

If you have played with it because you couldn't resist, you may need to repeat the exercise; or simply put the book down for a while to let your energy settle.

Assuming that old-time patterns have not interfered, this new time-energy will soon present itself. The sense will be like a ball of energy traveling up your arm, into this orb, and on to parts of non-separated, real, conscious knowing.

For some of you, the sensation will venture to a point behind the eyes; for others, it my sit at the base of your throat.

Repeat this exercise with the right hand. You will not even get a chance to tamper with the energy this time, as the transition will be immediate.

The results will mirror the previous ones, although for those whose energy has stopped at the base of the throat, the second orb will free itself from where it was stuck and gravitate to where it belongs.

For this next exercise, please plant both feet firmly on the floor, and clasp your hands in front of your navel. You will immediately sense two orbs traveling from the soles of your feet to the same point behind your eyes.

Now—or later on when you relax—you may sense a draining of energy. This is to facilitate a broader sense of self-perspective, so you can appreciate that perhaps there is more to you than meets the eye.

The consciousness you have received connects to an innermost knowing that opens many levels of consciousness and frees connections from interference. These levels may almost seem to stem from different regions within the brain, but the actual interference is way beyond this.

The reason you sense this in all the head regions is that the energy passing through alienates this overly sensitive area. It is overly sensitive because wrong current frequencies create a magnetic dragging effect.

This has quite an effect in this region, as it is a point of polarity—a little like the North Pole.

Don't think for a moment that we only have two points of polarity on our head and feet; we have thousands. But we will only touch on this at the moment.

The main point to concern ourselves with is this: due to old-time, restrictive energy movements, the head region is just more open to interference. These interferences are not something that you want to keep repeating, and your own personal guides are helping you to re-ground.

Align yourself with the sinking sensation to ensure that the separated consciousness is aligned with the strength of your self-purpose. This is where the self-will and determination comes from.

Put into terms we understand, this means that you desire to follow your spirit-direction, which is now integrated with your physical nature, so you know more intuitively what you want.

Now would be a great time to put the book down for a while and take a break. I do mean this. Take a break of no less than thirty minutes, please. Give yourself a chance to stabilise. That separated consciousness has been separated for quite some time. Give yourself time to adjust.

If you do persist in reading on, just read this chapter again until you stabilize; but the choice is yours.

No, I'm not joking.

Now that you have had a break, we can continue our discussion. You see, if you had kept reading, you would have undone the entire great work the source has passed on to you.

We are now able to reopen parts we discussed before, but also to just expand on the past understandings or add a different interpretation. This means that the energy that is meant to flow together will now have gaping holes in the actual flow. These are not actual portals, but the effect can be similar, in that unwanted interference is able to flow in.

To more clearly define this sequence of flow, imagine two flows, close together, but one is now more negative and the other is more positive. The current's polarity will push them apart. The result is this: unlike when you relaxed, interfering energy is now able to pop in whenever it likes.

For the next interpretation, imagine this opening in many layers under a real, open portal. Unconscious energy is now flowing out, so are you comprehending real anxiety, many types of fears, and lack of self-direction, which relate to lack of self-love and lack of self-strength.

This isn't the prettiest scenario, but it is something many people live with to an extreme every day. We all have the milder version somewhere, pushing a button we weren't expecting. The good part is that we also have some automatic restoring mechanisms, and these are what we want to connect to.

I'm just trying to open your eyes to how the source explained certain little inconsistencies of current, or why I sensed this or that irregularity.

Where does this lead us to now? I and my guides were connecting you to many activations to smooth out your flows. Would you like to see what we are talking about?

Hold the middle finger of your left hand just touching the top of your head for about twenty seconds. Now point this finger under your right armpit.

Next, move your finger up and down the length of your hand. Repeat this seven or eight times; then just hold your hand here a moment. Why?

Some of you will sense an outpouring of energy. This energy is a little dense and holds a few built-up emotions in it, so your head might want to drop.

Your hand will feel like it wants to let go, so let it. Of course, we now repeat this on the other side.

A couple of sensations may be evident—tingles on the face or the back, or perhaps a releasing in the neck region.

For some of you who work with energy regularly, a few new tones might appear. You will be reactivating energy parts in a more conscious way.

The whole idea of this exercise is to avoid an energy reaction, which is a good reason not to speed-read and miss these stabilizing tones that follow the reactivating tones.

Remember that law you learned in school: for every action there must be an equal and opposite reaction. This is to limit all reactions. It might only be interpreted by you as energy transference, but when this is interpreted deeper in the physical, it will be a chemical reaction at some stage. So, we are just avoiding the chemical effects—or the rebounding, if you like.

Any tool that helps with any kind of rebounding is more than just a precautionary measure. You may want to write this down as a reminder and put it on your fridge with a magnet.

Every time you have a healing, massage, or acupuncture, you are going to be releasing toxins. So, how are you going to get rid of them efficiently and minimise the side effects? If you don't release the toxic effects, you can relive the emotions through rebounding. This is something to think about if you're a healer of any description.

Rebounding undoes all the good work, effort, and energy that we desire to connect to and use in a purposeful way. Please have a go at this. It does work.

Here is the secret, which has also been recommended—much to our surprise—in a couple of other books. Cut up three lemons and allow them to soak for an hour with enough water to cover them.

Draw yourself a warm bath, add your lemons to the water, and have a good soak for at least twenty minutes. If you sense a little burning, take a shower afterward.

You will be surprised at how good you feel.

This also helps those who want to give up smoking. If I ever do really strenuous exercise, I usually make a point of having a lemon bath. The next day, I'm not even slightly stiff. It's a pretty cheap detoxifier, I would say, and one that really works.

Write it down now before you forget. Drinking lemon-water or juice doesn't have the same effect even slightly, so don't put it in your head that it will.

You may consider that I rave on sometimes, and I admit I do when I know something works. If I am helping clients with any emotional burdens, I will always ask first off if they have access to a bath. Occasionally someone may not have a bath, though they are usually tourists, so I almost insist that they come back the next day and use mine.

Even after I rave about the lemon bath, some clients have thought it unnecessary. They usually ring up to say how great they felt for a week or so, but they wonder why they don't feel good anymore.

The conversation is always the same. "You didn't have the lemon bath that I indicated you needed to release the toxins, did you?" They invariably say, "I didn't think it was that important." The amount of effort I take to explain things doesn't seem to register with some people.

Seeing as the detoxification is so simple and cheap, some do not appreciate it's worth. We should probably charge people and give them a little tub to take home. Then they would not forget. People are such funny creatures. If I told them it was a very rare and secret formula, they would be rushing home to try it.

This conversation on toxins and the like leads into our next topic, which needs a more solid foundation of elements and essences.

This is basically enough foundational strength to introduce you to your self-activations. Now perhaps you will be able to sense more where the new millennium is taking us in the next chapter.

# 8

## OPENING THE SECRET TIME TO
## THE NEW MILLENNIA

We opened our conversation discussing separations. Now perhaps I need to explain how many separations have occurred. This is such a large subject that we will discuss it in each chapter. However, there is one large, contributing factor that ties everything together: *truth*.

It might seem like I'm harping on and on about truth, but I would just like you to understand a different perspective of this rather large subject.

In the previous chapter, we discussed how to create real truth. But there is another angle from which to look at real truth: *if your truth has immense worth, then so do you.*

Ponder this statement, please. If your truth has immense worth, then so do you. If you have immense worth within all self-presence, an absolute wealth of worth is reflected in what is created with all self-consciousness.

We are talking about a life full of worth. You may be financially independent, but money is never the only focus; it can restrict our life with family and friends. I can create huge stress on our health.

I would like you to consider one word used before: *restriction*. Every restriction of truth creates a separation. This seems a little too simple doesn't it.

How does this separation occur? Imagine truth to be a current, which it actually is, or perhaps you could think of this current as a link. Now imagine a current that flows through the soul and heart first. Then imagine that truth is restricted, either in a negative manner or an overly positive manner. What happens next?

The current will change form. Is this important, or does it even matter in the slightest? It's only a tiny bit of truth; it can't impact my life that much, can it? Well, surprise, surprise. It does. We consider this tiny bit of current first, because it is an actual link.

You see, this is a true form of life with enormous amounts of power flowing through it. Now think of a power line being lopped off in a storm, and all the damage it does to everything in the vicinity.

For a start, we have a new scenario to contend with. Also, the extra current is diverted through to the other links, so they fray off as well. These frayed lines keep swirling about and end in a tight coil, restricting and constricting. About now, you probably think I'm over-emphasising how this takes place. But am I?

Remember, I am only talking about the sacred spirit at the moment, not the physical. So let's just back-track a little to where the current link was first severed. There are a couple of ramifications to consider.

You might be wondering why I elaborate on how restrictions of current affect us. Isn't there just some quick antidote to fix us up, pronto? I guess you think my guides will come in now and tithe an affirmation to make everything better. Well, you are correct, but there are a couple of small indiscretions to get out of the road first.

There are a couple of things that really need to be understood before we take the antidote. By antidote, my guides mean taking out the anti-part, the part that is against truth. You may or may not be aware that we can sense rather than feel this part. It is not related to any emotion.

Because we are revising a couple of steps, let's consider the current and what it is made from. Current on this level is, and can only ever be, made of consciously aware current, because you need to be conscious of all that you are to restore. If you are not really conscious of something, then it is impossible to restore all that is vital to your everyday needs. You simply will not be aware that this aspect of your life needs restoring.

This is not hard going, because on so many levels you will be aware of any separation.

At this point, I think it is important to have a clear image of separation in mind, where you had your soul in the left hand and your heart in the right hand. Imagine all the connections that have separated from the soul and are unable to communicate with this vital point of our self. If this occurs, all matter around the soul becomes dense.

For this exercise, all that is dense is in the left hand, and all that is current is of course in the right. Please weigh up the two gently. Perhaps even close your eyes.

Did you notice that as you weighed the two up, the left hand soon lost its dense weight? You automatically wanted to turn your hands to each other and let the energy balance. Clasp your hands together now as you ground this intention.

If we consider the ramifications of this little exercise, you might surprise yourself at the conscious connection to your consciousness, which you are now integrating with a new ease. You see, it made sense not to hold on to dense energy. You will find that this intention has flowed way beyond where you are consciously aware. This will be highlighted for you soon enough, but perhaps we should redefine the heart first.

The dense matter is in the right hand, and the appreciating, balanced energy is in the left hand. Once again, as you gracefully redefine your desired flow, please close your eyes. This is becoming automatic, isn't it? Your clasp already wants to ground and balance. You may sense energy moving from one side of your body to the other; this is your soul and heart communicating.

To sense this a little more intimately, remember that this is *your* energy. Close your eyes for a moment to sense this activation. For those needing a little more time to settle, take note of where you desire to return later on.

On returning, hold your hand over this page to sense the vibrations. Remember that everybody is attuned to different senses, and you might see energy folds integrating. Please remember, though, that our many senses will becoming conscious, and this is what all the exercises are about—to wake up our awareness to forgotten senses.

Following in this line of thought, a different awareness is asking to be unravelled. You see, just by appreciating that consciousness is needed, the affirmation that will be tithed to you is going to work differently. How so?

Think about it a little. Is your answer a conscious one, or is it one that you plucked from your mind? Don't think for a moment that I'm taking you on a wild goose chase, running you in a circle, feeding you tidbits of information so that this seems like some ritual or secret consciousness linked to many old terms you might find in any book shop. Right from the start, I and my guides have desired to open you to just a couple of very relevant thoughts.

By now you are able to appreciate that real, sacred truth needs to be considered as such—that it is actually aware and able to be connected to your real energy.

Conscious awareness adds up to conscious truth.

Consider that simple truth, as it exists, needs nurturing, and this truth is connected in many ways. We also need to consider also that truth is made up of a conscious spirit that is also connected by consciousness.

Sounds a bit heavy, doesn't it—all this talk of consciousness. Don't worry. I'll lighten up a bit in a minute, but it's not just me writing this, as you can probably tell. My guides have quite a few subjects, aspects, or items that they want me to cover in this discussion, so please remember that in some cases, I am only passing on a message. While this may be true, don't think for a moment that I don't use all that we are discussing. I most certainly do.

In the opening dialogue, I confessed that I used frustration to identify when something wasn't working or to sense when a self-aspect was missing something important. We have just discussed the fact that, without senses, we simply aren't able to connect. At that moment, a rather large key was opened in your subconscious, asking to be consciously connected in an aware manner in the future.

This meant that you desired to release all unconscious reactions that led to frustration, but you were unable to sense your own response or reaction to what you where consciously sensing—because it was blocked off.

So you see that you are using each and every particle of consciousness that you pick up along the way. Nothing is wasted or consumed. All that is shared must be vital and useful, contributing to our future. With this sharing contribution in mind, perhaps it is time to revisit a previously opened exercise that now needs strengthening.

Please start this exercise by remembering when you were asked to place the flat of your hand in front of yourself. What is it that really happened? You connected; but you also connected in a different manner. This isn't hard to comprehend, because your consciousness is now responding to energy of a higher vibration and frequency.

This means that you will be moving on from using responses and reactions to using denser energy or matter, but remember that you need to become reacquainted to working is this manner, because it needs to become automatic. This higher vibration frequency reacts and responds in a totally different way that you were unaware of because you aren't used to this new response yet. Isn't this worth putting in the memory banks? Indeed, it is.

While you were not completely aware of this, you were also reconnecting to a sense that was already known to you in a way you were unaware that you had forgotten.

This unawareness meant that you were unaware of all that you were thinking about in this life. When you're not presently using something, it's very easy to forget that at one time you were quite efficient at using many different aspects of yourself in a totally aware manner. So, instead of thinking that you are being introduced to a new phenomenon or learning to how to interpret in a new manner, please think of this as remembering, because so many of us do.

Now that you can respond to a more automatic reaction, your senses are automatically telling you what are conscious matter and energy.

Remember, this is another aspect to the new millennia: the vibrations about us are challenging us to remember all that we used to be aware of.

I have trouble believing that everybody is just walking around in a state of bliss, even if they are aware. They would be blind to the amazing potentials opening all the time, or they would be in a blind, stagnant awareness, no matter who they are.

Yes, I am content, but I know that there are so many self-abilities waiting to be rediscovered. I want to ensure that I live out all that my potential has at its disposal. I never wish to throw away or dispose of any aspect that is truthfully connected to my self-consciousness. However, I do desire to dispose of energies that are not truthfully connected to my own self-current.

This statement was really tithed to me years ago, so I was able to consider all energies that flowed about me. This we have discussed already, but it is an area that needs many different understandings. Without the correct awareness, it is hard to discern all that is truthfully of your own energy and what is just unused, unaware, unappreciated energy of others, floating about.

It seems a strange scenario that others' energy could just be just floating about, not really doing much, when, at the same time, it is capable of interfering with your own judgments and keeping your self-consciousness from being aware or used for the purpose it was designed for.

This is another reason for exercises: to wake up self-awareness to the activations of energies that are not only in you but also surrounding you.

These change according to the consciousnesses that people around you attract. Isn't this worth considering?

All exercises are intended to open your consciousness—which is now able to respond in many ways that it previously could not. This is what happens when you learn to re-sense a response that was unable to become active. The source opens conversations because they work.

If the majority of people about you are not using their full potential of awareness, then the probability is greater that you will follow this same pattern. Remembering how we forgot isn't quite as mysterious as it would seem. The guides desire to outline this over many chapters, as there are a couple of different ways that we may have been coaxed to forget.

This issue of how we have left our senses behind has turned into my life's work. At times this has been very enjoyable, but sometimes it is oh-so-frustrating. It's as if a person I am healing is not responding. It's even worse if this person is somebody I love or am related to.

Questions open doors that need to be found. Yes, we are mediums, but all the same, we need to ask our guides in a correct manner to receive the correct question in order to open up a correct understanding.

Now, I know that you don't comprehend this bit, so please bear with me, as it will help you to comprehend things a little differently. It will also help many things to automatically make sense. As your frequency rises, you connect to more understanding.

Please remember that we have had many lifetimes. Multiply this—and only this, so as to not make things too complicated—by the many points of separation we have. This alone adds up to a tidy sum of missing senses—the missing senses that we will be considering in our journey.

All your senses are made the same way, and they add up to how relevant you are. Senses are made of multiple consciousnesses. The source refers to us as being made of a collective consciousness. There is nothing new in this; it's just a different term. Because we have many senses that make up this self-collective consciousness, imagine for a moment the effect on us as we lose senses. What do you think happens?

When we lose a level of consciousness, we forget it, and after a few lifetimes, we are not even aware that it once existed.

Does this make sense to you, or am I just a little bit weird? I don't know about you, but I don't want to miss out on anything. After is was pointed out to me, I figured out that I was missing out on so much, and I wasn't happy.

I felt like a car that had gone through the assembly line, but I seemed to have missed out on both the optional extras and many of the parts I needed to function daily. Since finding this out, though, I have found ways to put many of the necessary bits and pieces back into my vehicle.

You might remember that this conversation was also about living a wealth of worth and about how it is possible to reconnect to this and many other forms of wealth by linking up to senses of our self, which then link to all conscious matter.

Also, now would be a good time to remember that it helps to know about the bits missing. If we're aware of their absence, we won't be left in the dark. Before we find out how to appreciate and connect to the missing bits of consciousness, the source will begin with a new focus to unlock hidden potentials. Unlocking these potentials involves exploring places that perhaps you have never ventured into before.

Finally, we will look at an element that unlocks many new types of self, which means that in this life, very few people are aware of them. If this concept sounds strange, remember that this is relative to the new millennium. Also, consider the fact that in a new time, many things might need changing or rectifying in some manner.

The source points to something it wants everybody to appreciate.

You are all moving to a time where spirit desires that there be no secrets, that all humanity becomes conscious of the immense ability that each and every one of you possess.

Earlier, I mentioned the need to connect to a correct consciousness in order to heal somebody I loved who was not responding. Remember that if you channel the source, you expect to receive all the answers and questions that unlock the reason somebody is incapacitated. Add to this situation the fact that the person I needed to get to was not even in the same state but a thousand miles away. Worse still, this was many years ago, and I knew only a fraction of what I know now about how to connect.

The person in question was my father, and I am never embarrassed to admit that we are a very close family and enjoy each other's company. Luckily for me, I have a sister who is also an intuitive healer who channels, so when I first heard that my father had been put into hospital and was in a coma, I was concerned but not beside myself, as my sister Julie was there to help.

This, however, was about to change quickly. An hour after my dad went into hospital, my sister went to pieces, which is fair enough; she knew exactly what Dad was up against.

This was when I found and opened a strength that I was not fully familiar with, one that I had never fully comprehended. While I had always been grateful that I could channel, I was about to unlock a potential that surprised me.

As Julie began to unfold the circumstances, I instantly knew that she was unable to communicate with Dad simply because of the state he was in. You see, without conscious communication, she was not even able to sense how Dad really was. This was something we had not encountered before.

So all of a sudden, unable to communicate, what was Julie's conclusion? That we were not prepared for Dad to cross over.

All I can say is, thank heaven for angels. While I had channeled for years, nothing I experienced on the phone with Julie had ever come close to what I was about to sense.

All of a sudden, Jesus came through with this message: "Julie, you are about to receive an immense presence of consciousness. This is an evolved activation through your evolved selves. I now open, at this time and in this space, a love of purpose to create this conscious connection. Julie, the complete love you witness in this space about your self is bringing the absolute god-reflection to a space of gratitude throughout your now-complete self. Julie, witness this love that you sense and now see as a blue radiance. The strength that is to grace you and your father will open all relationships of yourselves."

The next translation from Lady Mary carried the same strength of consciousness: "I bring to this love an eternal grace, as the heart nurtures each soul-presence, with all that is to be tithed this day."

There was at this time no emotion, but an immense strength was transferred though me, and this was clearly evident. The change in Julie was instantaneous, and she was then able to help Dad.

In simple terms, the consciousness connected by both of us needed to be passed on to Dad through his comatose state of conscious. Dad's consciousness was in a state of confusion. Once Julie connected—not just with the strength of consciousness from Jesus and Mary but with her own strength—to let Dad know he was loved and needed, his confused state of consciousness was released.

I have since seen this same state of confusion in so many clients, simply because of the separations we were discussing earlier. All self-love had been lost.

By the time I arrived home, Dad had changed considerably to our way of thinking. The doctor in charge had told us to make arrangements, and we had told the doctor with no bedside manner where to go and that our father would walk out of that hospital.

Next, we received a doctor who comprehended and had empathy for spirit, as did all the nurses who kept visiting, even though they were now with different patients.

As Dad gained strength—and of course this is the short version—all of a sudden his healing stagnated. Why?

If you're a nurse or have loved ones in hospital, please use this, as I found many people in Dad's ward doing this same thing.

Earlier on, I related how I receive a lot of direction through activations. So when I noticed a load of Dad's energy traveling out of him, I needed to ask why. There are a few reasons why this happens, but there is also one large reason that you can counter.

At that time, Dad was barely conscious. We can help those in his condition by simply telling them to stop healing others and to put their energy to use on themselves.

There are also a couple of very evident factors that I have not mentioned: the affirmations I relayed to Julie worked differently. They contained many conscious connections that caused strength of consciousness to be created and to move energy. This movement of conscious energy is activation, and this can only be connected in a conscious manner.

This is why I was able to see Dad's energy going out from his body, as he was doing this in an unconscious manner and his own healing was coming to a standstill.

Is it possible that at this moment you are doing the same thing in an unconscious manner? You see, deep within your self-energy that has lost conscious connection, you are unable to exist as the energy of a complete collective-consciousness.

Imagine some part of your energy only working at sixty percent of its capability. This relates to one huge fact—that we are all great at giving but absolutely terrible at receiving. This also has to do with past lives, but I'll revisit this area later, as there's way too much explaining to do.

So, why did I bring in a story about my family? So I could explain a couple relevant insights and how they have reflected not so much in my own life but in how I use them to work. But there is so much more to this than my work.

There are a couple of items my guides have asked for you to be able to reflect on. First, my father walked out of hospital. Next, the affirmations helped not only our faith and belief but created strength in our selves in a conscious manner. This strength of consciousness released any restrictions in perceiving truth—our truth that our father would soon be well—and nothing was going to separate our belief from this becoming a reality.

Another sign is how the strength of real consciousness moves unconsciousness. Release the unconscious element, and many aspects of the self heal or gain strength.

Remember, real gratitude and appreciation are not just emotions or feelings; they are living, conscious matter.

Some of this may seem a trifle tedious, this constant conversation with consciousness, but when you break down a couple of misconceived thoughts from the past, your thoughts will free up.

In the first chapter about how this book came about, an extract was given to me: whatever exists in reality exists in illusion. This isn't about me harping on and on; it is only about one subject, really—your ability to discern between illusion and reality in an aware manner. This is so you don't miss any opportunity in life because of inability to tell the difference between the two.

Remember this idea that Gabriel passed on. "If you repeat some annoying part of your life time and time again, why does this happen?" he asked.

"I have no idea," I answered. "What question should I ask?"

"Perhaps you should consider why mistakes agitate you so much."

"We repeat life patterns when we do not have enough senses to recognise that we are doing them unconsciously, over and over," I said.

This helped unlock a rather large, misconceived thought, something we hold as a knowing. I have often been told that in heaven, time is inconsequential and does not relate to matter. I have also had it rammed down my throat by many that everything around us is an illusion, no matter what we look at.

I am not for a moment saying that you need to believe what has been interpreted by my guides, but are you open enough to even consider a different outcome?

If I have learned one thing in life, it's that when my guides indicate that I need to question some aspect of life, I do so immediately to find out why. This also ensures that I am never following blind faith or believing that something is correct just because somebody has said it is so, no matter who they are.

If you desire to connect to sacred truth that is relative to the new millennium, then perhaps you also desire to release old-time, reoccurring constrictions that limit and consume some aspect of your potential, life after life.

The following affirmation concerns activating potential and is brought through language that unlocks as well as reaffirms. It comes through a collective consciousness rather than one solitary source, unlocking all new-time understanding. These are not my own words, of course.

Any content that I sense is hard to grasp or fathom, I will do my best to evaluate in our language.

Before I extend this to you, hold your hands in a clasped position, if you would. You will soon sense stillness and your mind will quiet. This means that any interruptions of energy not connected to your own consciousness will not be tolerated.

This tithing affirmation is to restore all self-space in this new time of this evolved self and to open all fortunes in all of your real future.

"I am Lord Matreya, and I am here at this time in this space of gratitude to unlock all that is of a new-time collective-consciousness presence.

"All of this self, which is now designed to equate to real time and to a real function, is to be revealed to all who truly desire to reform all that, at present, sits in an old-time existence.

"All of your total self is simply of a non-consecutive synchronicity, meaning that at present your synchronicity sits in many dysfunctional levels of your self.

"To prevent this from recreating in all future selves, we tithe this new time-activation to readdress much of your lost wealth from this living, life-fortune.

"All illusion kingdoms of repressed, unconscious representations are released, allowing a strength within the sacred soul, the sacred heart, to unfold to the now-natural self-nature of true belief.

"This, beloved friend, will be sensed as appreciation, and hence you will sense this activation between your soul and heart, as the all-new purpose of self-awareness reactivates all self-reactions to real self-truth."

In our language, this means that you will sense all this as an unfolding between your soul and heart.

We are truly seeking and desiring to be free and to see clearly where we are proceeding and what we are able to be. There was a limitation where your soul and heart were unable to communicate, whereas now you are opening many conscious levels of self. In Lord Matreya's words, please use this new strength to create a balance that you are now able to receive.

You may be sensing a strength of self in the right-hand side of your self. This is a self-strength that this self has never been connected to in this lifetime, but it will be needed in all new times.

For some of you who are used to sensing energy, an unwinding sensation might be felt sometime on the right side of your body. You will find that this balances your daily feelings.

"Please enjoy all light and love tithed with a purpose, with true purpose, to connect with real joy to a real wealth of self and to love of all source."

As your hands unclasp, a sense of release might be experienced, or your body may feel like flopping, now that conscious energy is able to connect in a new way.

The ideal introduction to such an affirmation probably doesn't exist, but please don't get too freaked out if you think it's a bit intense or over-the-top. This is probably a different type of affirmation than others you have already encountered.

One idea that perhaps you could take on board is to use an affirmation as a tool rather than using sacred words. No disrespect is intended or desired in all that was forwarded in this extract. Also, isn't my own idea but the source's, so please don't shoot the messenger.

Remember that every word is more than just a word, when it sits in an activated affirmation. No, I don't just mean that it is linked to enormous amounts of understanding on many levels of consciousness—although, of course, it is.

One meaning for the word *activated*, is "alive and moving," and this movement happens in many different ways, which we will be discussing. Consider, then, that each and every active word relates to a vibration, a frequency tone, or harmonic.

"So," I hear you say, "there's nothing new here. We already know this." Well, do you also realise that each and every sequence of vibrations works in a sequential manner on many levels, activating or deactivating on many levels of consciousness, all at the same time?

If a vibration activated in an old-time formula was to move—and we are not talking quantum—we would be describing how it was actually able to move. For any matter to move to a set formula, time needs to be relative.

No, you don't need to be smart to figure this bit out. Why?

Everything depends on one thing, or so our guides tell us, but I would like you to check it when you get to the next part. If you have seen the energy streaming in, then you already know.

How do you confirm what our guides are about to divulge? I guess the chapter of the title gives this away, but I do implore you to please check it out, especially if you doubt. Use the *muscle test*. Please remember that this isn't my synopsis; I am only passing on the theory as it was unfolded to me.

First, I'll outline a couple of the steps used to explain this to me, and then you can make up your own mind and check.

Consider the first statement that for all matter to be created, a divine synchronicity must be able to relate to an exact time, an exact place, and an exact equation. Then, we must appreciate that for all of this to manifest, time is an essential component and must always be relative.

Now, I'm no Einstein, but even I could figure out that without some form of timing, synchronicity wouldn't even matter or, for that matter, even come about. You can check by muscle-testing now, please.

In your left hand is past, dense time, and in the right hand, real time is connected to a real sequence through your sequential spirit to real collective-consciousness synchronicity.

The energy in your left hand is heavy and weighing you down. In the right hand is your self-strength of purpose. Point your hands to each other. The energy that now dissipates was never of your own purpose, so it will cease to be.

Sense how both hands desire to come together. Let them. Those who are very receptive may instantly sense a change of mood to a lighter, happier one now that the past-life, dense reaction has been released.

This repeats a separated-consciousness pattern where one is unable to sense the real future—only the past with a minimum self-future—or real sequences that connect to real synchronicity. Does this make sense?

There is also a larger issue to consider. If parts of your conscious energy have separated, then these blocks or cycles of energy are no longer connected to synchronicity.

Perhaps we could expand this equation by considering that any separated energy could also throw out how the remaining energy is able to synchronise. Now, perhaps, we can understand why, for so many, time seems unimportant.

The only item we have discussed thus far in the affirmation is time and synchronicity. It's now time to discuss another.

When I was first shown the importance of a word's vibration, I learned that it has a reaction, not just to its own vibration but to many vibrations and frequencies—or even a whole group of energies.

This may have looked like a play on words, but I missed a larger picture, and this is why.

First, consider that in all forms of humanity some people consider themselves to be of more importance than others, and please don't bring the ego or Karma in to confuse this conversation—not yet, anyhow.

I hope you won't consider this a bit too tedious to read, as my guides desire to make a couple of points understood.

Many words might seem as clear as they can be. They are only words. How can a mere word possibly have any impact on my life?

In the previous affirmation, the term *illusional kingdom* was used. This simply means that some person thinks you should dedicate much of your wealth of energy to them. We are not even talking about assets to be given to them, just energy.

This also means that you don't mind limiting your potential in life, so immense parts your energy can be directed to them. When you follow this form of unconsciousness, you are also limiting compassion for yourself.

Don't take my word for this. I'm only interpreting it, so straightaway you had better check on it before we go too far. You see, every time you check, something else is happening besides receiving an indication of what is correct. At the same time, synchronicity or the conscious connection to synchronicity indicates where unconscious energy has been going.

Surprise, surprise, surprise.

This affects many aspects of our everyday energy, each and every day.

What a pain—and yes, it really can be, if you think about it—that this limited energy limits areas of both spirit energy and, eventually, physical well-being. The lesson, interpreted, means this: when you lose the strength of your consciousness, it has many repercussions on your everyday life.

This loss of energy also means that you could unconsciously lower certain parts of your life expectation, as you would be unaware of what the lost energy could have created.

The source has also indicated that each time we are made unaware of a certain situation, it is not something negative. The source simply desires that we all create a strong consciousness. Remember—and this is as plain as it was relayed to me—that consciousness holds every aspect of your self that exists or has ever existed.

Unawareness of the self-conscious strength means allowing your conscious to separate; then all will follow.

There is another line of thought that perhaps you may desire to consider.

Link into this separated consciousness, and all who follow this separated thought will also follow. This is why at times we follow like sheep, I guess, and why advertising works so well on this separated consciousness. This also explains why—if you follow an unconscious direction toward what seems to be important for happiness or joy—it can seem so hollow when attained.

Consider a couple of other scenarios. If you are following an unconscious direction of joy or happiness that you created in a conscious part of you, it may go undetected, as this is a direction of self that you are not focusing on at this moment.

All of this we have found to be correct, but once again, please don't take my word for this. Check and double-check, as this is a foundational point in comprehending separation of any consciousness.

Please take a little time to ensure that this is authentic, a real vibration and not a contribution to an illusional, consuming, de-creating element that takes away from life.

I guess this puts a hole in the theory that he or she who has the most toys wins. But it's your choice.

While there are many other parts to the affirmation to be discussed, I guess it is time to open you to a couple of other insights that relate just to time.

Imagine this scene. I'm standing at the bottom of a mountain, waiting for the rest of my ski class to load on the lift. I have started a conversation with a lady on the lift who asks what I do. She says I'm a bit different. I don't take offence, but I fill her in on how I work. She then goes on to tell me the most intimate details about how she has been raped, and she asks for help.

This lady wasn't in my class; she was just somebody I met on the lift. But she had asked her guides for help. Yes, I gave this lady a healing on the side of a mountain, but the point is that there are many different types of synchronicity, if you are open to receive.

This is the whole point I am endeavouring to make: the right time can be staring you in the face. I thought about how brave this lady was to give out gruesome details to a stranger.

The other point to be made, of course, is you too are brave enough to ask for help or to admit to yourself that you need a little help. Perhaps it is time to ask for that help right now to solve some small or even larger issue that has been attracting unwanted energy.

The lady on the lift had also asked to free herself. She confided to me the following day what being free had to do with her healing.

This is a little exercise that reflects this desire to be free. In your outstretched left hand sits a sphere. In this sphere, you begin to collect dense matter that is blocking many points of consciousness. Take a moment to sense this, please.

In your right hand sits a sphere to release the dense matter or conflicting energy. If you take time, the hands will fell different from each other. If your senses are blocked, your left hand will seem heavy and the right light.

Next, point the contents of each hand toward the other. Take a few moments, and endeavour to sense how this activation feels.

As you bring both hands together, the arm that was so heavy with dense matter is suddenly released, freed.

This is an exercise to stimulate the senses in the real self. It asks the connected consciousness to grow strong again in a free manner without the same constrictions. This will then facilitate the release and signal that the now-dense matter connected to the separated bits of conscious is no longer desired, as it was not your real, free desire.

Some of you who are asking to release something a little larger may even have sensed energy dripping down your arms. As this sense releases, some of you may sense the whole of your body lightly vibrating. Those who see quite easily would be surrounded in a purple haze. As this haze lifts, a you have a freeing sensation. Please clasp your hands, as you now ground with new freedom.

Perhaps it is time to repeat this exercise. Remember, you have grown a little since you first attempted to open some new senses. This exercise is really asking your self to become more cognitive, to create depth using many new vibrations at once.

Please ensure that you re-ground by clasping your hands. That grounding sense will be stronger if you stand up. When your knees feel like buckling and your hands drop, this is an indication that all is grounded and complete.

The grounding exercise is worth repeating daily or each time you hop out of bed. Why? Because you are living in an ever-changing, personal self-environment, and it makes sense to align to your own environment.

Perhaps I should now clarify all that has been affirmed. If you had your very own personal environment about you, this would be an energetic reflection of your own self-collective consciousness. This is all that you have and all that is possible. You are not refracting what is impossible. You are consciously using all of your consciousness, not focusing to use what is of an unconscious nature.

More simply put: you focus on what you *do* have, not on what you *don't*.

You see, the source is indicating one thing. Before, you were focusing on both scenarios at one time—what is connected to consciousness (so it is really possible to create this) and unconsciousness (so it is not possible).

This is another example of what are two truths: you are true in one conscious time or in an illusional time of unconsciousness.

To put this as simply as possible, there is one underlying fact that all who connect to guide you desire to be underscored. With this outline, we consider that all that is possible to be created is reflected by us.

Thus, we create an environment that reflects no separation or illusional unconsciousness.

This environment gains our strength, as this is something we desire to create, and we know it to be a reflection of the whole collective-consciousness of all that exists—the god-presence.

Are we having a light bulb moment now?

I hope that you understand the relevance of what has been outlined, because as we connect to and create a strong environment about us, we are not going to be as susceptible to denser or lower vibrations. Thus our self-frequency is able to evolve.

Please remember also that this releases the contention or competition within the self. Thus you create ease, peace, and a harmonious environment. Are we hitting the nail on the head at this moment? This is only able to be accomplished with conscious awareness.

Now that we have redefined true awareness in a different way, as the source desired, we had better return to the previous conversation.

As you reconnect to consciousness that hasn't been used for a while, there are many different connections to be added on to make it work. The energies need to relearn what, how, why, when, and to whom they correspond.

Please consider that for energy to move, it has to be told what to do. Remember, this is your energy. It's all you. If this is your energy, then you need to take responsibility for it and for your energy responses.

Perhaps you could compare this to losing a leg. Instead of receiving an artificial one, you graft the old one back on. You still need to learn to walk again—or relearn the senses lost.

Gabriel and Uriel have a connective consciousness to facilitate. This is not only to open the consciousness but to activate connections. Then the many vibrations and frequencies you have connected to are able to communicate and respond. This is a bit like reconnecting all the severed nerves of the reattached leg and slowly relearning the capacity of this leg.

It also means relearning many new capacities and finding many abilities that you haven't been using.

Here is a tithing about connective consciousness. To open all that is efficient, all new-time guides now open all consciousness to connective consciousness. This opens all elements and resources to new-time, sourced activation. This creative presence is to open all facets of your once-limited potential. All receptors to this immense potential must now open to living a life potential, not a life of old-time existence.

I am now free to sense love in a free, natural self-nature that equates to my own self-environment.

This affirmation is about opening yourself to a future. Although your senses are unable to sense this, many abilities of your self are simply suppressed. Perhaps you can relate this to being able to reactivate parts of your brain so your memory works more efficiently. In many ways, this will prove to be a reality. It won't happen overnight, but it will happen, as a type of *reintroduction*.

*Reintroduction* is a word that needs to be explored, but for now, remember that you have been tithed a few different affirmations and, in truth, only the surface has been scratched.

With the impact of many suppressed reactions releasing, you have begun to connect in a different manner. It is like opening the floodgates to that which you have been asking for. Previously, the message just couldn't get through.

It is also like wanting to connect to Facebook but not being able to, as your computer is linked to a telegraph cable. This is the reason a new-time approach is needed.

This chapter is really about a new direction for many parts of your self. In some parts, things were a little tedious and repetitive to ensure that the unconscious and subconscious aspects of your self, which are not used to communicating, didn't get lost.

I would like to share how what has been discussed works in a healing or in a reconnecting meditation.

Imagine that you are moving through consciousness in a meditation. Serene stillness has moved you through many layers that you never really reach. As you move, all aspects and activations are very apparent, as is the depth of conscious you are communicating with.

The next awareness is of how conscious you are actually becoming. You haven't shifted the depth of consciousness you are communicating with or retaining. You are using this depth constantly each day, only now you recognise that you are returning to your original point of consciousness. Still, you are totally aware of all the vast connections that you have just made.

This means that you actually retain this level of consciousness on a daily basis. Now imagine the awareness that also comes with this new capacity. Then imagine this reconnecting of consciousness repeated many times; this is the reconnecting our guides are talking about.

I hope it now makes sense as to why the source goes about things in a certain manner. You might want it to hurry and get to the point, because you are changing an old-time point-of-view that sometimes resists without you being aware of the resistance.

This, of course, is twofold; it impacts both your spirit self and your physical self. We will explain this in more detail in the next chapter on a new-time instruction manual for a completely new time.

# 9

## A NEW-TIME INSTRUCTION MANUAL

Don't think for a moment that an *instruction manual* means doing exactly as you're told. This is more about how you have dismantled many parts of your self unknowingly, or how others have caused you to think you didn't need self-worth or that many aspects of your self are of no worth. It is about ensuring that all aspects of your self stay in a direction of worth.

Speaking of worth, you may be wondering why this chapter isn't at the beginning of the book. Would you have appreciated then what is being shared with you now? You needed to receive the information in a new way in order to create in the collective consciousness matter that only reacts to a sensory manner.

We have also opened our self to and discussed an absolute wealth of worth, and this aspect must be connected throughout the entire book.

Please consider the value of the next sentence carefully.

There is always one reflection worth considering. Every time you connect to a new knowing through energy activation with a conscious, complete connection, it stays with you. Therefore, there is no need to reaffirm an affirmation over and over. If you are actively conscious, you have been affirmed.

If you are able to create in a continuous, conscious manner, all that you respond to is going to be already active with a firm, conscious connection.

Therefore, using connective consciousness, you are learning to actively use and reaffirm the forgotten source connection between your own personal collective-consciousness and the source's collective-consciousness of all that exists, or god-consciousness.

This is very important, especially if you are a healer of any description. This means that every activation of energy you've learned happens automatically now.

This is the outcome. Consider that each and every day I receive what is like a lesson. If I had to repeat every activation that I have learned to help somebody, it would take weeks to finish one healing, so I would never move on. Everything would be limited.

As some energy becomes conscious, everything becomes automatic, so that all this conscious energy reacts, responds, and balances in an instant. This is what senses are—conscious responses, conscious reactions, conscious balances. It's why the senses are so very vital.

This we will reflect on from time to time, but our emphasis is on moving forward in a conscious manner. Then everything becomes automatic, of a natural self-nature in a present environment, which is a preparation for all things future.

This is sort of a reflection on what was outlined before. We make the correct foundations for the present and the future, as this is what many self-activations have been doing in an unaware way or manner. It is why the source asked us to consider our energy in a new and aware manner. This does make sense, doesn't it?

The other redeeming facet of connecting through a connective consciousness is that, should you ever desire to pass on some particular element to another person, your connection can help them immensely—and automatically.

The source passes on many tools to help, and some of these are keys and codes. These come in many forms with many different functions to simplify the unlocking of this aspect. I was asked to paint a few pictures—real, physical pictures, painted with many layers—so the finished article often didn't resemble how it started.

On some paintings are what appear to be hieroglyphics, but they are in fact nothing of the sort. Every aspect is associated with light. So you end up seeing something like neon lights unlocking, or perhaps there is the sensation that something is freeing up. Then you are indeed connected to a key with a wealth of worth.

This is why, when you place your hands in front of my pictures, that many unconscious parts of your self will vibrate. It means that a certain aspect of your self desires to contribute in an aware manner, not an unconscious one. The source desires to pass on how, why, where, and when this has affected your own self-purpose. Releasing the effects of artificial sensations releases complete reactions to emotional feelings without a complete reasoning of self-worth.

In our language this means that we have been responding to reactions that were not connected to a self-conscious sense—what the source considers a waste of energy.

Another facet of this opens not just new understandings but source activations. Become aware that there is so much more to us than emotional senses.

Please enjoy this harmonious redefinition. If you have been unable to sense real worth of your self, it has been eroded away from your self-atmosphere or the real senses of a real, living life. You will be free to experience actual activations throughout this book if you so desire. An activation is similar to having a healing.

Please consider that, as you are first shown how to connect to this wealth of worth, quite a few new potentials need to be unlocked. As you grasp a new concept, you will be shown many different ways to actually use this concept. Also consider that to use a different concept, you need to be fully aware and coherent, definitely not in a state of unconsciousness.

You may be aware that all you have just read is grounding throughout yourself. It is a good reason not to speed-read.

Grounding activates denser conscious to actually lighten up or come back to life. If you are coherent, you will always be aware of what you open up. Then, while conscious of a source tithing, you are open and able and free to receive. Straightaway, a key has been provided to release or free up a restriction that normally you do not desire to connect to.

Most of us are fantastic at giving, but we block ourselves to receiving. The main reason for this is that it's actually how we are wired, and there are many parts of us not communicating properly. To make sure that this doesn't happen in the future, we will be provided with a means to reconnect everything, to put the many disconnected parts together again.

One of the largest problems—and please consider what our guides desire us to comprehend—is that we are totally unaware that this problem exists. This is where we left off in the previous chapter, discussing energies surrounding us that we are often quite oblivious to.

If the wiring or the connections are not there or intact, then how the heck can we connect all this fantastic potential? How can we connect to so many aspects of our self, if we haven't got the connections to connect in the first place? Luckily, we have now been provided with this faculty, and it sits in a place where most would never look.

I have to admit that when I unlocked this—and in truth it was actually my guides who did it—I had no idea what miracle was unfolding for me. What unfolded was a form of connective consciousness. I don't just mean a consciousness. It is an energy in its own right, and its potential is so vast and unlimited, you might wonder how we ever missed its potential.

Please don't dismiss this as just a connector; it has the potential to free up many misinterpreted aspects of ourselves.

This whole scenario becomes more apparent, because there are many different parts of us that have never been defined. This connects to what was outlined for us previously about finding new truth that hasn't been exposed to us.

Unlocking this new truth adds a new dimension to connective consciousness. We learn to sense what this energy does, where it does it, how, and why. How much new truth about your self do you think this would unlock?

Our guides want you to check that this is true as you read. I will explain how to do this in a moment, but first I would like to introduce you to a couple of tools that make everything a little easier.

Keys and codes do, of course, unlock, but it is *how* they unlock that's important. Please remember that this an instruction manual to help you find aspects of you that were not apparent.

This is where all conversations in the following chapters are heading.

Consider this chapter a content outline. You are going to connect to the direction, so the unconscious part of your consciousness doesn't get lost. You may think the source is joking about getting lost, but of course they are not.

Also, as you open something that may seem small and inconsequential, consider that it often ends up being something you have looking for your whole life but didn't know it. This all adds up to finding some new truth and a different understanding about yourself. Always reflect on the smallest awareness. Join these together, and you access life-changing moments that you will reflect on for the rest of your life.

Over the years, our guides have challenged us to ask questions, to question the status quo, and to never take absolutely anything for granted.

The point is that part of the truth doesn't provide the whole picture, and without the whole picture, we aren't able to focus on the real truth.

This was pointed out to me, time and again, to indicate that consciousness was missing. Understand that some of the largest points of the direction we take in life have been missing. All these points have affected us in the past, so our future has no points of direction missing. With new and different reasoning, we are able to conclude that no points of direction are missing, so we don't miss out on all the points to living. We are able to see the whole picture—that life really is worth living but perhaps now with a new focus.

I hope that this makes sense to everybody, because it also unlocks another major point that could go unnoticed. If we don't fully register the worth of the self without a full connection to many points of consciousness, then all of our senses will also be missing out on the big picture as well. Perhaps we should consider contemplating this more complete picture.

When the senses don't get the full picture, we are debilitated in many senses of our whole self. Therefore, it is not possible to rely on our senses all day, every day. Senses tell you're consciousness what is going on.

Straightaway, your analytical mind tells you that your brain connects all the senses. That's what I used to think too. It's why I ended up missing out on so much. I was never conscious of so many things going on around me, or if I was, it was in a limited capacity.

No, I am definitely not talking about noticing all the starving people or the great things around us. Please don't take this direction; all I am talking about is everyday senses in a real manner.

What I never contemplated is that our intuition has a massive spirit component interwoven into it.

What I never also contemplated is that the spirit component actually gets the brain working more efficiently.

Before you think that this is just some sort of ploy to get you more spiritual, I guess I need you to check that what I've passed on to you isn't crap. It isn't something I simply made up to sell books or to be contentious.

For this reason, I will remind you of how to check for truth. If you have already reviewed muscle-testing to stimulate self-awareness, then you will be aware of this exercise.

Because this and the books to follow ask the reader to think outside the square, I was getting a little frustrated. How could I show people that what I've been passed on is relevant, correct, and works in real life?

After being directed to get everybody to check for truth, I remembered the kinesiology muscle-test. I was told to ensure that you were able to test the physical and the spirit at the same time so that nobody misses out. Otherwise you would only be testing for physical truth.

I now ask for all senses of truth to flow in a new-time, evolved manner to every evolved receptor of real senses. This affirmation helps bring together senses that would normally stay apart and opens up different parts of intuition as well.

It is time to link those hands together and ask for absolute truth. As you do your hands become firmer. Check it out to make sure, please. If something is affirmed, the connection is firm; if it is not affirmed, nothing is firm.

This may seem like a play on words, but in the new time, the source is asking us to be very firm on all that we connect to in the future. This firm aspect of our self relates to every sacred and true reflection of our spirit and the foundational structure that exists in all humanity.

The breakdown of this foundation is the reason that so many aspects of our self are sitting in an existence separate from our self, unable to retain all that is of self-strength. Without this absolute strength, we are just flopping all over the place, not resolving any of our true desires or intents.

This all adds up to what our guides have been passing on for ages: take nothing for granted, ask for the whole truth, never settle for just part of the story, and strive for every aspect of your self to be connected and sensed in the same manner.

Perhaps now is an opportune time to check that this is correct. Remember that a couple of previous points seemed open to interpretation; this is the whole point. Also check to see if other points of understanding need to be reinterpreted to be appreciated or to get the whole picture.

Next, if we discuss briefly the instruction outline of keys and codes just to put you in the picture, then we can return to the point where their functions become more integral.

Keys not only unlock; they are also integral in linking large bodies of moving energy together. Moving energy has strength; it is actually working and not stagnant. Please remember this, as so many people are unable to decipher the difference between moving energy and stagnant energy. This understanding is vital. It is one thing to connect to a consciousness, but you must be able to tell if it has any capacity or current moving through it or if it is stagnant and doing nothing.

Detecting what the activations are doing can tell us much. Think of them as energy moving around and flowing in a particle of matter. If current is going through the activation, it goes without saying that the consciousness is active and moving.

Activations help us fill in the full picture. If we comprehend this, we will be able to unlock so much else that is missing.

Don't take my word for this. Please check it.

I hope you understand why it might seem that I am going rather slowly. It will enable you to unlock so much that we have all missed.

Your source connection is being tithed a reason to respond to senses that you are unaware of, and it is asking you to use them. As you probably gathered, this is how the source interpreted this to be translated. When it comes to detecting, we need all the help we can get. No contribution is too small.

Moving on to the key instructions, always remember that we will simply be looking for where energy moves—or where it doesn't. This key is in the process of unlocking a constriction or restriction of energy.

Unlocking with a code means bringing a balance to enormous amounts of our complete selves, so everything that was put into perspective doesn't fall apart. This is also a way of integrating some energies to add stability.

Keys and codes, which are in your spirit blueprint, help detect real spirit-truth. Keep this in mind, as eventually the spirit blueprint opens the physical blueprint, but they both need each other.

To make this as easy as possible, the source had me paint a few pictures. Inside each, there are—for want of a better description—different levels of conscious messages. These are presented at the start of each chapter to sense the vibrations of how they work.

Hold the flat of your hand to your screen, but not too close. Perhaps you can try standing even farther back. Some screens are a meter and a half wide, so they seem to give a wider perspective, I guess. They also work as a perspective to future, so they help when synchronicity presents itself.

You may by now have noticed that some things are repeated and that many sentences contain the word *yes* somewhere. If some part of your mind needs extra wiring to help it work more efficiently, this is where the word *yes* comes in.

Think of the *yes* as an activation to a certain consciousness to start looking for a real flow of conscious energy to connect to. So I guess it's worth persevering with it, yes?

This is all part of the source equation, and it's much easier to pass on in person where parts of your mind are re-stimulated.

Don't worry. The source always has a solution. This re-stimulation will take effect with the aid of affirmations and the activations connected to them. This enables many of the same old mindsets to be released from areas that have a type of restriction on them.

Another important fact is this that without re-stimulation, there is no possibility for you to really sense.

If you are unable to really know what is going on, there will be no sense of knowing and understanding the feeling. This means, then, that you leave yourself open to the feeling and the emotion but are missing out on the scenario.

Why? Because not all the connections are in the right place.

The frustrating part is that even when we learn that we are missing out, a part of us will sabotage us, telling us that what we desire is not really what we want.

How this happens in so many different ways will be outlined as we endeavour to break down barriers. How? Remember that energy is attracted by those around you—friends, relatives, workmates, other shoppers, and neighbours. It's quite a list, isn't it?

The "how" part, of course, reflects on the previous chapters and is involved in learning different communication skills. The how also means that the new communication skills learned will enable you to interpret the truth. Now you don't miss out on the whole story.

You see, I was struggling over how I was going to get certain points across, as I have said before. Certain points of view don't follow normal interpretations, or they may seem a little out-there when they relate to the relevance of interpreting different energy.

To allay any misrepresentation, my guides suggest going back to basics and getting everybody to muscle-test.

See, I told you I would remind you in a conscious manner—only this time, we also need to consider the future.

Because it is so important that we reach real truth, the source has provided an affirmation for now and for all the future.

"I ask to indicate all paths of self-efficiency and truth, to align to all new-millennium reality through all spirit aspects to all physical purpose.

"All that is of this purpose, and only of this purpose, and of this real self, may be interpreted.

"I open this tithing in order to open every intention in the direction of real self-future and self-resources that unlock potential and appreciate real love, with gratitude for real self-reflection and compassion.

"I now ask that all efficient manner of life potentials now be complete and always present."

This tithing is just to make sure that you are able to interpret spirit messages more efficiently.

There are many books outlining how to connect to a certain consciousness, but new-time connective-consciousness works a little differently from the old-time methods.

If you desire to connect to the source and to ask your angel guides for help, doesn't it make sense to do this in the most efficient manner possible? By *efficient*, I mean, to ensure that your message doesn't get misinterpreted.

Opening your connective consciousness is the same as unlocking your angel wings. Are you aware of this? Bit of a surprise, eh? I used to think you only got wings when you passed over. I also thought this because of certain fables and stories that make us think you got your wings to help you ascend to heaven.

We don't come with a written instruction manual, do we? So we make lots of assumptions, and we forget to reinterpret them once we grow up.

All I'm saying is that a lot of what we know or assume to be of spirit is open to a lot of conjecture, yes.

This is, of course, why source desires us to get into the habit of asking questions—so no old fables or old wives' tales are ever misconstrued as reality. This is why we have never explored the immense potential of what actually lies inside our wings. Why, whenever we meditated, we were in too much of a hurry, thinking we could get to heaven with them and then unlock lots of secrets of the past.

You see, when I said that we don't come with an instruction manual, I wasn't quite accurate. Please don't think I'm talking about the blueprint; I certainly am not.

This reminds us of a human trait relating to how we have treated our angel wings: we were in such a hurry to use them that we missed what they are actually for.

Just like a good mystery, our guides are going to keep you in suspense so you can't just skip to the good bit. Don't worry; it won't be at the end. It's got too much work to do.

I may prattle on a bit over connective consciousness, but there is one enormous reason: I know how much potential this unlocks, and to the unaware and unknowing, it seems to be a very ordinary energy.

Why? No matter how, why, where, when, or with whom you desire to connect, this enormous tool enables everything to happen. It is an immense vehicle and vessel that has sat undiscovered for ages. It is like a secret passage to the self-wealth of worth or—as one of the chapter titles indicates—secrets to a new time.

Another interesting fact is that many people are already hardwired, so to speak, with this amazing asset and are not even aware of their gift for efficiently connecting with this asset.

When many people are asked how they channel, they will simply tell you that they were born with this gift. Surprise, surprise! You were too! Do you understand that I just said you actually channel? Everybody does. Nobody is exempt—nobody.

The only difference between us is that I have remembered how to channel, and your abilities are just a little more suppressed. They haven't gone anywhere; they just need unlocking.

This doesn't mean that you can straightaway channel your guardian angel's messages. We all need to relearn how to crawl before we walk, and everybody is rather impatient and wants to go straight to running.

This also means that you need to learn the responsibility of how to channel efficiently for your own self-direction, first and foremost. This is something I could write a whole book on.

Everybody needs to understand that channelling is a more refined version of intuition, so in a way, everybody needs to be more connected to their intuition. How is this possible? Through that amazing vehicle, connective consciousness. We will be discussing how to use this ability throughout the book.

So, now that you have been enlightened about your massive potential that exists within your innermost possibilities, perhaps it is a good time to reflect on the key aspects of things mentioned earlier.

The keys and codes open up your highest self. Instead of saying "highest self," what if we just said your "highest activating vibrations and frequencies" or your "angel-consciousness"? Okay, are we all on the same page here? Please don't get lost in what is unfolding. This is way too important.

Once your angel-consciousness is opened, it is also an angel connection, yes. Now imagine how clear your connection can be to your own—and very present—guides or guardian angels.

This one aspect unlocks so very much. Now I hope you comprehend that what seemed like me raving on and on was just to get us to the good bit, so it may have been worth persevering.

Please appreciate that failure to fully comprehend the worth of this aspect would have slowed the opening or even stopped this information from unfolding altogether. There is a method to my seeming madness.

Also, please appreciate that this isn't *my* desire, but that of my guides. I pass on what I know actually works; then and only then will the source also desire this connection.

There are so many reasons why everything must be fully appreciated and known. Truth must be in the clearest form possible so that what I pass on is correct.

This is one of my main reasons for wanting to write this book in the first place—not to say that I can channel efficiently but so I can actually and hopefully help somebody with new information that will make his life a little easier.

Please also consider the fact that I have experienced everything I write about in some way or form. Nothing is secondhand. If I haven't found real relevance in something, I won't mention it.

I guess there is quite an amount of explaining to do about angel-consciousness and about how I channel—which leads to one of the biggest birthday presents I could receive.

Getting down and intimate with one's own experiences isn't always liberating to me; it's just a reminder to pass on, as best I can, certain tools that worked better than others for me.

I have always channeled, but not exactly as I do now—unfortunately. The way I channeled as a child has always made helping indigo children easy.

Children are such closed little cherubs—how they heal themselves and all that they are able to see—but the most interesting aspect to them is how they balance and communicate.

A child who openly tells his parents all that I have described is a rarity, and I can only speak for the ones I have treated. Such children usually come to me because they can't sleep or are becoming very agitated.

Parents are often amazed that after I ask their children a couple of questions about their abilities—which in most cases they have never divulged to their parents—I can tell what they easily connect to.

Once they are able to communicate with somebody about how they connect, it is like opening something that has been bottled up under immense pressure. They just blurt everything out.

This is the surprising part for parents. I then show the children the part of them that is stopping them from sleeping, and their relief is instantaneous. After that, many of their abilities unfold.

How they connect and what they connect to needs to be reflected on. A large amount of consciousness is separated, with the right or wrong connections connecting exactly.

We now have the separated consciousness connected and working, and these children they aren't even slightly afraid to look at the scary aspects. Why would I show them a scary bit of energy? Simply so they can see and then sense the release.

You see, when sensitive kids know that dense matter has been annoying them, it's not enough to just release it. They want to make sure this aspect is gone for good, because once they sense this, there are no more problems.

As a child, I couldn't get rid of the dense matter until I was much older, so at times, ghostly figures would return. For this reason, going to a hospital was murder for me. I'd just about run out the door. Isn't it natural then that sometimes I would sort of turn off for long periods?

Eventually, I was able to switch this off—until my early twenties.

Then, along came one of my worst insights ever, something I didn't want to know—when my best friend's mother was going to pass over. Waking up crying and seeing somebody pass over wasn't joyous. Neither was telling my mate, insisting that something was wrong and that he needed to ring home at once. This led to me shutting down, except when a ghost of somebody would present itself where I was working.

At night as I relaxed, I still had problems shutting off completely, so I just went back to the stuff I did as a kid. This kept me stable, but I didn't openly channel.

This was to be interrupted, though. I had bought a concrete truck. In case you don't know, they have a high centre of gravity, and when off-camber, they roll over easily.

I was happily driving along one day on the highway, when all traffic came to an abrupt halt in front of me. Coming up very quickly were two people on push bikes with large packs. At this point, I had the choice of either running these poor people over or going over the embankment to where a new road was being built. Of course, there was no decision, and over the bank I went.

At that moment, I was not driving that truck. I saw my grandfather driving, and I was looking down at the hopper, which is where all the aggregate goes in, wondering why it wasn't falling over. Yes, this was a complete out-of-body experience while driving. Imagine that.

Next thing I know, I'm on the next road with the brakes on and not a scratch to the truck—and unable to fathom how the truck never turned over.

I admit I was a little in shock after my out-of-body experience while driving, not to mention seeing my grandfather at the wheel. You know what my first reaction was? After a couple of expletives, I realized that my grandfather had never driven a truck. He was a printer. And then I just laughed to myself.

Then, of course, it hit home what had just happened in a spiritual sense, and I have to admit it was mind-blowing, to say the least. The experience was enough to ensure that I asked a couple of questions about what had gone on.

*Use your gift*, was the message to me. It was like a bolt out of the blue, but I was ready.

I was aware that a lot had changed in me, but I decided to give it a go. The only problem was that I'd been disconnected for quite a while, and you forget relevant stuff, don't you?

For quite a few years this didn't matter, until all of a sudden it was as if I could tune in to the conflicts that people around me were thinking.

This turned into hell. I couldn't turn my head off; I couldn't sleep, and to say I was a mess was an understatement.

I tried getting help from all kinds of healing modalities and books, but I was unable to find any resolution.

Help does come when you ask for it, though. This I can vouch for.

One night when I was able to sleep a little, I was awakened by the bed almost shaking, but I was unable to move. Yes, I was at first terrified, and then a sense of calm came through. This was followed by an immensely bright light that engulfed me. At this point, there was absolutely no fear, just a sense that I mattered.

This lasted no more than a couple of minutes, but it was intense. The message I received then was, *Now you will understand.*

From that point on, I seemed to recover overnight, but I was fragile when I thought about channeling again. I did have a lot of questions to be answered, though. Why did I need to comprehend what I had gone through? What was I meant to understand?

I didn't reconnect, but I asked many different mediums and clairvoyant friends about it. Much the same answer came back every time. My experience was meant to help unlock how this happens to many people and so I could help those with anxiety or fear-related illness. Neither of these prospects thrilled me in the least.

Months went by quickly, and I was back to being strong, not just in body but in mind. At this point in my life, I was more concerned about what the tide was doing or if the weather looked good to go fishing than I was about doing any spiritual reconnecting.

This, of course, was about to change quickly. My beautiful, deep sleep was interrupted by an energy that took me from being asleep to being instantly wide awake. It's not like I got a shock; it just felt like something was about to happen. No, the house was not burning down. Then came the message: *It's about time you used those skills of yours, David.* I wasn't quite ready for a message out of the blue like this.

I did, of course, start to connect again, as I had so many questions to be answered, but I also asked to be secure in the knowledge that all I channeled was truth and that I wouldn't accept any crap.

*Then you need to comprehend all that you have received, ye*s, was the answer I got.

I did receive many insights as to how, why, where, and when everything I had experienced was to make sense. Once again, this is definitely the short version.

Basically, I was to be instructed in a couple of new insights that boiled down to asking questions that would form a sequential understanding. My first insight added up to what I am outlining here, since I have found it to be oh-so-correct. My experience opened up an insight for me, but I also saw how it affected other people in many ways.

The largest surprise came from the source, which explained the fact that we all channel in some way, that none of us is exempt.

You had better check, please, that this is correct.

Why is this so significant?

Basically, my realisation boiled down to something that I could easily interpret and comprehend. Simply, if everybody channeled, then everybody could be affected the same as myself, and even indigos could be affected with separated consciousness.

Then the self-realization was: *Ah, you idiot. It's not just that everybody channels; it's that they aren't aware that they do it, or that they do it unconsciously and in a wrong way. I've got it.*

For me this was like a bolt of lightning. It explained fear anxiety, restlessness, stress—right down the list to depression. Then I was shown how this affected the physical, not just the mind.

Now I was able to comprehend what all clairvoyant friends and my sister Julie had passed on to me, but what they had described was an understatement. It was a bit like the weather forecaster saying we might get a bit of a shower and a category-one cyclone comes along.

I couldn't wait to telephone everybody and relate why every new connection made so much sense. I knew this was only the tip of the iceberg, but—*wow*—everything just fit together.

The fact that everybody else related in the same way with the same understanding also made a lot of sense, and I was able to comprehend the huge potential.

Everybody's enthusiasm got me more than a little excited. At last I really could see the direction the source had pointed out to me with a bit of logical understanding.

The next logical channeling similarity is *intuition*, and it's just a different way of channeling, in that we do it unconsciously. And I was easily able to ascertain that many of us do it wrong in some way.

Had you ever contemplated that we all channel? I definitely hadn't. Have you checked to make sure this is correct?

My next instruction involved being shown many different activations of energy. This explained how I was able to interpret some very negative thoughts or the states of others' minds and to positively control my thoughts.

This introduction was to change my life forever, though at the time, I just thought it was sort of fun to sense. The fun part soon opened up the conclusion that it really was showing me how conscious energy moved and how unconsciousness moved or could be moved onto us.

Finding all these unconscious elements soon added up to why we were unable to sense what was really going on around us. I awoke to how this affected our everyday thoughts about what we think we want and how we want to be. The list exploded.

It was easy to correlate this to the emotions people were feeling, and a good deal of this was simply interference.

The next lightbulb moment showed me that people's feelings are not all that is reflected by their emotions. Now I knew why I felt great one minute and crappy the next, without any reason. Yee-ha.

The next revelation was how this related to all physical matter and why it constricted the flow of current to relevant bodies of energy. My elation was quickly kicked down, as I realised what a huge body of understanding lay in front of me.

I comprehended how this related to me and how this whole interrelated problem could be solved—and that it could also be solved in the future for others.

This wasn't one day's understanding; it took many months to create what my guides called a real point of foundation that all our understanding could work from. Each foundation then needed unraveling to find out how we had complicated each simple understanding.

A decade after starting and then completing the last draft, I am attempting to ensure that every interpretation will be current throughout all of the new millennia.

My desire to be so very correct needs a little explaining.

Consider that the source has been telling us for quite some time that we need to get to know exactly what we have a spirit-body for. No matter what books we read about self-help or new age, no matter the theme, it all relates to us getting to know what our spirit-body does.

The message is loud and clear: we need to be open to thinking a little differently about what it entails to be in the new millennia.

Without seeming to be to way-out, most of us are also aware that the energy about us has changed somewhat. The energy now basically enables us to do lots of new stuff, but the best part is that it enables us to free up parts of our spirit-bodies that have been unable to communicate properly or connect to this wonderful energy.

Even a decade ago, every energy coming to us was quite different. For want of a better description, I used to call it "fairy-floss intuition." That energy didn't facilitate us to be firm or to challenge what is correct. It meant that fewer people were open or inquisitive about what didn't stack up correctly. We knew there was more.

We have only scratched the surface of being able to get the whole picture. So let's add to the dynamics of this pictures focus, shall we?

Now that you have learned that we all channel in some manner, there is one small revelation our guides would like opened to you, yes. And this is rather a large yes as well.

Consider one enormous fact that many are aware of, but not too many. If a consciousness does not have current flowing through it, there is no possible way it can decipher what is true or relevant.

I know we have discussed this before, but you are able comprehend more now.

Consider a speck of separated consciousness. It cannot detect all that it is receiving, as no connective consciousness is connected to this separated particle of consciousness. So it's all on its lonesome.

Well, it's not really alone. This particle is still able to contribute. It's just unable to receive a full message from us. The energy from us has been constricted or restricted. This is where the lack of current comes into play; it is simply consciousness without the full current flowing through it. But remember that it can contribute in a totally incapacitated manner.

How would this effect you? Imagine you're that having a brilliant day, when all of a sudden you have a crappy sensation. You think to yourself, *Why would I feel this? Everything is just great.* Well, now you know your contributor. Better check, though. Yes.

Now, continuing in the same light, I need to direct you back to a new understanding.

In the old millennium, we had two contributors of truth—the one with all the correct connective consciousness and the one that's incapacitated.

Now you are able to comprehend the source's desire for a new millennium with only one truth for everybody.

So, if we are all on the same page, imagine how easily conflicts would be resolved. When you consider all the enormous self-potential that has been untapped, it's clear that we use only a limited portion of our capacity.

Now do you comprehend the need for a new millennium?

Since everything is out in the open, I hope you comprehend why every tiny facet of information needs to be comprehended properly and unsuppressed, free of the old thought processes of the old millennium. Better check this all out then, yes.

Do you comprehend that having your energy linked to both processes at the start causes us a little havoc? Well, do you? Think about this.

We have been receiving two sets of emotions, feelings, and intuition— and that is just on a couple of levels. This opens a whole plethora of connotations.

Now that this can of worms is open, it means that we all need to be able to comprehend the real differences between the two.

At this point, I'm nearly ready to switch camps and ask my doctor for a pill to fix all this, but I don't think he would understand. So, I guess I need to ask the source for the pill to fix this dilemma.

You see, when you don't know about something, you sure as hell are not going to worry about it, are you?

This is why a lot of people take medications to mask a wiring problem.

Demographics doesn't change the problem either. Every country in the world uses something to escape it—from cava to drugs that are stronger than any prescription.

This hits home another reality. When in the world's history have legal and illegal substances been taken in such epidemic proportions? When has mental fatigue ever been so prevalent? We need to wake up to the duality we are living in and ask why we are living in it.

If we first understand how and why this debilitates us, then it is easy to determine where and when it is no longer going to be an infringement in our daily lives.

Once again, there is the other option, of course: to put our heads in the sand and pretend none of this exists.

Thank heavens that so many books on the new millennium have already been written to stretch our awareness. Some have already started us in the right direction. Appreciate that they have all asked plenty of questions to unlock many limitations and to challenge the status quo, so our next steps aren't so daunting.

Remember when we were told that we come with an instruction manual? That is what this chapter is about: unlocking the secret of the manual's location and—more importantly—learning how use it. This will unlock your true senses that haven't been used to their potential. It will also open up true potentials that go untapped but are needed in the new millennium.

I hope this is making sense to you. To help you understand, the source will be opening up many tools to make deciphering truth much easier.

I do have a favour to ask, though. Please don't speed-read or try to skip chapters. Not only will you get lost; you won't experience or reactivate all the keys and codes.

You might now see a pattern emerging: you need to comprehend much new "knowing" before you take the next step. It is easy to formulate this new knowing or new truth, which then stimulates all current to be compatible. With compatible current, you are then—and only then—able to facilitate the use of the connective consciousness.

So this section is a little like being in a large department store, purchasing all the bits and pieces to help make everything work in the new millennium.

Of course, you have received many parts unconsciously, as they are the bits we have been preparing, and these need to come from the unconscious to the conscious. If you haven't appreciated them, they have become separated by now. These self-aspects and abilities are waiting for the sequence that will connect them to the synchronicity. They are waiting to be told that they are needed now.

Sequences of your self can relate to another time sequence or a new-time sequence—the presence. The presence time-sequence releases the impatient self, the one wanting to run before you crawl. Without presence in the correct questions from the source, I wouldn't have progressed very far. I also encountered many indecisions in my early days of trying to comprehend new-time truth.

With this dilemma, I guess I will be asking you to check that everything is correct or okay—or whatever language you identify with to ensure that consciousness is flowing through the truth.

Yes, in truth, this is the only difference between the two. All you need to check is whether or not a real consciousness is flowing through whatever you desire to know the real truth of.

Now, do you understand why our guides have at times taken us a little more slowly? It is to ensure that we comprehend first that we have actually been receiving two truths in many different ways.

This is also the basis of all duality—a real truth and one not so real or even slightly true. This might seem too simple an analogy to represent duality, but it's the misrepresentation of duality that is complicated.

Again, this isn't my own translation, so please check that this is a reality and not something I or my guides made up just to make things interesting.

As the source pointed out to me, those who desire to control real truth are those who desire it to seem complicated. This is also a point of contention, so perhaps before considering this statement, you could also ask if this is correct, please.

Now that you have avoided the consequences of taking any statement for granted, was the translation on this point correct? And was it also correct that many who desire to control the truth make every aspect of spirituality seem very complicated?

Consider as well, according to the source, that when spirituality started out, it was very simple, with no complications whatsoever. So, if the spiritual aspect of life seems a little complicated, what has happened?

It's just so easy to predict, isn't it? It is the same scenario as taking our cars full of computers to a mechanic now. If something is a little complicated, we leave it to those who seem to know best or are meant to have our best intentions at heart.

This is another of the new millennium points. With new connective consciousness and all the other good bits, you will know instantly if the person you are sharing your evolved intent with is truly of the same ethics and virtue as you.

Imagine a political arena where politicians actually keep a promise, as they are reflecting the same intent and desires that all people seek.

In the past, those who were directly responsible for being connected to spirit also controlled just about every aspect of daily life. This means that in the future you will be able ensure that your future is correct in every aspect of your daily life.

It also means an end to the why-did-I-do-this-again cycle where something isn't what you wanted.

There is also a larger picture to this scenario, as we might expect. As I said, I have had an immense amount of help to unlock so much that I had been questioning, and I appreciate the help that the source has extended to me.

We do need help, and this is another aspect of receiving. With a connective angel-consciousness, the correct message that help is needed on a real matter is likely to actually get through.

The source once again recommends that you check the truth of this statement. When you do, you reach a new depth of consciousness within your soul that you have not accessed before. This is to open yourself up in another way. The connective consciousness is opening a whole new opportunity with your new angel-consciousness to connect on a more full-time basis.

We discussed before how you connect to your innermost self when you relax or, most often, when you sleep. Well, this is a similar connection with your soul—or to be more precise, your spirit-soul. The only difference is that this is going to be more full-time than part-time.

Imagine how much more in-tune your intuition would be with a full-time connection rather than a part-time one.

But hold on a minute here. Haven't we always been connected to our soul? Yes, you have indeed.

So how am I going to be *more* connected?

It's a different soul. Sorry, I'm not trying to confuse you, but I am about to remind you that your spirit-soul and physical-soul are in fact two different energies.

Does this also explain self-separation? The same is true for your heart as well.

For this to become more complete, we need a little help in searching for a conscious aspect of your soul.

There are more ramifications to this dialogue than perhaps you ever considered. What the heck do I mean? Well, before you would want to connect to your soul or heart on a more full-time basis, there are major considerations to ponder.

You are going to be more actively aware of an actual connection to your own spirit. This is a major foundational portion of your innermost, real self.

You might actually find out lots of things about yourself in there. You may even find bits of you that need changing.

Can you actually cope with this? Eventually you're going to have to find strength in yourself that you didn't know existed. That's the easy stuff, because this isn't going to happen overnight.

It also means unlocking, yes—unlocking new, innermost, real desires with a new intent. Did I mention that this innermost self has a source aspect to this energy? This source aspect helps to connect to the real, collective consciousness of all sources of source consciousness.

Yes, I know that's a bit of a mouthful, and it is a lot to think about, especially since you're so used to going around in cycles in the old millennium. Yes, I thought a self-source aspect might scare you off.

Imagine that you want to actively be in contact with your own spirit-soul of origin and eventually your spirit-heart of origin.

This has immense ramifications throughout your whole self. It means you desire to check out what your soul and heart have been missing out on, have never connected to, or have been separated from.

You will also be defining large parts of you that actually exist but have never been contacted.

Much of you is actually present but unrelated in an unconscious manner or present and unaccounted for.

So, while you are contemplating whether or not to connect to an actual part of your source-self, we'll move on for a moment.

Okay, you've had your moment, so I guess I can continue to open up a source-aspect to connect to the source-aspect of your spirit-soul.

This is a new-time tithing to connect to all new-time soul-spirits. This evolved tithing of this evolved new time is to open freedom to all self, innermost knowing, and wisdom.

I now open in all self-presence all innermost equations of this evolved life to free all old-time programming and to open all true, living, life intuition.

This evolved freedom is to be always present in this reality of all new-time intuition of presence.

Connecting to this evolved part of your spirit-soul opens to what really exists in your spirit-soul, not what has been programmed by limiting the spirit soul to an existence.

This guided message simply means to connect to the knowing, understanding, and comprehension that exists in this soul, or to find out what is really going on and what you have totally been unaware of. I was going to highlight this, but it is already contentious enough.

When the reasoning of self-consideration in the soul has been so limited, all self-compassion and gratitude is now able to contribute. This is so you can connect many new aspects of intuition to this knowing, understanding, and comprehension.

This will be slowly filtered into your intuition. Otherwise it would become a little overwhelming.

Please remember why this is so. Your energy would change too rapidly and perhaps even reject what is a real evolution. Perhaps we should consider how many times this may have happened in the past, and we were unable to evolve for this very reason.

Seeing we are on the subject of energy, perhaps we should keep following this line of thought, and I should introduce you to how I came across activations.

I would like to explain a little bit about this one phenomenon, because this is something I comprehend very personally. While this affected me because of different circumstances, the results are something I easily comprehend. This is one of the underlying reasons I was able to interpret where and why myself or others were separated. So this part is back to a more personal part of my experiences, I guess.

At this stage of our conversation, or at this time in my life, I have connected and reconnected to roughly the same amount of consciousness, except for a couple of extra ones I wasn't aware I had connected to, as I had forgotten.

Please appreciate that having a spirit-guide and having a physical—and spirit-guide combined are very different.

Some understandings take months to unlock, but when we heal, this understanding is passed on in seconds. This is the automatic part I was outlining before.

Now, did you receive the connection? As we heal the spirit, we pass on how to heal the physical to release pain.

At the moment, I would like to concentrate on all things mental, as this is quickly transferred to physical.

This is a short version of how I was easily able to see how to combat anger, anxiety, fear, and most energy associated with an emotion or feeling.

I reasoned that if everybody channeled, they were open to interferences from many levels of separated consciousness. Perhaps you can appreciate why there are thousands of books endeavouring to help us sort out our different emotions and feelings.

Do you think that this might be made a little simpler if we were able to comprehend that our emotions had in a way been receiving two set of instructions? Is this worth considering, do you think?

Imagine the conflict in your emotions with two sets of truth. Add to this equation indifferent feelings, and we are gathering quite a concoction of experiences, aren't we?

Does this paint a whole new picture for you, or did you see the implications of two truths straightaway?

It's funny that, as soon as you mention emotions, everybody begins to take things personally.

Now imagine being able to sense all these separated emotions and feelings of others. It is easy to see how your own emotions become a little confused. This is what I had to learn to switch off.

I guess this is the same as anything: experience something personally, and you have immense empathy for others who may be afflicted with the same pain.

This is my personal reason for writing this book. The source just wanted to add quite a few extra bits and pieces. I guess it makes things more comprehensive.

A couple of months after learning many new aspects of my angel wings, my innermost spirit was reintroduced to an awareness of the world of activations. This opened up many logical understandings, reasoning, and cognizance to change my entire insight.

From this moment, you could postulate that a whole new self-strength was evident, but I was still fragile for a couple of weeks until my real self-intuition kicked in. Luckily, now I can pass this connective angel-consciousness on without the fragile component.

I was aware that many things had changed that I simply wasn't able to put my finger on before. But in every part of me, I just knew—as did family and friends—that so much had changed.

I need to put my sister Julie in an entirely different bracket. While we have always been close, we have always bounced our spiritual understandings off each other, so my appreciation of this is probably beyond your comprehension.

When you are working way outside normal thought, things can get a little lonely. Also, you need others' points of view, as you might have missed something that they easily see. Not everybody has this same advantage, and there isn't a day I don't appreciate it. Because of this, you can understand how much we have hashed out over time. Having the same DNA helps as well—and sometimes hinders the outcome—as you are so close.

The significance of this working relationship of understanding was about to change in a completely new manner.

The following describes an activation that opened a new world of understanding energies.

I started my night with a meditation. As soon as I hopped on the bed, I noticed a different grounding. I was unable to move. Not only was I grounding but unfolding. I received what is like an automatic affirmation: *This I will open to you later.*

Then I received my instructions: "David, you are to transform somewhat, my friend. You notice on your left-hand side many guardian angels that you have never reconnected to in this lifetime, yes. I, my friend, have been in contact always, yes, and you remember my energy, yes.

"David, you are to be tithed an insight, which in truth you have asked for. By now you are noticing the omnipresence of yourself. This is to stay with you as you open all understandings. You will also be aware of a new state of body. This you will use to comprehend your new destination.

"David, notice where all self-energy sits please. Now notice where all mind portals sit, yes. You are noticing all self-energy. Release through this, yes."

All of a sudden I was becoming very agitated, as I sensed all my energy release. I was easily able to ascertain that this wasn't good. Throughout this, I was unable to move or reply. I could easily see that a lot of my energy was escaping straight out the top of my head.

I could then see this energy become very dense and dark and flow into what looked like solid-gold orbs. Then, all of a sudden I was very much back to being guided.

"David, you sense that all is not well, yes. This is where all your separated self is going, all your separated consciousness, yes. You know this sense, yes. Now you instantly understand, yes, the emotion of loss, of total emptiness, loss of any self-strength, any self love. All have dispersed in an instant."

In the next instant, all was flowing back in, with no sense of the dark or dense matter I had seen. The important part is that I recognised where all my energy had gone and how it was able to come back. But I will return to my meditation.

"David, you recognise that this was your consciousness, your self-consciousness, now separated from you, yes." My only thought was, *Wow, this happens to everybody.*

"David, you have reconnected to your grailage and your own direction of your omnipresent prophecy. David, this simply means that you desire to stay present, be in contact with your consciousness, and be conscious of your direction, nothing more."

I was more than "having kittens" when this was directed to me, and I spoke plenty of expletives. It just seemed too much to take in. I mean, I wasn't exactly expecting this and I had no mental preparation for what I was receiving.

I did remember a bit of prayer for some reason, not that I was at all religious and still am not. "For all which we are to receive, may we all be truly thankful." It's easy to understand now, meaning that you need to be able to receive before you give.

I'll admit I was out of my comfort zone in the first part of reconnection, but everything made sense. Everything just felt comfortable, like I was home at last. More importantly, for once in my life it didn't seem to matter that I always felt like I didn't belong.

This was so much to take in, in such a short time frame.

"You will soon understand." This was the last message of the night, as I came out of the meditation absolutely exhausted but feeling good—except for the last answer.

I now easily comprehend so much, especially about separated consciousness and how the effects debilitate and incapacitate you and make life intolerable.

Instantly, I remembered a couple of different ways I used to balance as a kid. This helped me reground, as I didn't feel grounded until I did. I couldn't wait to pass on my learning experience to Julie the next day. I showed her what had unlocked many different healing potentials that we both could use.

But as soon as I had passed this on, I instantly felt listless. What the heck was going on? Julie checked, but got nothing.

Timidly, I reconnected. "David, Julie needs to pass on a point that at present you both do not appreciate." I told her that we needed to hold hands and that we would pass on to each other whatever was opened to either of us.

We both went into a massive spin, unlocking, with our guides holding us everywhere. Our right sides went numb, experiencing the same energy as last night. Then automatic knowing or recognition popped in, and Julie couldn't stop smiling.

What had taken place? This was our answer.

"My beloveds, you have experienced a change in how you are to exist in all future time. You have both experienced a balance to pass with every reactivation you are to unlock. You both sense that you are centred in a completely new manner, in a completely new form, and of course in a completely new flow.

"My friends, both of your energies were needed to compile this understanding that has just unfolded, yes. At this moment in this time, you have reconnected to real, androgynous synergy, an element that needs to be reintroduced for all new-time."

The only reason I kept parts of this unfolding in this chapter is to help explain to you how things started to unfold so differently for us. You see, there is a large component of androgynous energy in every freeing activation that is ever to be opened.

I could just as easily have said that I had a life-changing experience and was guided to get rid of some separation of consciousness. However, the vibrational energy that transpired and connected to many levels of our consciousness could never have been passed on.

One of the last changes to be revised was the androgynous self. Don't get too up-tight. This doesn't mean that all of a sudden you will be over-appreciating the opposite sex or having gay tendencies. This does, however, start to unlock many constrictions and restrictions that will be indicated as we proceed.

This is the explanation for an androgynous self, as I have interpreted it. Because we have a spirit-body and a physical one, there are certain allowances that we need to get used to. There's nothing new here. There are so many books reflecting this line of thought, and many of us are aware that the self-spirit body, or the one we take from life to life, has a couple of aspects to it. Perhaps we don't know about these aspects, or we have forgotten they exist.

Another term related to androgynous presence is *omniance*. This is all about balance and ensuring that no one uses gender in a controlling manner.

However, omnipresence is one of the aspects we freak out about when first linked to. This is simply terminology or translation and is not associated with our physical being.

How we came to disregard this term with our own spirit has a little story attached to it, and if you think I will pass it by, you are wrong. It has quite a few insights in it.

This understanding took months to unfold, so you are getting the abbreviated version. Please be grateful, because gratitude is able to be restored in a present time, not in a past "now."

To comprehend *omniance*, I was directed that I would also need to understand *afterlife*. This connection wasn't totally apparent to me, either. I was asked to think of the many monuments in my life that I held sacred. Okay, that was fine; but what did it have to do with after-life? This is the conversation that transpired.

"David, imagine that you wanted to create a message in the time of the pharaohs. You just built something large, with pictures that depicted a story, yes.

"All kings needed to pass on messages and promote their self-importance, and the only way to do this was to turn themselves into gods. None of this is new, of course.

"Life in this age was a little shorter than it is now, so the length of one's life was a daily focus. The priests of the day talked up the after-life and the wonderful life that existed if you followed god's will. This, of course, was easier for the king, who was also considered to be a god. This part is also nothing new.

"So, the focus of life in many ways was on after-life—not an eternal life, just after-life—and definitely not a *living* life. This is an example of how changing your focus on a real life affects your consciousness. This part you have already comprehended: that our consciousness holds us together and, if not manipulated—yes, manipulated—it gives us a correct focus.

"Spirit-consciousness lives forever. This is the bit that we take from one life to another. Most of us relate to this, don't we? This consciousness is therefore omniance; it is of the highest consciousness. Well, isn't it? Check.

"This consciousness holds all that is true—and all the mistakes we have made, as well. It is also a vehicle to connect to all that exists, everywhere, as a whole collective consciousness of absolutely everything of a real source matter.

"In theory, if we use a connective consciousness, we should be able to connect our spirit-consciousness to an absolute collective consciousness of all that exists in a true reality of presence.

"If we were to modify this to all the spirit-consciousness that is complete at this moment and not separate, then, using a connective consciousness, we would still be able to connect to a more limited version of a full or complete collective consciousness—or god-consciousness or source-consciousness or whatever term you choose for this complete consciousness."

Is this worth knowing, and is it relative to allowing us to be whole? Better check for yourself.

Now we have ascertained that we are making headway by learning to connect some very major parts of our consciousness together to create a stronger and more efficient self. The tithings you received earlier as an affirmation are all linked to what you have opened.

In the opening affirmation, think of the presence of worth as wealth. It is worth finding out where this consciousness is heading. The direction is intended to introduce an omnipresence or true direction that is present on a full-time basis to raise your real self-consciousness.

There is also another consideration that will be presented in the next chapter: the gift. Without it, how would you know if you are in fact connecting to real or separated consciousness?

Remember, you can also only connect through the real spirit to real collective consciousness of all that exists. This is all about using your original soul-connection, your point of origin. With this ammunition, knowing that only real collective consciousness connects through the spirit, you can now understand the extent to which all guides have gone to ensure that all spirit-consciousness is understood more completely.

Let's hammer this home. *Spirit* is where your original soul and heart exist. If you integrate these in a real manner using connective consciousness, then a strength of self-spirit is created, which is the vital foundational component of our true self.

This whole section might seem unexciting and rather tedious, but it also works on subconscious levels that you are not fully aware of. And if you are unaware, then you probably aren't going to be too excited until the real relevance unfolds. Consider parts of this to be preparation for eventually putting together the unconscious, separated bits and pieces in the correct manner.

In a roundup of this chapter, we have identified a couple of elements of your self that are a way for you to become the facilitator. This is so you can interpret your unidentified parts that belonged to a past consciousness and—depending on how they came to be—are now sitting as un-consciousness or in-consciousness.

We also discussed the ramifications of these sitting separated, thus rebounding many illusional emotions and feelings.

*Rebounding* is the effect felt as withdrawal kicks in. Remember, you are used to not functioning at full capacity. The other connotation of this is that you are used to the conflict of duality—two emotions being thrust upon you at one moment.

Why did I recap? Simply because I know the effects this separated spirit causes, and many are unaware of them. It is hard to reflect on some aspects that are only of an in-conscious or un-conscious nature, as you are unaware of their everyday abilities and potential.

The reason for writing this book is to ensure that there is no reason to accept separated consciousness as being normal. That separation limits you from all real potential.

So that everything is released with ease and with the grace of guiding guardian spirit, a new sequential synchronicity is to be tithed—with all gratitude, compassion, and appreciation—to open all self-elements of real love.

To facilitate this, the keys and codes in the next chapter open these opportunities to be more of a free self without the conflicting interruptions in our lives.

These are tithed with purpose so that real love is present in each and every self-moment of a real, living life.

The following are not my words, of course, but those of Sordlion and J'spirin.

# 10

## KEYS AND CODES TO OPEN A NEW-TIME CONSCIOUSNESS

To facilitate this small understanding but rather large activation, we are going to need the help of a few friends.

Sordlion and J'spirin are star angels, who, along with many other vital contributors, have opened so many new-time understandings for us.

They have pointed me in directions that, quite honestly, I would never have found on my own, as they desire us to break new ground and not simply rehash the past comprehensions.

I liken this to thinking that the world is flat and finding that it is in fact round. They have pushed my boundaries to look outside not just one but many square boxes.

These boxes have turned out to be rather large, orb-like bodies that we simply haven't been using. How could we, if we were not even aware that they existed?

"Looking outside the box" is a good simile, as we were kind of boxed in and therefore unaware of everything on our inside that was not reflected. All that was indicated to exist within us never added up to the reflection of our auras, chakras, or meridians.

In other words, once I was aware of what the energy and the emotions were saying, nothing added up. I needed to find out what the emotions were *not* telling me as well.

To help this come about with ease and to help me look outside my comfort zone, I needed to feel comfortable—not rampaged with energy that was connected to others rather than myself.

This is a point many people identify with. Have you ever wondered how much the contributions of other people's energy affects your own everyday thought, comprehension, or self-decisions? This is an area we will be discussing at length later, but my guides have asked to set up a little bit of groundwork first.

Imagine an area of your own energy about yourself that is like an extra aura but many times larger. Not only does this reflect all that you reflect now but all that you desire to reflect in the future.

While I have found this to be a vital help, especially in these changing times, it is also an area I forgot about for quite a while. Why? I and my guides kept me rather busy, exploring the many boundaries that are shown to interrupt our daily lives.

You see, if I had received the new-time environment straightaway, I would have had little appreciation for all the conflicting environmental interferences that were disturbing my energy. What is to be shown to you is an extra environment. The reason for this is that you are much more expansive than what you probably give yourself credit for.

The other facet of this is that it grows as your strength does. Not only are you protected from feeling your self-growth; others are too.

Why is this an issue? Because a brighter light attracts more attention. If others are also growing in spirit and in their senses, they can be intimidated by a stronger energy. Yes, you don't mean any harm with this revitalized energy, but if your self is also working at a higher frequency, you can interfere with others' energy.

This simply means that your energy would annoy them, just by your being around. So, what if you are married or in a steady relationship? Now am I attracting your interest?

You see, just the reverse is correct also. Where before your relationship was harmonious, now this person just sets you off. Please consider these consequences carefully. While this is a significant factor, so is the reverse; denser energy of others can also interfere in our own growing, conscious energy.

Perhaps if you sit down and think of how this energy has affected you or others, the awareness becomes quite significant in your daily life. This is rather a large problem now, especially if one partner in a relationship is growing while the other is rather stagnant for the moment.

Simply, this is meant to help stop the spiraling divorce rates. While you grow in consciousness, your partner is not upset, nor are those you work with or come in contact with. This maintains a harmonic level of peace for you and others.

To put everything into perspective, you are about to grow another self-environment, which stabilizes your present self-consciousness. This then helps the stabilized self to take in only the new consciousness that is of a harmonious nature.

So you are setting about creating a future for yourself. It is all about living life in the present rather than the past and not worrying about your future or becoming preoccupied with the after-life aspect of things. Right now, you might not be aware that your actual self is reflecting these elements in every part of your self, but you are.

Earlier, I mentioned that the spiritual nature of our self was, in the beginning, quite simple and uncomplicated. When I first desired to unravel this maelstrom of disconnected equations that the energy was not reflecting, I noticed two scenarios.

You may find this word *scenario* repeated somewhat. Why? Well, in the last chapter we found that there was a different explanation for duality, yes. We found that because of separation, we were interpreting two sets of truth—sometimes both at the same time.

We then discussed an expansion of this first scenario on a truth factor, where we found that we had our own self-truth contribution. Then we found another scenario where others' desires or intents caused interference.

Put simply, we had two truths: one involved only the self, and one involved ourselves and others, and the aspect of others could easily become complicated where many contributed.

Consider this complication over many lifetimes where, instead of being occupied with many contributors, we just lump them all together to form an imprint or pattern that ends up being a separating schedule. This simplifies the equation to fix everything up.

This makes sense, doesn't it? Otherwise, we would end up on a wild goose chase. Add to this equation the fact that many have been contributing for many lifetimes.

We also discussed how the "now"—yes, the now-time—also refers to a time without presence. This means that many are inflicting on us their presence of what they were unable to resolve in their lifetimes.

In such a case, our past relatives are just being generous. Don't forget that we have done exactly the same to them, life after life after life. Do you see now how after-life is relevant? Another way of thinking about this is that our relatives also desire to see how we have resolved or are resolving the same problems inflicted on them, yes, life after life.

Let's reflect on something important my guides shared with me while I was touring Siem Reap in Cambodia. The conversations we shared are too long to reflect on, but what I interpreted can be boiled down to understanding that many life schedules are being repeated. We end up being separate instead of complete.

Being of two different self-truths means that we are unable to be whole—not of two minds, not of two memories, not of two consciousnesses, and not of two separate bodies of conflicting energy.

Before you read on, please stop and think about what has just been outlined to you. Consider all real outcomes, contributions, and conclusions and how they all add up. "I would just think about that a little bit longer," my sister always says.

In the following chapters, we will be discussing how and where to find these debilitating aspects. At this moment, you need to be aware of the *why* and *when* factors. You see, the annoying fact is that this was outlined to me fourteen years ago without the *now*-component or the concept of repeating the past in the now.

Our complete consciousness is unable to be present all at one time, but all sequences, if joined together, become synchronicity. Why then are we unable to join all these sequences together to recreate synchronicity and move the interfering past life-schedules into the now?

With these schedules now able to be released, a new self-presence is able to be created through your present and activated soul and heart.

These *how* and *why* factors are the preparations of what you are to receive—once you have learned a little more about how to receive in a present state of simply being.

This reflection is concerned with a new and different, natural self-nature. To start this ball rolling for me, I needed to learn how to reflect in a different manner. I needed to change my concept of having keys and codes. When I first interpreted "keys and codes," I thought they were a type of lost scrolls. I took each little mark that looked like a hieroglyph as only having written meaning.

Yes, if I looked at any of these strange-looking markings that I saw in many paintings, I could give a definition of what they meant; but this was actually being short-sighted.

Each one, if looked at a little longer, turned into a working light, where a limited, dimensional aspect was being reflected. I then found that what was translated and interpreted by our guides was a whole new equation of what or how things really are.

This is a small transcript of our conversation.

"David, you are beginning to sense and see differently, yes. You are able to determine that all is not what it seems to be, yes.

"David, the interferences you are interpreting are the afflictions of separated consciousness. Over the coming months, we will open the causes of this disability.

"David, you have also found many interferences that are simply past life, which people interpret as multidimensional energy, but which in fact are only past life, yes.

"David, this infliction is, in fact, holding many people from being able to be at peace and to be present with their self. This aspect also means that many people will then internalise or constrict their own nature, yes, and this will then debilitate all self-growth.

"David, this will then be reflected as deactivating or separating all forms of real spirit. This is basically represented as being self-resentment of a balanced self-worth.

"David, you have realised that this means that people will only be able to focus on the material aspect that is not reflected in their everyday lives, to focus on synchronicity and why their spirits have been broken in so many ways.

"David, have you thought of focusing all your energies on why people are unaware? People are so unaware that in many ways they do not desire to find truth that might be confrontational or to find real reasons for their absence of reasoning.

"David, in truth, you thought that this paragraph was a little too confrontational, yes. This is simply because people are not able to be at peace; they consider looking closer at the self to be confrontational, yes.

"David, what may seem unorthodox is simply a paradox, and many at present are unable to see the potential of new reasoning, yes. Why is this statement correct? Simply put, if you are receiving two sets of truth, then you are in confusion and thus unable to reason, yes.

"David, this means that there is no reason or truth available to use. Most will either follow what everybody else is doing or do absolutely nothing and stay stagnant. This is then going to be reflected in all energy cycles. This is how you saw a schedule, yes, or an imprint or illusional blueprint for afterlife, repeating in a continuous cycle, yes."

My guides don't mince words; they are to-the-point and take any indirect interpretation out of the equation. The old-time alternative, as I have said, is the "fairy floss" version or the don't-worry-my-beloved-one-day-you-will-find-your-true-path version, yes. This is easy to take but resolves no misdirection of self; no outcome or reasoning is resolved.

In a way, this was a question I didn't desire to answer. Have you had a few of these yourself? Now imagine a whole stack of these questions that actually need answering. Our guides are endeavouring to show that once you strengthen the self, you are strong enough to look where once you might not have dared.

As you grow, your awareness becomes stronger as well. This means that when something is irritating you, you are seeking a resolution, not just fobbing it off.

The whole point of this conversation is that if you are able to create a new-time environment, then you are able to resolve one major issue. If you are able to concentrate on just one truth for a moment, how easy it will be to move ahead. If you desire it, a vehicle is being provided for you to look at yourself without outside conflict.

This is why we desire to resolve one of the largest and most contentious issues, where your consciousness sits outside your own environment. Yes, that is correct. It's right outside your aura or self-energy zones. That grounding effect you are sensing will facilitate the reconnection of this—after a couple of other elements are also connected and comprehended.

I start at this point when healing any new client, and every time I'm just flabbergasted that every single person I have ever met has this same debilitating element.

I will be going over this in a few different ways, but to start with, it always looks the same. This seems to stimulate certain senses deep within the soul and helps recreate certain strengths.

What does this look like? Well, that depends. If you look now, it will look like a mess of matter; if you look through a stilled aspect of yourself, then that is a different matter.

In the next chapter, I go into more depth on how it appears to me, but for now there is one more pressing engagement. All guides are ready to de-stimulate those areas of yourself that have been overworked and overstimulated and are likely to break down or overreact.

This overreaction is also one of the largest contributors to our own reactive, instinctual feelings or emotions.

Our emotions seem to conflict, but they are simply reacting to two sets of truth. They are unsure which truth you are meant to follow, so in a lot of cases, both are followed simultaneously.

This also is to be tackled shortly with awareness exercises for those who sense overreactions to this element of yourself. You may sense that your head wants to drop. This is grounding your desire to release this self-issue.

This is another reaction that interrupts the flow of our sequences into our synchronicity, yes. To help ease this situation, perhaps we need to discover why some of our elements react, while others are unreactive when they need to be.

There are many receptors that contribute to the efficient nature of our soul, which is where all foundations of our self start from, yes.

Perhaps it is time to think for a moment longer about this statement and to check that all foundations of the self start in the soul—no ifs, buts, or maybes. These foundations are the vehicles, vessels, and structures that facilitate all self-abilities to follow a soul-direction of your soul-self rather than the abilities of others.

Let's totally clarify this statement. We can't afford any wrong interpretation here, as these are to lead into some vital energy exchanges in a present manner, in all natural environments, and in your future.

Perhaps it is time to check, though.

A soul-presence is the only way to clarify a real direction, so with this in mind, imagine your soul flowing to any region of your spirit-body. This flow connects to soul-receptors that have been rather dormant. Now they are facilitating a response to a soul-question; energy is being sent out, and a response is detected and comes back to the soul.

Your soul and your self-collective consciousness are one and the same body of spirit, if the collective consciousness is actually whole. The only reason that the soul-collective consciousness may appear not to be whole is that not all of the soul-collective consciousness is able to connect to the source collective conscious.

Your soul can't fully talk to the source collective consciousness of all that exists. We need to follow the energy to understand why it can't and what impact this has on our soul-self.

Earlier on, I was expanding on the vital components that make up the collective consciousness. Really, my guides were asking me to open people's awareness about how consciousnesses move around or communicate with each other. What is present in spirit is then going to be present in the physical, so your spirit-body is the real self-blueprint, one and the same.

Now that I have said this, I must also say that this is the *complete* blueprint body. If the whole soul-component is not integrated within the blueprint, then the blueprint will appear outside the body, not within.

As you might be able to predict, we are recreating whole bodies of self-consciousness so that each body is whole and able to activate, to move in every motion it is meant to, to connect to every receptor it is meant to. Then there is no emotional reaction to a sense of being incomplete, no space of consciousness filled with any unconscious matter.

Each single consciousness is like a whole body and acts accordingly. If appreciated in a grateful manner, they will respond with compassion and gratitude.

How does this relate to us? Well, as we keep our connection to vital components of conscious matter, they will then be active, yes.

Consider that this analogy is only how it was interpreted to me, which I have concluded as correct and without constraints of understanding or interference. However, you need to conclude this for yourself.

Early on in my quest, I found that the majority of all problems seemed to stem from connections. Please let me clarify this.

The largest problem was not being able to discern between what was needed and real and what was made to look real but was only interference. Interference is the many forms of conflict that we mistake as reality. I needed to ensure that I was never connecting to the how, why, where, and when of this interfering nature.

How did this come about? The one true self-nature I counted on was my soul—my intuition, if you like. We have a built-in knowing that is the reliable aspect of our self-resources, something to be counted on.

I'm just going to blurt this bit out, as I have found it to be correct for another matter. You can take it on board, use it, and save yourself the long journey. Please get out a pen and paper immediately. No, I'm not joking.

Do yourself a favour and write this down and put it on the fridge, on the mirror, in the dash of your car, or on the computer screen. Just do it.

What I want you to write is such a foundational strength of our self that everything else revolves around it, but because of the simplicity of this self-awakening, it may go directly over your head. As I said previously, all spirituality was simple at the start.

We all place so much physical and spiritual importance on the heart, yes. Do you realise that every component, every resource, every element, every essence, every current, capacity, form, and function start with soul-content, soul-communication, and soul contribution? When you integrate all of your soul, then a presence of soul or soul-consciousness is always going to be present with all the correct connections to the correct matter in the correct way.

So what do you need to write down?

*I am of soul presence.*
*Therefore, each and every aspect of myself desires to be real*
*and of absolute source truth.*
*All of this self reflects the true, creative self-nature through*
*all self-environments to be my complete intention.*

This is the base formula I have used. I will, of course, augment this abbreviated version, as perhaps you are unable to see the innermost workings in front of you; are unable to see all the trees because of the forest.

All that is represented by a physical nature is the pivotal point our lives circulate around, so we tend to think in terms of our heart and soul. This then means that the heart in our self is considered to being the pivotal point of our desires and intent. Consequently, we are not releasing from our point of self-strength and all that is important to our makeup.

This also means that your physical matter will always become the driving factor, so you are always going to separate self-belief, balance, and harmony from the core.

On the other hand, if this shortcoming has been pointed out to us, then we might consider changing this to soul and heart or, to be even more precise, soul *to* heart. Either way, a conclusion of the soul—appreciation, gratitude, and compassion—creates immense strength.

This could then be interpreted as the current of every self-collective consciousness and the connection to the consciousnesses of all that is of the source and combined in a relevant manner. This is a load of current in a balanced gravity and in harmonious balance with every environment that exists in reality.

Another way of interpreting this is that every consideration of this current's strength is only going to be used without affecting others. This immense power to affect others is how we create self-strength, but it is only to be used within the self. This is the blue energy that you may see throughout yourself.

This soul-energy is also the energy that has broken down, and the separation has affected us in many debilitating ways. How has this happened?

We were considering how much strength and power was once within what is considered to be a self-collective body. What actually happens to this powerful self-strength? The whole self-atmosphere and the radiant, blue self-energy break down. We have all done this in some manner, many times over many lifetimes.

With the breakdown of this energy, all self-consideration is placed toward the heart, which is like the physical, connective-consciousness connector, so this becomes the main sense of what is to matter most in our lives.

The next scenario to be considered is this: not all connections to the heart are actually broken, just some of them.

The largest and greatest scenario to be considered is this next one. Forget about all that we just considered. Look at the whole forest and the many different scenarios taking place all at once—but without vital awareness of each other's existence or the place we exist in the real vitality of living life.

Years ago, I considered what had been translated to me as a play on words, as did my friends, and we missed many vital points. Each and every word is made of a frequency—a vibration, modulation, harmony, balance, gravity, aspect, element, and essence—so each word comprises vital communications about so many different senses.

Now, imagine that one of these vital senses is unable to communicate. You wouldn't have a clue what another person was talking about. Please keep this thought on the back burner, and don't let it go out.

We have been considering the atmosphere and breakdown of the spirit-body, which is then passed on to the self-environment. This basically means that we are unable to reflect on what is actually vital to our self-strength.

This inability to consider what is vital means that our foundational self-abilities are also broken down and separated.

Many books and movies on the subject talk about separations, but they don't explain how we end up as we do. This means that we often focus on what we *don't* have instead of on the things we *do* have that are complete and working. We are sort of preoccupied with what we have lost—the where-the-hell-is-it, I've-just-got-to-have-it scenario.

When we comprehend how our energy has dissipated, then the simplicity of fixing our self returns—without falling into complex scenarios. We are really just figuring out what is real and what is illusional crap.

Please take these next few sentences slowly, and certain self-knowing will unfold.

If we started out whole, then as the strength of the soul-spirit waned, we would still have many complete soul and spirit connections. But as the environment wasn't strong, parts of our unconscious soul and heart lost their gravity to the self and ended up orbiting it.

We are considering then that certain parts are correct still, and that the once strong and conscious parts of our physicality and spirit are now moving away from our self-gravity, as they sense that they are now not vital, yes.

Consider this breakdown of communication within the self. The strong bit is working overtime to make up for the unconsciousness that is now unable to communicate properly on a full-time basis. This scenario also means that others in the same boat are able to contribute to your energy system, as it is wide open in many places.

As we begin to receive contributions from others' energy, the spirit breaks down further. We need to develop a new defence mechanism, now that we are receiving contributions from many energy sources that are also disconnected.

We are also doing the same to others. Imagine parts your heart sitting unprotected. How easy would it be to receive contributions from others? Very easy, yes?

This is why I was able to know what was going on in others' thoughts, and why I knew that many parts of us were not receiving the truth—or, to be more precise, not receiving truth in a correct manner. Does this clarify things somewhat?

This statement might at first seem to be conflicting, but later it doesn't. This explains much, doesn't it?

Awareness is such a key. Do you comprehend why my guides at this moment are asking me to follow the energy, not the emotion?

There is another reason also. The emotion may have a multitude of contributors, which is easy to ascertain now, for without certain awareness, we just follow the cycles of the environment around us.

The alternative is to fix all environments and atmospheres that are reflected by the whole self, which requires eliminating interferences. We are then able to communicate with our whole self, never being separate.

Can you imagine communicating at this level of awareness? How simple communicating would be. Imagine how many levels of awareness we would be communicating on. The spoken word would be minimal, but the senses would be able to communicate, which would be phenomenal.

All this reflects our desire to have a new time where we are not separate from our foundational abilities.

When everything is weighed up, we are, at the moment, a little suppressed in many areas for all the reasons outlined previously.

Consider also that as we follow the whole self-spirit with a soul-core appreciation, we become stronger and thus more aware of our abilities. It all boils down to living a life with purpose that is reflected by the self, not others.

This would then imply that perhaps there are many parts of yourself that, life after life, you have not connected in a full, collective-consciousness manner. Perhaps it is time to check, yes?

Throughout this whole chapter, you have been receiving many types of energy to help identify where your strengths presently lie and how they can be integrated to create a strong direction—to create a more whole you.

This whole you then opens your self to finding real joy with a real future. The following chapters are only concerned with your natural self-nature.

The outcome of this—and this is in my own words only—is that you begin to see yourself in a different light. Then, as strange as this may sound, you get to know yourself in a new, appreciative manner.

The hardest part about this explanation or any other I could convey to you, is that you will not fully comprehend when you are at peace with who you are. Please don't link me to any group of hippy, religious, new-age, or way-out people. Please don't.

If what is outlined helps you, then this is all that matters. You are to just be, to be comfortable with yourself and not worry about how or what others think of you. What you think your image is and the way you act are reflected automatically and all of the time. Had you considered this?

I guess we should digress a little and remember that whatever is in our soul is then reflected through our heart, if we desire this to be so. Have you ever reflected on this thought?

I'm opening a can of worms here, especially if we consider our true reflection and the image that we would *like* to reflect. The reason this is such a can of worms is that we have often reflected the environment in which we exist rather than what is in our innermost self.

Put into our language, this simply means that when we are surrounded by a group of people who are consuming, they can ask us to reflect their intentions. Often this is so subtle that we may not even realise that this unintentional programming is occurring.

If our own reflection is not strong, we will take on the images of others. This means we feel stronger as a group, as this reinforces our self-worth and our ability to feel strong.

This then reflects many good, illusional points of view. We may desire to be an image of strength, but in our innermost self, we simply are not.

This means that you are not afraid to have your own point of view, reflected from your innermost soul. Therefore, it is not a reflection of an image that you have consumed in an unaware manner.

Be aware that I made no reference to your aura, as this is simply a reflection too. Actually, it is a whole lot more, but is it plain to see how our self-image has sometimes been a little conflicted.

The reason for not solely reflecting on our self-aura is so we can sense all that exists within. A strong image from within creates a strong environment and atmosphere in which our aura can exist at peace.

These, of course, are not simply my own words of conclusion, but ones passed on after reflecting on them. Perhaps your own guides can help you to see a more true image of yourself through them if you so desire.

This tithing is of self-image that is to be reflected in a true, self-nurturing manner. Before this tithing is brought forth, may I just outline what may or may not be experienced?

For those very aware of their own insight, this tithing may seem as though you are focusing through many sets of eyes.

The moving in and out is your consciousness moving from unconsciousness in order to be conscious of many new self-images. This depends on the level of your frequency, the tones, and the harmonics that accompany the way you ask yourself to receive. They send a true message to the image you desire to create.

This also means that there could have been quite a bit of interference between the real image that was sent and the image received. That interference was simply unresolved self-images of past-life desires or the images with which others have distorted your perception.

I am now able to restore all real-life perception in a true manner, with all true self-reflections to be restored.

This tithing is to help you automatically refocus all insights that you have ever received in the way they are intended to be perceived. In our language, this means that we are able to ascertain more clearly what many insights meant, as we may have received a limited version, thus distorting the whole meaning.

Those of you who are able to sense your eyes might feel them rolling quite quickly at the moment. They will be visible once more as all integrates into one self-reflection.

This tithing helps you to understand the content of the upcoming chapters. It doesn't stop now; it realigns through all of this lifetime. Perhaps it would be a great idea to remind yourself of this.

Your dreams may reflect limited insight. Then the real capacity of your strength will reflect a greater potential. This awareness will soon open each day. Please notice that your thoughts are less constricted, and your logic is becoming vast.

For this reason, it might be a good idea to write a reminder note to ask yourself to be aware of all new perspectives that expand and extend self-insight of your day-to-day logic.

Please take a break for at least an hour before starting on the next chapter: "A New-Time Gift."

# 11

## A NEW-TIME GIFT

Opening presents is always fun, if you allow yourself to accept them. You may consider this a strange analogy, not wanting to accept presents. Actually, this is much more common than you realise. I know this because I have had long chats with clients and have asked questions in or after a group meditation.

You see, every year since I can remember, birthdays have been a chore. I have always pretended to be happy to keep everyone else happy, trying to seem appreciative and never being insensitive.

I wanted to enjoy birthdays, but even doing affirmations from many people and sources never helped. You could fill an encyclopedia with the questions I asked to remedy the situation. I knew the problem was an issue of acceptance, because at Christmas I was as happy as a clam.

The remedy was to come, but it had a few parts to it.

When we talk of omnipresence, we are talking about a part of us with a long memory. We discussed this earlier. We also discussed how the connective consciousness was integrated in your angel wings, yes. I also opened up on a more personal level, sharing how things had unfolded for me.

Now I would like to share the opening of angel-conscious on a more physical level. Remember how I said that a spirit blockage can cause physical pain? Keep this in mind, please.

On this particular morning, my guides wanted to discuss the different parts of omnipresence. I have to admit that I wasn't feeling too open to conversation. This was many years ago, and I had not even been really aware of following activations at that stage of my life.

I guess I was unaware of the different energy I was about to encounter. In fact, my thought was, *This is all just great, but can you get rid of this bad back? It's killing me.*

"Well, David," was the response, "be patient as all is unfolding."

I would like to remind you that in years previous, I knew when somebody was passing over, but I had no indication of what was about to open. Please keep this in mind.

I had just begun to interpret what my guides identified as omnipresence, and then I was going back into unconsciousness—a state of self-unawareness. Just as I was going back into a deep sleep, my back exploded with energy. I asked what the hell was going on.

"What do you think they are, David?"

"I have no idea, but they're flapping," was my reply. Then it dawned on me. "Are these angel wings?" I asked. No, this was not a fairy tale, and yes, I was wide awake from a depth of consciousness—too wide awake now.

"Yes, they are, David."

Before waiting for a reply, I said to myself, "Christ, I'm going to die. You can appreciate why I was hyper for a moment. I had only been relating omnipresence with afterlife, so you can understand why I thought I was heading in that direction. I can laugh now, but you can imagine what I surmised and why I had a moment of concern.

Before I reflect on how these insights are all related, I will shed a little more light on this very different night.

After being reassured that this was quite natural, just a different activation, I immediately calmed down. *Now I understand*, I thought to myself.

"David, you can embrace all the senses being extended to you, yes, to pass on."

I felt like I was opening up everywhere, and yes, my wings were flapping everywhere. I was quickly informed that the serenity I had sensed earlier had been a result of the connective consciousness that is my wings.

Now I understood. This linked everything together, and I felt like a Sara Lee commercial, with layer upon layer upon layer joining within myself. "Wow!" was all I could say.

"You are interpreting all activations, David, yes." For me, this was an explosion of knowing that flooded into me everywhere, but it was very pleasant rather than overwhelming.

This new unfolding was very intimate in that I was at ease and able to sense so many different energies and—for the want of a more descriptive word—to diagnose what was happening and where it was happening. This was very surprising stuff. What else could I call a sensation beyond my limited comprehension? With so much happening, I needed to write down every aspect of what I sensed in order to bring some understanding.

After using this energy for years, I grasped just how much potential had unfolded this morning. Thank heavens, it was the weekend, though. I couldn't have moved if I needed to.

Let me start a quick roundup, before exploring many of the possibilities of angel connective consciousness.

This omnipresence was a conscious key that opened a desire and an intention. I desired to bring the spirit and physical-body energies together, so I received a lot of help.

Actually, one of the real openings occurred a little later while affirming the androgynous consciousness, and this balance sits in all omnipresence. I didn't know at the time how vital and relevant it was, although I soon would.

Each activation that unfolds has one or many affirmations within the activation's presence, but one thing never wavers. When it comes time to bring spirit and physical together, the androgynous element is always present.

Your self-consciousness and the source's are integrated.

This is an area my sister Julie and I check on continually, to ensure we are balanced. Neither must be more of a strength than the other, and the energy balance must be exact. Even when we are in different countries, we need to catch up. Texting or using the computer is fine, but once a month, we need to actually talk.

This has the added benefit of showing us if a vital part is missing. Even if we haven't talked, the other knows this instantly. Now perhaps you understand why we rely on each other.

You are probably wondering how my birthday misery fits into all this.

The split between the physical and the spirit has one debilitating effect, one that perhaps many have never considered. Self-worth is greatly affected in many different ways. More precisely, it limits the potential for self-worth to be recognised.

Early on in my journey, I was given this advice from Jesus. The whole conversation was actually about tithing, but it also expounds on lack of self-worth. Most of us are fine with giving, but receiving is another matter.

There is also the other blockage to consider: if you are unable to receive, you can at times have problems in different areas of your life with giving in a tithing manner.

There is a reason why this comes to a head so easily in each of our lives. Consider that if you continue to give and never receive, eventually the cupboard is bare. All in life must be tithed, and all must learn to receive before giving.

When this was relayed to me, I didn't fully comprehend the necessity of receiving before giving. I needed to think in a different manner.

You see, we always think materialistically. We forget that we receive in spirit first, and then the energy follows.

In simple terms, if we relate this to ourselves with a tithing from all guides, one simple thought can change this whole, old-time programming and processing.

I am of an evolved spirit.

Therefore, all self-presence is always current.

Therefore, all-self representation is only able to be represented in a totally free manner.

Therefore, this soul is only able to be reflected in the heart in a true manner of self-faith and self-belief.

I ask to restore all self-gratitude, all self-appreciation, and all self-compassion to a real self-capacity.

This equates to the self-soul always reflecting in one's self-heart only, for I am only able to sense all that is true and correct according to my self-abilities and awareness.

In plain language, this means that you are only able to contribute what is true if you are actually aware, if the self is free of programming and processes that do not constrict. This means tithing freely, without programmed conditions, to empower the giver by restricting the receiver's freedom. This also means being able to receive without controlling the receiver's gift or restricting or humiliating the receiver's self-love.

All tithings must be free of all controls; they are never to deplete the receiver's loving nature or the environments they exist in. This can only be achieved by using a new, natural equation of soul and heart.

Why?

The soul component is how your heart was created, otherwise it would be like putting the cart before the horse. If we place the heart before the soul, what does this do to our self-energy? It constricts and restricts it. Simply, it causes self-confliction.

This is a base cause of all humanity's self-conflicting nature.

To save us pain and suffering, I will also translate how this wise piece of tithing applies further down the line, when this parable of life becomes so significant.

Essentially, this breaks down to your spirit-energy receiving all activations to create a destination for a physical matter.

There is one, huge potential that until now I haven't opened. I was deep in unconsciousness, and then I became automatically conscious of all that I had never responded to before. This means that I responded to self-awareness and inner knowing that, until that moment, had been blocked off.

Another way of thinking about this is to bring the unconscious part of us to consciousness and awareness, using the foundations of our self all of the time.

In the end, this means that if you are more aware and available to respond to base foundations of your unconscious matter in a conscious way, then all of your self-consciousness is present. Well, isn't it?

Now that you are able to be present and aware on many levels of consciousness, please consider that once you were unconscious too.

Doesn't it go without saying then that your sense of reasoning must change the way you think daily? Well, doesn't it? We reflected on this in the tithing in the last chapter.

Perhaps you should also consider another thought about this statement. What would happen if this was repeated many times over? Imagine your self-awareness. A multitude of new reasons of self-belief would appear. Well, think about it. This is correct, isn't it?

Knowing your own self-faith, you would be following it rather than relying on others to tell you what you should or should not believe.

In your innermost self is your soul-presence, your creative soul-presence, and their extensive and expansive aspects desire no limitation of their potential. This is to be reflected with the strength of this intention into your spirit-heart.

This potential can then be grown in a real self-environment, using your own natural abilities and those things that bring joy to your life.

In simple terms, this strength is a spirit-reflection or base foundational component in your personal self-environment as well. It is repeated as this spirit-definition is integrated into the physical soul and heart. A very special self-image is then created—of you!

Remember, only you know what really makes you happy. Yes, we all share a base collective consciousness, but we all have our own special abilities to nurture. How can others appreciate these, if we have never shown them to anybody—often, not even ourselves. Is this worth thinking about?

Massive self-potential sits dormant in most of us in an unconscious manner.

There is one wise phrase I have found to be true, and it reflects these insights. We all need to find our base foundations that we have been unconscious or unaware of. Once these are in place, all our self-abilities automatically flow into place.

If we nurture our special abilities as we create, we ensure that there is no division between our self and our true abilities. I hope this makes sense to you, as I will be exploring it throughout the book. For now, though, it just breaks down to following your real spirit-destination so you won't get lost. Not only do you get to the destination; you also get the how, why, where, and when of getting there.

So ask to receive your spirit message.

Julie was, of course, the first person I was able to pass the angel-consciousness on to. Connecting to this angel-consciousness turns out to be quite easy to pass on without any trauma or drama, when you know what is going on or are simply aware.

I went through every aspect before passing this on to Julie to ensure that she had no surprises in store for her. During that time, I once again opened and received a new-time tool and vehicle that I have never stopped using.

As soon as Julie was able to connect, I was more aware of how this angel-consciousness and all activations connected an where every aspect was going to integrate in a more true form.

The look on Julie's face confirmed all that had been connected. The process was working and was helping her to interpret in a whole new manner.

It may seem incongruous that the vibration of two words could have so much meaning in the way energy can be moved. When the affirmation reflects a harmonising tone, these two words also help to release, which is something discussed in the earlier chapters.

Tones are a pitch that some of you have already been experiencing. I don't mean any energy sensed by the body. This is only experienced in the head region, most notably, of course, in the ears.

At other times, we refocus behind the eyes, nose, and even on the roof of the mouth; all are high sensory points.

Our guides make the point here that there are many different focuses of balance.

These tones come in when you begin to settle or just switch off a bit. If you are very comfortable in your environment, then it will not matter if people are around—except for one tiny problem. We all need to find out about the important stuff, and this means hands-on learning about how spirit influences our daily life.

Even with very direct direction, I need to experience every spirit to physical effect just the same as you. The reason I am bringing this to your attention is that tones automatically create many balances between the spirit and physical parts of yourself and others.

Now to explain this as best I can.

Everybody's consciousness is made up of minds and memory in a spirit body and in a physical body.

Please concentrate a little to ensure that you comprehend this part, as this understanding relates to every foundation of your consciousness.

Absolutely nothing is separate from this core of every level of yourself. This is beyond significant, yes. It basically means that you don't have just cellular memory; you are far more expansive. You have it in every particle of your body.

You see, there are in your physical body lots of conscious points, and we are not talking about the brain.

Before attempting to move ahead, I need you to check that the conscious significance of what was relayed to you is correct, so please do so.

Spirituality is the same as everything else; grasp a couple of core foundations of understanding, and the rest comes easy.

So too, if we miss a couple of core understandings and nothing fits together, everything becomes frustrating or complicated. Once again we reflect on how important awareness is.

Be assured that after grounding these couple of items, we will return to learning how to connect to your angel-consciousness.

When I first got my head around separated consciousness, I had a lot of help from guides to fill me in about how everything was relevant. The hard part is that guides talk a totally different language. How often have you been to a meditation and not fully comprehended the messages that transpired?

This also means that everything you desire to connect to needs a new relationship to connect this understanding.

Your physical nature is not the only priority of your life, and the angel connective consciousness helps to make sense of this world we are living in, even if you have been on the journey for some time.

Eventually, this is a little bit like waking from sleep. Loads of stuff have been going on around you that you never even noticed before.

Angel-consciousness helps you to grasp the few formulas that open your intuition to all that is not revealed and enable us to open certain understandings automatically.

So, how do you think this is going to come together? Do you think a miracle will help and that this is what you will receive?

Imagine a certain aspect of yourself that has a little fear in it. This is probably in an area that you are already aware of, as from time to time this aspect has reoccurred. We now know this is because there is a little bit of separation in it.

Even this simple appreciation helps, because we know a resolution can be found at some time, so we are not so insecure about it. Still, you desire to be free of this.

Now, I did mention that there are a couple of formulas. Let's go back to imagining the aspect with a little separated consciousness, because the mind and memory are also working on separate matters, which, if truth be told, is not what this particular consciousness was designed to do. This is how consciousness came to separate in the first place.

Now we have a separation. You might think we need to know exactly why the mind and memory split from the conscious. Well, at that the moment, no, we don't.

Earlier, we either talked about or received an affirmation with all the parts that make up the miracle formula, so everything will now work automatically.

You may have been totally unaware, but this doesn't matter either. Why?

Consider an earlier understanding where we learned that activations are conscious movements of matter. All of a sudden you are able to find out if the mind's or the memory's activation is moving in a real spirit manner, or if it's only working in a physical manner as a past physical memory. Automatically, the spirit-consciousness is able to determine what, where, when, or how all energy is really moving, and it is able to fix where it is not moving.

Let's look at how you would have reacted in a past scenario, so you can see what needs to change. If you repeated a past-life cycle, then you would probably try to fix this problem in the same way you did in the past in an unaware manner. Does this make sense?

The only problem with this is that you are in a totally different environment now, with different conflicting energies, yes. So, do you also understand that this would then become confusing to you?

This is the reason behind bringing a present presence of consciousness to help release the confusion. Simply, this means that you would not be joining present times to your past lives to find a resolution, as this would be asking to repeat past-life experiences again and again.

This means that you use your own spirit in a present presence of source guidance to resolve going over and over past conflicts.

You may be aware now that this is opening as a flow through your physical veins at this very moment.

This sharing gift is perennial and will connect when needed to the celestial collective essence to free all inhumanity within the self that desires to block any presence of self-purpose.

In our language, this sharing is going to be way more significant than you are able to interpret at this moment, as this frees self-aspects of yourself and all connecting abilities that need to be free, to resolve the purpose of why we are here at this moment in time.

The grounding effect and the tones you are receiving are testament to how serious the source is in sharing all tithings to free up humanity's collective consciousness and to open a strength and share it with all humanity.

As you ground, the sensation of peace begins to flow, connecting, and is available to be sensed. To enhance this, just close your eyes, please.

As you raise all conscious essence, flow is also rising in frequency. This is to stabilize the flow of energy between your spirit and physical consciousness, thus make all of your physical self a structure of conscious matter.

Once again, please clasp your hands. The combining energy may be noticeable now, but it may become more pronounced as your energy strengthens and stabilizes.

As we return to our discussion of the presence of time, an element is needed to facilitate the change of a past self-atmosphere that created stagnation in all spirit-flow. We were talking about past conflicts in our selves and that if we sense this conflict in others, it will remind us of those in our selves. Now we will discuss what has been released, yes, released.

Please remember that finding a solution in the past resulted in your sensing what could simply have been brought on by your feeling this same reaction in some other person or a certain situation.

This is correct, if your environment and atmosphere were open due to lack of spirit-strength. Another person's energy in conflict might remind you of how something good turned out bad in the end, so now every time you feel good, you feel that something bad eventually must happen or follow.

How? Through unconscious memories and issues that we feel we have never resolved. This means that we will always have an identity crisis cropping up from time to time.

Why? Because the self was unable to identify what we were unaware of, yes. This also means we are unable to identify what is truth and what is not real.

Where? In the unconscious and subconscious mind and memories, because the mind and memory are unable to communicate.

When? All these consciousnesses of spirit and physical self are not present in one time frame, or they are all in separate time frames.

This is simply because we are unaware of the illusional dimensions that are just separations between lives. We have never been fully conscious of, all that has been unresolved or unconnected to truth in all past lives.

Now, do you comprehend this? You really do not want to repeat a certain life pattern of illusional truth.

Remember, all that has occurred in each life environment has been remembered in your physical-self and in your spirit-self.

This is what your soul does. It is omnipresent. So doesn't it make sense to make every part of your spirit and physical matter present and communicating with your own personal soul of omnipresence?

I have said that sometimes we need to think outside the square, and this is one of those moments. Please let yourself be present.

Previously, we were reminded that every energy must be a conscious movement of matter, no matter how large or seemingly insignificant. Perhaps you would like to recheck this. Why? Because every time you check, you are reactivating parts that have sometimes sat dormant.

This means that the activation tithing exercise is freeing and then reactivating a presence response for all repressed flows of this self-aspect to be restored. Once again, you may have sensed the self moving or being active, yes?

Why? Because you are asking yourself to be always present—no ifs, buts, or maybes. This is because you are sending current to a once-dormant area. Remember, you desire to open up your connective consciousness and get it moving again.

By now you have seen repeatedly that we desire to resolve things simply and to release complication and confusion. Remind your mind or memory that this is important and is needed to make you whole again.

Remember why you desire to become complete, why you need to become strong in your own self, why you once again desire your intent to become significant. This is why you sense the relevance to this simple understanding.

It's not complicated, just straightforward. Why?

At this moment, the connective consciousness is opening you to angel language or self-spirit language. This happens on levels of yourself that you will soon be reconnecting to. Keep in mind that you are easing yourself into this and reconnecting sequences.

This is to ensure that you stay comfortable with reconnecting. Otherwise, parts of you would reject the parts you need to reconnect. This we also discussed earlier in this chapter.

Remember that you are now going to continuously—all day, all the time—use parts of yourself that were once unconscious. How can you tell that this is happening or that you are really connecting?

There are always preparations to properly connecting to large, working consciousness. Otherwise, it is too, easy to sabotage what is really desired.

Remember, this is what the instruction manual was about: preparing you not to follow controlling or conflicting energies.

You naturally feel this as anxiety, fear, or emotions that relate to being separate from the truth that relates to your soul. Please keep in mind that this truth is the foundation on which all self-heart-energy is created.

This works in a couple of ways. I endeavour to open one way, then straightaway I open another. You will be able to use both of these ways forever, if you desire.

This again is a preliminary preparation designed to make life easy, so please don't think of it as more stuff to do. Yes, it is a bit like doing homework before the lesson, but then the reasoning in the lesson makes more sense, and you get the "aha" moment or the lightbulb effect. When you have a destination, you don't get lost. Each chapter works this same way.

Consider that as you gain parts that were separated, you also gain strength in yourself. This we discussed a number of times. Imagine this energy that you regain as a whole.

You are beginning to radiate so much more energy on so many levels. Had you even thought of this prospect or the implications of simply being in possession of a stronger, more energetic self?

Another thought is that with each conscious reconnection, your frequency, vibration, and many parts of you are now much higher and lighter.

Yes, the tones you receive will automatically balance you, but in a way you are a different person now, especially to people who are used to the energy level that you usually work on or vibrate at.

Is this worth considering? Absolutely.

Human beings are funny creatures. We can sit back and observe ourselves or those we know whose natures we are accustomed to. Ask any coworker or relative or anyone with whom you've had a long relationship, and they can tell you every little trait you have, good or bad.

That image you reflect changes as your frequency rises.

I know at times I have a weird sense of humour, and sometimes I need to keep myself amused. When I was driving a concrete truck I met all types and lots of groups; some were family-orientated, and others were hard nuts. I live in an area with extremely rich retirees, so my demographics age is varied.

I took it as a personal challenge to win these guys over. The first day I met them, I knew what I was up against. I didn't say a word; I just worked with them.

Within a couple of encounters, they were joking with me. Now, time is money in any business, but when they had a hard job, I didn't push them; I just tried to help. After a while I would be in and out of jobs quickly, but the pushy guys would be stuck for ages.

So what the heck has this got to do with getting spiritual? Just this. We can't do much about the people we have to associate with, but we can turn them around. Funny thing, you'd be surprised how many of them opened up to me when they were having a hard time—I mean, about topics like a child being run over or someone dying.

They all found out about the other kind of work I did, which was a strange conversation, but even those guys who would rather fight than hug never gave me grief about it.

In fact, I got much more grief from a spiritual meditation group, when I was just trying to find some like-minded people, than I did from those I healed. This group, like most, represented quite a kaleidoscope of interests, and most members did not know I channeled. I just wanted to connect to somebody else's perspective. I wanted to learn.

The next week, I was informed by the facilitator that some people were a bit afraid of my energy. I just said okay, but I needed to find out why. My image was a concern. I will also admit that this was way before I found out about tones and a stack of other information relevant to this subject.

I consulted another healer I had befriended, and he just laughed at my predicament. This is how he explained my situation to me, and perhaps you might be able to use this.

"David, you have had a bit of a transformation. Your energy has just sky-rocketed." Yes, I understood this. Then he said, "You asked to protect yourself, but you didn't ask to protect others from your energy becoming lighter or stronger." I needed to know why the hell I needed to do this. It didn't make sense.

I was then informed that these people were afraid my energy was getting lighter than their own energy, and this challenged their self-balance. This explanation did the trick, and I have passed this wisdom on to many who were surprised at its results. Who would have thought this?

And then one of my guides explained how jealousy or envy creates many unconscious barriers.

So, even though you now have tones to help you, do you understand why I asked you to be aware of your energy before our guides connect you to angel-consciousness? This is then added automatically, every time you are balanced.

My guides were insistent on this. Why?

As you become more complete, you will need to become more aware of your actual energy. To be aware of this self-energy you need to be secure in who you really are.

I am of a self-presence. Therefore, all that resides within this self is only of this self-atmosphere, environment, and reality.

All self-purpose is refined to react with all realities of freeing god-consciousness.

This self-purpose is the creative current of life. Therefore, no fear exists within these boundaries of expectation, for myself and all humanity.

—Shared with the love of Gabriel.

This affirmation helps us to raise our own vibration while never excluding others. It also allows others to raise their vibrations in their own time. Is this essential? If you consider the spiraling divorce rate among those seeking enlightenment, I would say that this is imperative, wouldn't you? Remember that our conversation is about self-stability and security, so helping those we love is just as important, isn't it?

We will be discussing this in the next chapter. As before, we are just opening your subconscious to all that is available to be connected to.

In addition, the source is ensuring that your focus is now firmly in the future and not dwelling on the past. You're becoming aware of real currents. This is to evolve in the tithing you now receive so you can link all angel-conscious aspects of yourself together. Yes, there are many.

Please enjoy this opening to your angel-presence.

This tithing is brought to you by all guardian angels that specifically guide you—and only you. How does this work? The tithing is facilitated by a star-angel collective that guides guardian angels.

While there are many guides that we communicate with, Sordlion and J'spirin are the androgynous translators I usually talk to on this level of connective consciousness. I am grateful to these and many other guides. Their guidance not only helps us but also opens all that we desire to know and understand, including how much we have all been missing out on.

Please remember that each source-tithing is also a sharing of conscious energy that, when complete, is conscious love. Hence our guides help us reconnect to a capacity of potential that perhaps you do not realise yet.

This tithing of this evolved time of this evolved space is to openly illuminate all self-possibilities.

This tithing—which all guiding guardian angels now affirm as all-present selves with a creative sense of evolved desire—freely open.

This evolved capacity, from this moment, is never to sit separate from all self-angel-capacity in this time of presence.

All are simply to be part of this evolved presence for all time.

I open this love of real appreciation, of real stability, with all dynamics of ability.

This reality of gratitude now opens each and every possibility to every creative nature that exists within this complete and present self.

This complete self is to open each and every one of these capacities of real virtue and ethics. In truth, this self opens every self to the capacity of real self-compassion—in each and every nature—of my natural ability.

I now accept—with all love and with all angels who aspire to create real love—a creation that we desire all to connect to on a full-time basis.

Therefore, I am now able to create a full and meaningful life, which is able to exist only on this basis and never on a de-evolved existence.

With this reflection, then and only then will all comprehend how to create *real* love with *real* appreciation, gratitude, and compassion.

These ingredients must exist in each spirit and in each physical nature in order to be of real manner and real matter in all new time.

This true, living soul-presence is therefore complete in each and every self-purpose.

This is why a new-time presence is coming, and for many it is already here.

Love always, J'spirin and Sordlion

Perhaps you can check each aspect of this tithing for your own personal truth and for what reflects with you.

Now, I will do my best to translate this for you in our language.

Affirmations are a strange vehicle when you aren't used to working with them. So I have to take on board every possibility of every person whose time it is to read this book.

Remember, an affirmation is talking to many levels of your self. Also, take on board that these are selves that, at present, you may be unaware of. Nonetheless, these selves actually comprehend the real capacity within the intent and desire of each word. So perhaps you need to take on board that each word in an affirmation is working on many levels.

Another concept to understand is that you receive a level for this moment—and then for lots of moments in the future. Consider that at each moment, this present moment, you require lots of different consciousnesses, and all of them make up a complete consciousness. So, think of the presence as lots of complete sets of consciousnesses, okay?

The next thought to add to this spirit-equation is that once a consciousness is needed, you start a reaction of creating. Think about this a little longer, please. You start a *creative reaction*.

You see, for something to be of a real desire and intent, you need to have checked to make sure it is actually real on many levels of your self.

So, how do you check? By asking lots of questions to check its authenticity. This is why our guides continually and simply say, "Questions, not answers, create." Is this simple equation worth implementing?

The first part of the affirmation was your guides asking questions of your self, asking if you really wanted to connect to angel-consciousness. After all, everything is your choice.

The next part was about opening up the activations to make this all happen—connecting your consciousness to the correct connections on many levels in order to create a correct connective-consciousness.

So, this isn't hard to follow. The illusion that this is complicated is dissolving quickly.

Next, perhaps, we need to change the old angel-consciousness—that part of your soul that hasn't been used in a while—to become a superconductor and an ultimate connector. This is most important when we consider that there are going to be lots of parts to connect in the future.

People usually hate to admit that they often listen to unconscious direction. This unconscious direction is then made redundant, having a looser strength within the connective angel-consciousness. Then all consciousness that was real and never of an unconscious direction becomes conscious as your intuition or gut feeling.

Perhaps one other consideration should be explored. A stronger, real connection to more of the real direction means that your intuition will be more effective, more correct, or of a conscious nature.

Think about it. Doesn't it make sense, yes?

So, what else does this mean—besides not making as many mistakes? It means that in the future you will be cutting down the old life-patterns that never went anywhere.

The only trouble is this. In the past, in an unconscious way, we actually asked for these cycles that never went anywhere or created anything of real worth. I don't enjoy making the same mistakes over and over. Do you? Maybe this is a wakeup call that we need to make the most of. Be aware of what you connect to.

With these insights, it is now time to move directly to the angel-consciousness to free—yes, free—some of the old self-limitations. Please remember that this is an exercise in reconnection, with the purpose of sharing real energy foundations that exist in all humanity.

I now redefine all self-worth of the absolute self to include all self-angel permanent presence in this evolved time and real self-presence.

I am of this love.

Therefore, all of this self is of this love.

Therefore, all of this self is the creation of love.

This angel-consciousness is now ready to unfold at the correct time, when all of your guides sense you are ready. This also depends on when you are able to relax.

Don't be too concerned if your breathing slows down somewhat. You won't stop breathing. This is simply an indication to you that many levels of your consciousness are ready to communicate and work together.

Don't be too worried by the energy unfolding. At first, this is simply a deactivation to release energies that have been suppressing this most vital consciousness.

As the actual activation takes place, you will sense the freeing of this suppressed consciousness as a falling motion. This falling motion is your self connecting to many levels of consciousness in a different manner that makes them able to respond only to conscious responses.

While you are aware of this falling action, please sit still. Perhaps a few new perceptions will be sensed. For everybody I know who has been opened to this consciousness, the wing-sensation was always evident. This is really an unfolding of repressed soul-energy. To sense this a little better, hold your arms out with the palms of your hands facing the ground.

An unfolding sensation in your back will once again open, and you might sense that there is a density to the unfolding wings. You are immediately releasing this. Just move your arms in sequence with your wings; connect to them and sense them.

Your mind and memory of this consciousness will soon connect, so at this point, bring your arms back in and clasp your hands. Have you noticed that you are sensing much of this with your eyes open?

After reading this next part, please close your eyes to connect a little stronger.

Please hold your arms to the side, the palms of the hands facing the floor. If you are lying down or are sitting parallel to the side of the chair, turn your hands to face the same direction as your face.

At this moment, you are reacquainting yourself with the extension and expansion of your soul-energy. Soon your guides will be asking to connect to you. This will be evident as you ground this energy.

As you wait, you will sense the reconnection of this energy, and you will be reacquainting yourself with an ascending energy. If your arms feel like coming back to the clasping position let them. The energy motion will stay evident, as you now still your whole body, yes.

Please, relax and be aware that your breath is stilling. Don't worry; you will not stop breathing. Please close your eyes and let yourself receive with grace, ease, and synchronicity. Relax and sense.

You can use this exercise when you are in peaceful or quiet surroundings. The vibration of the words will help, though.

Welcome back. Those of you who have connected in this exercise will find it evident that you can use your mind and memory to flap those wings a little. For those ready to receive, remember that high-pitched tone automatically balances and protects.

You may sense this straight away or when you relax, some time later when you least expect help, however this is another consideration, which needs immediate attention.

Do not forget that all consciousness needs to ground. I will put this way. How many life times do you think this angel-consciousness has been sitting separate from the rest of your real conscious?

There are so many people who come to see me for the first time who just aren't grounded. What astounds me is that some people think this is normal. So, if you have been wallowing around, light-headed, this is why: essentially, you are not grounded. If you have a constant feeling of motion, then this also is a symptom of ungroundedness.

Tones automatically balance and integrate the spirit-body, but you actually need to physically ground and integrate spirit into the physical body.

Another way of thinking about this is that you are connecting your soul to be more present in your heart. Remember, your soul is a vital component in activating your heart and getting it to work in an efficient manner.

This is you, taking responsibility in a way that matters to you, ensuring that every part of you stays together.

If you have quickly read the last two paragraphs, please reread them. They are very important, yes.

This may seem a little strange, but please bear with me; this really works. Please stand and point your hands in a firm and deliberate manner to the ground. You are receiving help and can do so at any time in the future.

You will sense yourself going into the ground now, yes, with a sensation that your legs are buckling at the knees. After sensing your knees move, clasp your hands in front of yourself. The grounding sensation will once again be evident. Remember, you are being helped.

In a moment your hands will feel like dropping. Let them.

Please repeat this exercise now, and it doesn't hurt to do it each day to ensure a smooth day.

To remind yourself that you have indeed asked to reunite and reassemble all these parts of yourself, it might be worth writing down how to ground for future reference, yes. Even if you sensed your angel wings unfolding as you read, there is still more to unfold as you relax over the coming days, weeks, or months.

This is just the start of unlocking many parts of your potential each and every day, if you so desire. The choice is yours.

You may liken this to getting used to a new group of people moving into your house. You can't hide in your room and slowly get used to them, because they are in there also, and they are all you!

There is another prospect that is added to this new equation of connecting to an efficient consciousness. I guess the operative word is *efficient*, so this consciousness opens the way you interpret intuition, moment by moment throughout your day.

Unlike your usual thought cycles, intuition does not impede your usual thought patterns. In fact, quite the opposite happens. You release processes that have been passed on, processes that everybody thinks apply only to processed foods.

*Processing* in spirit terms is simply rehashing the past with a twist. Processing uses a question to find truth, but because you are using answers from many different lifetimes and scenarios, the real answer is impossible to find, as there are now thousands of answers to what started out as a simple question.

This subject of processing, which we will soon be opening up, involves being able to use a strength of consciousness. This in turn opens soul-intuition, which then quiets some parts of your mind or stops confusing chatter.

How the heck can intuition possibly quiet my mind? It runs at a million miles an hour all the time. I'm used to this, and I enjoy the thought process.

Well, have you ever thought about where all those thoughts come from or how many parts of your consciousness contribute? Have you considered that the conscious contributing to a thought may actually be separated consciousness attached to one of your thought processes?

I boggles the mind that an inferior source could be contributing to your actual thought process every moment—one that you're totally unaware of it.

In truth, we opened this discussion when we opened a conversation about how fear and anger became permanent. This is just adding to the reverse dynamics of why it can't work as efficiently as possible.

In another light, the source is simply identifying ways to get us up to speed. To do this, though, we need one of the largest tools shown to us.

This was completely unexpected and appeared one birthday. I hope you too can enjoy my birthday party.

Please don't think that angel-consciousness was my big birthday present. It wasn't. There is another rather immense unwrapping that is still to come.

This is the bit where I have been champing at the bit, so to speak, to bring through. Yes, there have been some very significant aspects already, but this chapter is something special.

This is like putting a Ferrari engine in your average car and then hooking it up to Microsoft,—if you get the picture.

At the very start of this book, there were quite a few references to the desires and intent of the source. Now the source desires that, somewhere in the proceedings, we match up with your desires or your consciousness, so we are all on the same page.

There are many potential capacities that exist, and this is where we are heading. The capacity of strength is the one potential that we and the source desire to focus on at present. How do we create this strength? All the steps we have taken thus far have moved us forward, but now we need to take a quantum leap.

Earlier, we focused on the soul and heart and made you aware that you do in fact have a spirit-soul and spirit-heart as well as a physical one. We also shed a little light on the fact that perhaps these two were not in fact working together or communicating.

So, if you have a spirit-heart, you can assume that the soul is replicated too. Therefore, there must be a physical soul. Indeed there is, and it sits in the physical heart.

Now that you have this piece of relevant information, I shall return to my party—or just a little before.

We need to be relaxed in order to receive, and this is a pain. I mean, I want to enjoy myself and not be uptight about receiving, so I asked for extra help.

J'spirin was rather early, as usual, but he brought lots of friends that I am always glad to see.

I had been asking rather a lot of questions and, in fact, blew a fuse when certain aspects weren't changing or healing. I was politely told that I wasn't asking the correct questions, so I asked for the questions. You see, this was a while ago, and at that point in the proceedings, I hadn't previously known that I could ask for the actual questions to unlock everything. I point this out because this is really about communication, isn't it?

Think about it this way. We have many different connections to our source angels that really haven't been used to their capacity. Our angels need our connections—which used to exist but don't now—to interpret what we are asking.

Yes, sometimes a real message gets through, just as sometimes their real messages get through to us. If you're not in touch with your real spirit-self, how the heck is your message going to get through except when miracles happen?

This is where our real conversation is heading. Because there are a number of things I have always done naturally, I sometimes assume that others do them too. This would have been a fair assumption at that time, but remember that this was years ago.

Remember our conversation about asking someone how he channels? When the answer is, "I always have," it doesn't tell you much, does it?

Because I had assumed that everybody channels, albeit inefficiently, it stands to reason that if I could channel, I had the right connections. My next revelation was that I must show others what they were doing wrong or inefficiently. I really couldn't help myself.

This little self-conversation had occurred long before my birthday, and I had made many inroads, but they left me stuck and frustrated. As I have indicated before, frustration often points you in the right direction, if you ask the correct questions and don't act impulsively.

I will now resume my birthday story. It was a bit past midnight on my birthday, and this is how the conversation went.

"David, there are quite a few questions you desire to be opened in truth, yes. We are here to assist, my friend, on your special day."

I remember being a bit peeved at being woken, as not everything was working out as planned, so I wasn't totally receptive. I was really ready to just go back to sleep. I don't mean to sound ungrateful, but talking to guides isn't anything new, so sometimes I was a little blasé. Also, remember that midnight is for sleeping, when you are used to getting up early. Add to this that with each new birthday, I was becoming less receptive, and I was probably rather grumpy at being woken.

"David, so much of your self desires to change, yes."

"Yes, okay. Can I go back to sleep now?" Angels have a way of getting your attention, even when you're unreceptive.

"David, there is so much that you are unaware of. You use your soul but little of your heart. We are here to show you your inception, yes."

The energy traveling through my body soon got rid of my crappy mood.

"Simply, we are making you more aware of all that you actually do have. Perhaps this is more desirable than all that you do not have. David, you just need to use all that you have more efficiently, instead of worrying about not being connected to this or that. David, let us show you where your true strength lies."

The energy was a bit like someone had put me in a vacuumed press. It was simular to every bit of me being sucked into my soul and heart.

"David, this is where your first point of separation occurred. All that exists here is of absolute truth. You can sense all this, yes."

I thought I had experienced a lot of knowing when I reconnected to activations, but this was bringing me alive again.

"David, this is all that you are asking for, and this has always been your life direction, yes. The integration of your soul into your heart is in fact so much more, yes. This is to unlock your understanding to the new millennium or to a new-time present and all that separates humanity from this new time."

"David, examine your newly integrated soul and heart. This is more than just the sum of your soul and heart, is it not?"

"I guess I've got a lot to figure out," was about all I could say.

Although it was two in the morning, I had to write this all down. There was just too much information to absorb or make sense of, and I didn't feel coherent at that moment. I just knew I had to write it all down.

An hour and a half later, I'd just had it, and I fell into bed, exhausted.

Nobody woke me too early, as it was Easter weekend, and my Easter bunny had come a bit early.

My nieces arrived and wanted to know why I was still in bed. They just wanted to play, as little kids do. At least the angels had fixed my mood, and I was able to relay to Julie what had gone on.

Julie was a little more sympathetic after seeing how much I had speed-written. This was more than automatic writing; this was really as if somebody else had been writing. This was also shown by the fact that the handwriting changed styles with each contributor.

There was some very interesting reading to decipher here, as a lot was condensed and needing the long version to be added, I guess.

That night of my birthday, I was ready for bed early. It had been a long day. No sooner was I in bed than, here we went again. This time it was more of an unlocking of what I'd received the night before.

This might be a strange description of energy, but it was light and clean, with lots of deciphering linked to every activation. Insight can be a remarkable experience when it's not just affirmations or activations but so much more.

The automatic writing must have once again opened automatic comprehension and clarity.

"Now, David, you have the how, why, where, and when to comprehend all that exists of yourself and all that sits separate. David, your inception indicates all that is sacred. This we opened last night, and this is also where your first separation occurred, yes?"

"David, this is all that you have asked for; the rest is your life direction, yes."

How much work this was to entail definitely wasn't indicated at the time, but knowing what was ahead wouldn't have changed a thing. Now that I had my new birthday present, it was time to unwrap it.

I mentioned earlier that because of all the stuff I did as a kid, it was easy to relate to indigo kids, and being around them helped remind me of other stuff I had forgotten about. This was to become invaluable, as I needed these senses to understand, interpret, and then openly comprehend the vastness of this unlocking.

I did fill plenty of books in the days after this—not just to get my head around it, but so that Julie could as well. Everything was very concise and needed a lot of opening.

A couple of days later, I sat down to all I had written. The translation of one sentence turned into twenty to thirty pages, so an hour and a half of writing took a couple of days to decipher. I also needed a different type of deciphering, and seeing we were still on the Easter break, getting out in my boat helped me digest everything.

What I really needed was a bit of "me" time, without thinking too seriously about all that had unfolded. This is something I often do after "download heaps." Essentially, I try not to focus on everything that has unfolded, or is about to.

This is an intuitional thing, and I do it for many reasons. I try not to take myself—or whatever comes in—too seriously, for one rather large reason. The balance between spirit and physical could easily become unbalanced.

Here is how my birthday present unfolded and how I translated this source interpretation in a new-time manner. By now you probably are not surprised that this involves a new way to interpret truth.

Before you comprehend the significance of this interpretation, I probably need to outline my inception. There was one tool I needed to comprehend.

In a conversation I had with Gabriel—who is, thankfully, a very consistent visitor—he was outlining how humanity's truth is limited, which is one of our largest debilitations.

After my birthday, I was asked if I would care to resume our conversation. I mentioned that now, at least, I had a better understanding of where I was heading with this conversation.

"Are you ready to start then? David, you have such limited comprehension of all that you have received, yes. Please let us outline things and ensure that all is correct."

"This is what I am asking for. Thank you."

"David, consider your strength of truth, or how much actual strength is held within your truth," said Gabriel. "So you have learned something. David, consider the strength of your truth before your birthday. You realised that the flow—or all energy that was actually able to connect to truth—was not only limited but that the amount of current that flowed through this truth was also minimal, yes."

There is a reason I have not highlighted this section. Some people just skim through books for the good bits, so to speak. What they fail to realise is that words can activate them. This is something I will digress on later.

Please be aware that the following sentence has many new-time keys and codes to help unlock parts that are able to contribute. For those of you who are aware, this may appear to light up.

These contributing parts, at present, don't have enough current flowing through them. This is to ensure that this capacity is asked for, yes.

Simply, this is to ensure that all who connect will appreciate it with gratitude and compassion, enabled to connect to real matter.

Now, ask your own angel-self very nicely to connect to this previous sentence, please. No, I am not kidding. Perhaps you can also reread it, please. I have attempted to keep this book very basic and at one level of understanding.

For this one moment, though, those more sensitive souls may see an immense blue orb interacting with you. This is to help your source presence in the future. For those who do not see it, do not feel that you have not connected or missed out. It is connecting to you as we speak. The tones to balance this activation will also accompany this.

You see, sometimes you can't tell how large or meaningful something is at first sight, but this we desire to change as of now.

My earlier words are a type of affirmation to stimulate your angel-consciousness. Now for a small realisation. Were you aware that perhaps something large was about to be connected or unlocked by them?

Please consider what actually exists within your spirit and physical soul and heart that you really know about. Also consider that, at the moment, all are sitting separate and not really talking to each other.

You see, as Gabriel was telling me, we use but a fraction of this potential. Why? Because we assume so many parts of us are all communicating, when in fact they are not. Most of our inabilities relate to this. Perhaps this one scenario is worth taking note of Gabriel's words of wisdom.

Unless the real strength of the soul and heart are combined, every single particle of matter can never fully retain strength. Remember, this is how you were created and are meant to exist.

If our real soul and our real heart are not always communicating and acting as one, then all self-sources will never be able to appreciate truth in a gratitude and compassion, which are needed to create real love.

"At present, all only represent a minute portion of real love. This is something most of humanity does not appreciate." You had better check this, as it is a rather large statement by Gabriel. So is the one that follows.

"How can all comprehend or understand this love, if there are no relative senses to awaken all to an awareness that this actually sits in the existence of all?"

These last statements are probably easy enough to understand, but I and all guides desire to release hidden meaning, which were meant to confuse us in the past. Consider the vibration and frequency of the word *exist.* This means a current and present presence, every moment in time that we have ever been fully complete.

Existence, of course, is the opposite. It is many levels of incompleteness and many unawarenesses that indicate past time.

This hidden meaning testifies to one large fact: for a long time, we have not been aware of what we are really capable of. So, as our guides stated earlier, when we unlock real self-foundations of what is not limited, we are then strong enough to not keep repeating this.

There is also one massive learning I need to interject and put into place. It is one of the largest separations, and I have found it to be disguised, time and time again. Because we care for each other, we often interfere—without realising that perhaps we are stifling or constricting another. This is most apparent in family situations or circumstances where people are trying to live their lives through others.

Instead of repeating past mistakes, we have now gained enough strength to unlock many new foundations—that is, self-abilities—so one after the other, with increasing ease, the foundations grow.

This is how we actually get stronger: we keep connecting to real foundations of truth or true parts of us that we are unaware of.

Using this integrated soul and heart as one, all this energy will flow as it is meant to, so we become stronger. And the stronger we become the more self-potential we open. This self-potential is designed to contribute, once we are strong enough, and strengthen all humanity.

Why? Because this raises the vibration, the frequency, and the harmonics to become lighter as you release denser consciousness or help others awaken.

What happens next is that your physical body does the same as your spirit-body; it works at a level of quintessence.

Does this awaken your senses to your most limited capacity so you can comprehend that you are of this existence? This existence means living in complete limitation instead of how we could live. There might be many other things in life that you are fantastic at.

Reflect, open your awareness, and open all that you need to be absolutely aware of. Then many others will once again do and say things that reflect all that will bring joy and happiness to your life. I am not speaking only of spiritual enterprises. I include everything from the smallest to the largest parts of your everyday life.

I have noticed that they all combine to create more meaning to what your senses are telling you.

In the early days, I admit that I was probably overly analytical, as I wanted to define the real changes or the changing understandings. I wanted to make sure I was getting a real joy by having a new, real truth.

This is a massive subject, but there is one other fact that is worth considering: how much real energy this has.

When your everyday self raises your vibrations, you will contribute only in a non-conflicting manner. Because of my job at the time, I was unable to share what was going on in my life, except with a couple of people. I was, however, becoming quite aware of the rising vibration that I was able to unconsciously contribute.

To give you an idea of this strength, I'll share this story.

The plant I worked out of was becoming increasingly busy, so a couple of extra concrete trucks were transferred in. One of these drivers was most upset as he perceived that his truck would not be earning as much, and he took this very personally.

One day he was just "spitting the dummy," so I said, "Did you ever consider yourself fortunate to be closer to home?"

That just lit the wick for him to explode, and he did. After listening to him rant and rave for five minutes, I said, "Are you finished?"

Yes. He was ready to rip my head off.

I asked, "How long did you spend traveling to work each day?"

"That's not the point," he quickly told me.

Before he could say another word, I said, "You spend an hour and three quarters each day. Multiply this by five or six days that you're not at home. Here, you're home in five minutes. Think about it," I said as I left.

About three months later, I was asking this same person about his weekend. He told me that while he and his kids were driving down the highway, they had said how they never used to see him before, and they never wanted him to go back to his old plant. He also went on to describe all the things they did together that they'd never had time to do before. He then described how he'd had tears running down his face and needed to look out the window to control them. But I don't think the kids missed the significance of their message, do you?

I have quite a few examples of changes in outlook over this short period, changes that really hit home to me, frequency changes that helped me and others.

To help with the total alignment of how to reconnect to this most vital part of ourselves, a couple more physical and spirit senses need to be felt.

While all previous tithing affirmations help with understanding, they really help when it comes to feeling and sensing the energy moving in true activations

You might be wondering what is the difference between what I am talking about now and what I said before, yes. Now I am absolutely aware, with the self-inception, of what is me and correct.

Next, I am aware of what is me and *not* fully correct.

Next, I am aware of what is not even slightly of my energy but is sitting in my energy.

Next, I am now aware of how to change this and grow all that is real and current and worth connecting to and to release all that is not.

Next, as you release all that is not of yourself, you are able to ascertain that a part of your self needs reintegrating.

Simply, the inception is a vehicle to allow self-awareness of how, where, when, and why it is possible to make the self whole again.

When this is all said and done, it lets you sense parts of your energy that have been missing.

Is this really necessary? Is this going to help me achieve everything in life I want to achieve? Is this going to help me find what I might like to do in the future?

This is about making you more aware and keeping you aware.

Why would you desire this? So you never miss out on an opportunity to connect to a life potential and a life synchronicity.

I hope this resonates with you.

Please join in finding the potential of your inception, where the true strength of your integrated soul and heart exist as one energy in one time of presence.

This point of presence is how we send a message to be received. It is then sent to be expanded and extended with all of your collective consciousness connections. Hence you become aware in a true manner to create real purpose in your life.

You do realize that when we said *extend* and *expand* we are talking about energies that have sat dormant or have only been used in a minimum capacity.

People I connect to this are usually more than surprised at the vastness of their self-energy—even people who have been on this journey for decades. This means that the message you have now sent in a spirit of consciousness from your soul is directly connected to a conscious manner of your heart.

You may not realise this, but with no interference between the two, you are now moving to change every awareness of yourself. You will then move in a consciously activated energy integrated as self-peace.

Yes, the previous sentences were totally channeled. Did you sense the change of vibration? All of your self is reacting to true responses, and this is how activations truthfully work.

Those of you who desire this awareness may sense that you are now moving through many old, stagnant times. Once you are at your new destination, you may sense or become aware that your self dropped and then was grounded.

Just close your eyes. You may sense that you are connecting to new activation. However, the choice is yours to send and receive what is truly of your own intent.

I now ask to connect to all true intent, which guides this self with true presence.

I am of this reality. Therefore, I am able to restore all creative natures to real self-abundance of self-faith and self-belief.

All true self-presence resides within the real purpose of spirit gravity, which my whole intuitive self follows.

Simply, I am of this reality, of creative love. Therefore, my incipient love always intends to be of self-presence.

This has been shared with the grace of Gabriel through the whole collective-consciousness spirit.

Perhaps you were able to sense forward movement. This signifies that you desire to seek direction to easily integrate self-faith and belief with true synchronicity.

Now we can extend and expand this gift in a new-time sequence.

You might feel a floating sensation as you move with ease through your inception. You are simply responding to all that is in harmony and is absolutely complete within yourself.

Please clasp your hands. Yes, you are grounding once again. You are in fact releasing the limitations of your incipient, sharing self. Yes, you are raising all expectations and thus all conscious energy.

Now you are raising all immediate, separated self-energy. It is possible to connect, now that this self-energy is present at a correct connective frequency.

You see, years ago I found that most separation was in the actual connection, not in the consciousness. This might be worth remembering, yes.

I guess this is my own very personal tithing gift to be shared. The significance of this statement I will now share in the following chapters.

# 12

## A NEW-TIME BIRTHDAY PRESENT

The actual receiving process perhaps needs clarification, now that so much of your self is changing or is open to change from the same old, routine thoughts.

This, of course, has been changed with the addition of connective consciousness, linking through your angel-consciousness to use your much-expanded consciousness.

The self-sending and receiving relationship of the collective angel-consciousness includes many layers of self-consciousness for your highest good.

Another matter to think about is that your self is now never excluded from your conscious thoughts.

In the last chapter, we discussed self-strength and the immense potential this opens.

You are now connecting to the affirmation in the last chapter again. In fact, you are releasing an immense part of you that doesn't accept your self-worth automatically.

This automatic appreciation is a reflection of your soul communicating with the essence of your soul and *heart*. This whole body of energy is reconnecting throughout many elements of your self-purpose with a new response.

This evolved response is to be a permanent feature of your everyday life, meaning that many of your receptors will now be open to freely receive love.

If you were to point both hands to the ground, ensuring that the flat of each hand faces the floor, you might sense that an overwhelming energy is pulling you over on the left-hand side.

This energy indicates the sex you use to create with. See how both are now evening out. Perhaps a freeing, new energy is flowing in both hands now, yes.

Simply and automatically, you are responding to an innermost reasoning that has been unbalanced, limiting your potential. Now you are just balancing this out somewhat.

Please bring both hands up to face each other. Another grounding may once again be sensed, a coming together of energies, but this is not integrating. Rather, it is combining energies. I'll explain in a moment.

As this energy grows, you are sensing an enhancing of frequencies. This allows a balance in the modulation of each self-vibration. If you close your eyes for a moment, you may sense this.

Did you sense stillness? This means you are not over-responding and thus are able to receive. Does this make sense?

If energy is unable to communicate, then both energies may become competitors. Thus they are unable to come together. Please focus on this statement and reflect how this could correspond to the limitation of your self in areas that you are totally unaware of.

Stillness enables you to open real senses. You do not respond now; you just allow all god—or source-consciousness to balance the self-harmony. Then you begin to reactivate as each and every part of existence energy starts to exist again.

This is then transferred to self-knowing, meaning that you comprehend the difference between the two senses, because you were sensing that you are sitting in a blissful existence, not in the blissful awareness that really exists.

Sense the shift. This is you, desiring a balance of self-humanity to freely exist in a permanent synchronicity of availability.

Comprehension of this statement is relative to the new millennium, so we understand what is synthetic or artificial. You may automatically be releasing this element that is falling off you.

Perhaps now you understand why so much was explained previously. No matter how tedious it seemed, it was relative to releasing much that the infrastructure of incorporated inhumanity is unable to sense.

I am of a self-humanity. Therefore, I am able to receive real, conscious, aware love, comprehended in every particle of this self and responding to self-respect in every self-presence.

To highlight what is possible, consider that the collective consciousness' potential is like receiving many whole self-bodies that have gone unnoticed. Because they are a part of yourself and desire to contribute, they must be needed and desired to part of the whole self.

Remember when I said that this seems to be a lonely quest? Well, connecting to all these bodies is similar to sensing that you are arriving home, which is exactly what is to be facilitated.

Also, remember that tones will be re-identifying those selves to reground you as you read. The whole of your self will be shedding dense limitations or dense energy as you read.

Now, please take note of how this unfolds. This is so very important and will reappear in every aspect of your life.

This is about a source solution to release the I've-done-it-again scenario, but wait to check, and our guides have information to disclose. Not only do they have lots to disclose; they have lots that reveal much of our past insecurities and why we are as we are.

Now, remembering that connective consciousness links your everyday consciousness, perhaps you need to redefine this. Your physical matter is now linked to your spirit on a more full-time basis—not just when you relax, sleep, or meditate, but every moment of the day.

To give a more personal account of this transition, imagine that you are in a deep meditation. As you keep going deeper, all of a sudden you open a new awareness that is quite strange and contradicts all that is meant to happen.

What is this new contradicting knowing that you are automatically aware of? As you go down, you are also ascending or staying current and aware of your present, conscious ability—or where you are connected in a totally conscious manner.

This is like going into the deepest meditation you have experienced and then, instead of going into unconsciousness, you stay totally fluid and able to explore all of your subconscious possibilities in an aware state of consciousness.

This also means that many other senses become apparent on a full-time basis—not just when you meditate.

This doesn't mean you're going to become all religious, get all funky, become a hippie, or lend yourself to thinking way outside the square. Nothing will change except for one thing.

More of your thoughts will flow freely, without the old-time processes, which means that the message you desire to be sent from your soul will be received in the correct manner in your heart, to create the correct matter for both spirit and physical love to be created.

When this is all boiled down, all of the self will become very connected, or perhaps relevant, to why you think as you do.

Add to this that you now desire with a present-now, not a past-now, to create a true time of presence.

This true presence of now has a totally different current and capacity, of course, with a combined capacity of physical and spirit-consciousness to not only stay more connected but to add all that is best for the self and all humanity. How?

Perhaps you can consider for a moment how the source unfolded this different translation. Using a connection with a connective consciousness, what is one of the greatest advantages of this aspect? You are opening a more direct line of communication. Yes, well, aren't you?

So, with more information, you are able to compile what is relevant and what is not, and straightaway a whole new thought pattern must emerge—a more lateral one, yes.

Does this make sense? Do you now realise the potential that could be unmasked? This is such a small step, but it is a step with momentous potential.

So, are you considering this outcome? Does it make sense to expand all opportunities and become a more lateral thinker, or should you stay limited and less exposed to many different sources of information?

Now are you ready to open a small insight that is continuously overlooked.

If you are opening to new communication—not just the same recycled communication—then you are open to receive. Yes, that message is able to be received. Now you are open to receive. Please check this truth. This is a message the source desires to be interpreted and translated.

Who would have thought that one word could have been taken out of context or interpreted or translated in so many different ways? This makes sense when we comprehend the breakdown from not being able to sense efficiently.

Does this explain how some separation occurred, and we became a little lost or misdirected? Now you comprehend how many misdirected life cycles or duality schedules were misconceived. Now you know where our spirit and physical were unable to communicate efficiently.

You had better check this, please.

Only now are we able to unwrap the present that changed so much of my life.

As I have stated in the opening chapters, so much is about finding out why, where, when, and how to open reason and real responses. Now we comprehend that the communication skills we employed were—or became, over many lifetimes—less than efficient, to say the least.

To increase this communication, I have asked countless questions. More importantly, I have been directed to the questions I needed to ask each and every day.

I knew intuitively that I was missing an enormous piece of the jigsaw, as everything just wasn't adding up.

You may think it's great being a channel, but if you ask questions, you also have to know when they are relevant or when the truth you are receiving isn't complete on a particular subject or level.

So, how do I actually know if my emotions or feelings feel conflicted if I am not able to embrace the three basic elements of real love—appreciation, gratitude, compassion?

You see, I asked this question for quite some time, until the reasoning became apparent. How do you think your heart came to exist? For the moment, we will be thinking outside the obvious thoughts.

To start this off, we are straightaway going to the unobvious, as we are concerning ourselves only with the spirit-heart, not the physical. The spirit-heart was, according to my sources, created through your soul.

If I switch directly into channeling mode, then the answer to this question will be a little more informative. The conversation would be with Gabriel, relayed through Sordlion and J'spirin.

"My dear, concerned people of this world, we would love to facilitate a new degree of understanding with open hearts and with what you would call open senses. At this point in time, through your real intuition, we would love to engage in new and meaningful relationship, and as a source recipient, all new-time equations will be automatically opened to your awareness.

"Please consider that to open oneself does not mean to open oneself to fear, if you are able to receive in a correct manner. May we please explain this statement? In the majority of the lives you have lived, you have opened your beautiful self to two dimensions of truth. This self-truth means that in the past you have prevailed with two opposing logics. The first of these you considered to be reality, which is, in fact, close to all reasons of truth but never complete.

"This we will explain to you soon at length, but for the moment, just please consider that the truest form of true communication is in fact limited. This you would have already discovered.

"We do desire to open you to how your self-direction has been guided by an interfering and challenging energy. This has meant a confusing time for you, and yes, we desire to rescind or fix this. Rescinding also means that we need to fix many misunderstandings that so many of you have held on to as self-truth, self-faith, or self-belief. This also means being in conflict with your own self, yes. Had you considered this outcome?

"The next problem is that your innermost self was fighting for control of whatever truth seemed the most logical. Do you see your dilemma? Please let us unravel this scenario so your minds are able to comprehend this unfolding of two-truth conflict.

"This initially has meant that you were able to receive controlling energy as well as energy of a complete love-basis of foundation.

"Eventually, my friends, you have tired of this duality. Essentially, you cut yourself off from receiving. This is only natural when you are unable to differentiate between conflicting energy and real love, yes.

"This then means that a controlling, love-based energy became one.

"To change this scenario, all guides desire to cease this dual existence as much as you do, for we are unable to help when you are unable to translate truth from illusion, yes.

"This also means that you are all creating in such a limited capacity that, in truth, as your population grows, the percentage of reality diminishes. Hence, it is time for a new time of being able to create in a fully conscious manner.

"This new manner of purpose means a new resolution of reasoning is needed so that all is not simply a rehashing of the same old information without moving forward in real terms. Duality stifles all future.

"In the simplest of terms, all guides desire a new manner of restoration and, most importantly, a new manner for all to be conceived with a true future, not a debilitated one.

"This new time of creation also means that you need to be able to dissolve all disharmony that sits within your very selves in a state of unawareness. Add to this infrastructure the fact that so few desire to be aware of all that really exists within. Most have only used a minimal percentage of this resource. Most of you sit in a state of denial of your real potentials."

Please, let me intervene here. If there was something conflicting in our innermost self, we actually just wanted to pretend that it didn't exist, and we hoped it would go away.

Now, imagine this inaction life after life. It compounds, doesn't it? Because this has been manifesting for years and is now of a more unaware state, we are not sure how to fix this confusion of having two truths. So the source is showing us a solution.

You can resolve this inner state of peace that resonates with the true opening of self-faith, self-belief, and a new-time activation, where your vibrations align with real, foundational frequencies. It is now available for all humanity.

Now we return to Sordlion and J'spirin and the Gabriel message.

"This, my friends, comes by way of a new-time tone. When all placed together, they create an active self-presence rather that a stagnant one of a limited future.

"This reactivation is to create a new purpose, for many aspects of your self at present go unrecognised, and they have in truth never been utilised, as nearly all are unaware that this self-potential exists.

"If, at this moment, you desire to open your innermost self to be available to receive in this new manner, in this new opening of reality, then perhaps a portal of real love can contribute to the real harmony of yourself."

You see, I could have facilitated what Sordlion and J'spirin desired to be passed on, but you would never have received the vibrations and frequencies needed, not to mention the harmonics. While this is essentially a reality change for so many, the reasoning for this change must always be evident.

For a new manner of spirit to form in the self, perhaps you need to understand why this equation must be explained. If you are totally unaware, then there is no way that you will simply open yourself to receive, yes.

Earlier on, our guides and I disclosed that very few of you, in fact, use the full resources of your soul and heart as one. The reason for this is that you may only be using your original connection to your soul and heart from many lifetimes ago.

Strange as this might sound, it is correct. This means that if you start off using the soul that created your heart, you then create spirit, yes.

This spirit is then used to create a physical soul, which then creates a physical heart.

We pray that you are paying attention now, as this is the moment where many of humanity have in fact opened themselves to disabilities.

How? The heart is the result of many points of creation. It is, in fact, the result of many collective consciousnesses integrating in perfect harmony, yes.

The reason for this outburst of self-emotion is simply that so many of you seem to have forgotten how you were created. You see, most of you have simply reversed the order of creation, yes, and started with heart and soul rather than soul and heart.

Once again, I need to translate in our language. This simply means that the self takes the heart as the origin of all self-resources, or we don't bother to go any further, or our self has been rescheduled due to earlier life confusions. Now, back to Gabriel.

"The implication of this reflection is that the soul and heart—or the physical heart and soul—are usually all you relate to.

"Yes, when you relax and sleep, most of you reconnect to the spirit for a brief period, but most people stop at the physical soul, thinking that they have in fact reached the point of self-creative desire, when in fact this is so far from the truth.

"My beloved friends, do you now ascertain what—through David's soul—we desire to translate to all?

"This is correct. At this present moment, very few people actually reconnect to the spirit-soul and heart. We would also like to remind you that this has also been a reoccurring image in each and every lifetime, life after life.

"This self-image further alienates the self or distances the self from all true origins. When you distance the origins, you distance the energy and all true future, as the ability to truly sense a correct desire will be but a fleeting connection as you sleep or meditate.

"Remember, David said that all guides desire to open all of humanity to a new, constant consciousness. Perhaps now you can understand the reasoning in a present-time manner, rather than through the many disrupted manners of time that do not reflect a true desire or intent."

This essentially ends the guided translation from many guides. The reason only one voice came through was to avoid disrupting the frequency or the message too much.

Channeled messages of this nature are completely different from when I channel for groups of people. While there is always an oriented content, the majority of a channeling is facilitated with a healing message as well.

The healing part of the message takes less concentration, because there are many contributors—guides or angels. This also means that you would be going deep into your consciousness while staying very conscious. You never need to miss the whole reason or reaction of what was interpreted when you stay conscious.

The other reason that translating in a meditation is so easy is that you use the whole of your body to translate with. You are able to use every particle of your body to reflect the message as it was received.

You see, initially the guides start you off using only your physical soul and heart and many senses within your head region. Then slowly you are introduced to many other facets of your body's sensory parts, increasing the consciousness of your self.

However, only when you give yourself permission to be free to re-access your real spirit is this possible. Then, and only then, do we venture into the original soul and heart. If you are not accustomed to using this area of consciousness, then you may have automatically closed down because it was alien to you. Perhaps now you comprehend why it was necessary to repeat so many unconscious notions?

Remember, I said we sometimes need to think outside the square. Perhaps now you can appreciate a little more how this point of view has evolved to release the old, de-evolved and stagnating energy symptoms of past and present interferences.

Let's start at the beginning, as I attempt to explain something that has been so automatically overlooked for so many lifetimes. The physical heart is like the last link to what most of us identify as self-energy. In a way, we send this area of our self to the most identifiable self-energy. Can you relate to how this occurs?

We then might move on to our physical soul inside our physical heart, but quite often, for most, this is as far as they venture. This is an unconscious blockage.

Those who have been on this journey for a while would have ventured here each and every day.

We now need to go back somewhat to the spirit-soul. This is more like the origin of our energy, the immortal point of our self. This soul was the collective consciousness's energy that created our spirit-heart. It is an extension and an expansion of our soul.

This soul and heart of spirit is the point of our foundation, of how we were created, yet we have forgotten this. Why?

Well, this is how our self-spirit is created, yet it gets forgotten as we lump our self-spirit in with all spirit. So, right from the start, we dismiss the self. Can you comprehend this?

Because this is then thought of as spirit, the fact that our original soul and heart exist in there is forgotten.

You had better check, though. As you check, please point both hands into your soul and heart before asking this most important question, so you will receive a self-changing answer.

Do you comprehend, now, that you are being guided by the source, way outside the square of old-time thought? I only received this equation of new thought because I asked for true answers to many questions that didn't add up.

The real foundations in life need each and every one of these elements, not in a limited or artificial capacity. The amount of artificial contribution that has been hindering our true resources has been beyond comprehension.

This last sentence defines why the source has facilitated us with the inception—the source—of our true self. Perhaps this is worth pondering on a little longer, yes.

Once you grasp a real strength in yourself, then you are able to really use this it, as it is all yours and has never been tampered with.

Please let this next part sink in, as this is perhaps going to open up a new way of finding what is real, and it will link you directly to the soul you were created from.

These things will happen not just when you meditate, but on a more full-time basis day to day.

If you join all the strength of your soul through your heart, then you integrate this energy and it becomes your spirit. We then integrate this with our physical soul and heart, and instant self-truth is available.

So far there have been a few tools for you to become acquainted with. One of the largest of these is the connective consciousness, and this is about to be amped-up somewhat.

Consider that when you meditate, you connect to a vast amount of consciousness that is not readily accessible on a full-time basis. This consciousness isn't just knowledge that you only use on a spirit level; it activates your thought patterns and body functions.

This statement will in the future unlock so many self-potentials that perhaps you may wonder how you missed it before.

It's strange that something with so much unlocking potential is unobvious and invisible, yet it holds so many potentials we're unaware of. The reason that the source is sharing this unobvious potential is that this one unconscious memory has single-handedly stopped many levels of conscious from integrating back to your strength. It needs to be defined, turning self-power into self-strength without any interfering power from others.

Imagine a vast amount of your consciousness always being accessible, always ready to use, day in and day out. Don't underestimate this potential.

If this vast amount of usable and very conscious energy was actually used, imagine the contribution it could make to your daily life. Imagine the stability your consciousness could contribute to the rest of your self by using more than ten percent of your conscious brain reaction.

Imagine creating a more whole self. Yes, remember that this is what nearly all books of this genre ask us to seek. With this insight or reasoning, a real response is going to be readily achievable.

Remember, the response to unawareness is a conflicting emotion. On a subconscious level, your energy is not moving the way you desire it to.

The source is in fact sharing much awareness that has just gone unnoticed for far too long.

Every book we read does this in some way. It is also a way of linking many conscious aspects together and using them so they don't all sit separately.

After this, a full-time *akashic* link can be added. This we will discuss later.

Remember, this is about connecting to our potential, and a vast amount of this is unexplored.

Another point can crop up in the inner soul and heart when they are neatly sitting together. When they become one, they work as one. The strength implications are obvious, so inner strength obviously becomes stronger as well. This depth of inner strength holds many capabilities and some not-so-obvious capacities of energies.

Also tucked away in this inner part is your depth of intuition or self-knowledge or capabilities; so this is a little mystery tour. Maybe you knew, or may be you didn't, but it most certainly isn't sitting on some plane doing nothing, unable to be reached or used. This may have seemed to be the case, after all that we have been discussing.

For myself, as you know, a different level of understanding is needed to comprehend an appreciation, gratitude, or compassion in the manner of some spirit or physical matter. Even when you relate this to just one word—*presence*—you could fill books and books, as I have indeed done.

I have asked a few questions that opened up a little differently one Saturday night. It was about two in the morning, not my usual channeling time, I can tell you.

Activations that wake you up are sort of intense. This was only the introduction, though. As the chapter title suggests, this was indeed my birthday, just a little past midnight.

Before I get too far ahead of myself here, I should indicate that a couple of months prior to this we had been introduced to a couple of rather extraordinary guides. I have already introduced Sordlion and J'spirin and the changes they helped precipitate. It would take many books to describe their contributions.

This is a basic unfolding of how we easily comprehended the changes in everything we receive. Old-time understanding says that energy consciousness sits on one level. This you can relate to.

There is also a diverse energy system connected to this, which in a way ensures that you don't stray outside this level. This conflicts with many thoughts, but don't think for a moment that we are all working on the same level or are unable to shift. Simply you are receiving a preparation to release what is like an old time schedule that keeps you in a limited capacity.

Before my birthday—or any large insights that have occurred—there has always been a lead-up or a preparation. This I have discussed in a limited way.

Yes, I am often surprised at the outcome, but without the preparations, I would have missed the important parts.

If I had missed *this* important part, what do think would have happened next? Actually, I would have been a little frustrated, as I would have sensed I was really missing out on something.

So this was it, for a start. Then I would want to know what was going on and why all of a sudden I felt crabby and everybody was just annoying me. Then, perhaps, I would be crabby with my guides and say, "What's the use, if I can't get a true answer." You sense the scenario, don't you? Whether you channel full-time or not, the result is the same.

I was asking for a question to be answered, but I didn't really have all the questions in order to create an answer. Then I needed to recycle, as I was unable to work out an outcome. So I might do a small or large cycle until I comprehended a real result—not just an answer but something comprehensible and understandable that I could relate to.

Does this sound familiar? How many times have we repeated some cycle in a lifetime when we were just seeking truth. How have we ended up following a certain schedule while we missed an opportunity to connect to ourselves in a more complete manner or to make ourselves more whole?

Years ago, the preparations were not easy to notice, so many surprises cropped up that I wasn't ready for. The source desires that this not happen to you, so I will continue.

I was looking for an outcome, a resolution to something in my life. I desired to either release or create, not simply find an answer. So, why did I end up doing the same old cycle over and over? Because I didn't have the correct preparations.

There is another outcome equal to this that could go undetected if all the relevant questions weren't linked together from their different levels of consciousness. That's right, many thoughts on different levels of consciousness, never linking up. Better add loads of questions on different levels to the answers as well.

So the real outcome, which links both these scenarios together, is this. How do you unblock many levels to link all questions or conscious thoughts together and create a conscious outcome that is easily understood and totally comprehensible?

This, of course, will be a preparation to start with, and it needs energy to link all levels of the real self together as needed, desired, or intended. Each of these must contain the real truth and nothing else, and then there are no distractions that later revise the past over and over again.

To cut to the chase, so to speak, we are now in a present moment, connecting you to many spirit parts of your self-spirit, so the original soul that started your own creation is to be reconnected.

Remember, because this soul or heart of origin is thought of as spirit, the real importance has been overlooked as just some bit of spirit helping us. Is this hitting home? The crucial link of our self has not been used except in a subconscious manner.

The other point to consider is that this soul and heart were being used in a separate manner, never together, even through the subconscious.

I may have prattled on somewhat again, but when I have been explaining this to clients and friends, I can tell if they easily understand the significance of this or not. It takes a little bit to get your head around, especially the significance of what this means in terms of connecting to all real self-contributions.

In person, I am easily able to reflect what works correctly with a client's consciousness, as I talk actively to your consciousness through all guides, and I know when you need help. Needing help is an issue of your connective consciousness, as this is where most deactivation happens.

In a meditation, groups of people needing the same help always seem to sit together, and they help each other find reactions they might have missed. When I look at these groups, they are all illuminating differently. If a correct, connective collective-consciousness is able to share what all guides are reflecting, then all move with grace, ease, and the sequences to create synchronicities as needed.

We are about to combine all the aspects that we have discussed in all our conversations and translations to many areas of yourself that are not communicating. We are about to change this. Then you can flow into that self-potential immediately.

The *inception* is, of course, the integration of the initial self-soul that is to move through your initial heart in a creative manner.

This is how strength is created. This is the intent of self-desire. You are asking all of the collective consciousness to be active and to become as one. Remember, strength is balanced current without separate power.

As this exercise progresses, please factor in that you are receiving, and take your time to ensure that you miss nothing that is intended for you. Remember, hurrying means not being in a sequence of presence and able receive.

This exercise means that whichever sense you use, you will receive the sensation that the whole energy of your head is flowing into your body. Whether you see or just sense, this will be correct.

This sensation will be repeated a couple of times. Close your eyes and connect to this, please.

This is like energy just flowing into your head. Then your head feels like dropping.

This is bringing an unconscious self-energy to become current. Now you will ground this whole sequence of consciousness.

Your eyes will now roll to facilitate a new insight. Now a grounding sensation will be evident. Please close those beautiful eyes again.

The depth of consciousness that you just reached was also evident as your stomach contracted, yes.

You were aware of the depth that you reached, yes, sensing how that consciousness is moving through your complete self.

For those who are a little more aware, you may notice that you are surrounded in a blue light. This is your self, asking to access self-strength.

If you are unable to see this, hold the palms of your hands away from yourself as if leaning flat against a wall. Sense the energy encompassing you. This energy has started from your initial soul, and you are reconnecting this energy as a resource of self.

Before closing your eyes this time, please take note of the depth of consciousness that you reach and retain it as you open your eyes.

With your eyes wide open, notice that you are still receiving. So much is still flowing into you, yes.

Before we move on, hold the flat palms of your hands over your body. Sense that the body is now becoming not only more active; it is becoming alive.

This exercise is about to repeat and bring so many aspects of unconscious self-ability back to your self.

This exercise should be tried tomorrow as well. Remind yourself with a note so you don't forget. With your eyes open, consciously drop into the depth of yourself with your eyes open, yes, with your eyes open.

This depth of consciousness that you have just accessed is what you are constantly aware of now. How about that?

Now, imagine this repeated thousands of times. Imagine how aware you would be or how in-touch with your intuition you would be.

This depth of intuition, of course, leads to many other aspects of your life, many other potentials and possibilities. That flowing sensation you feel is to open yourself to this evolved activation in a manner of your future self.

Put simply in our language, this is to activate a future, as this is something attainable. Creating in past tense is a waste of energy. It's unattainable and creates interfering emotions.

Some of you who have been on this journey for some time will feel a different sensation of moving into your self, as this is what you are actually achieving.

To bring balance and harmony to your self-energy, some of you may once again hear tones when you relax. To help ground this energy, please stand and point your hand in a deliberate manner to the ground. Some may sense that they feel like flapping about, but eventually they will calm down.

Those hands are probably not the only sensation. A buckling of the knees indicates that unconscious consciousness is now presently grounded throughout yourself.

Over the coming days, you might sense that you are a little more aware of all the smallest things in life. As you become familiar with these smallest senses and keep yourself open to them, your senses grow.

Remember, from all small things larger things will grow. So will your awareness to the larger aspects of life.

This means that you will see new purpose in many things that you now do. Of course, this will be what our next chapter is about—purpose.

I appreciate purpose. Therefore, this life evolves with absolute purpose. Therefore, I am able to open every self-ability in a free and true manner.

This self-reflection simply means that I am free to be me in all that I desire to be free.

I know that there have been an enormous number of affirmations in this chapter, but they do show you how to use connective consciousness, yes, to use this long-lost self-ability.

# 13

## NEW-TIME ABILITIES

An ability that comes naturally but has not really been explored is the focus of this chapter.

We are going to be making a little more use of some of the awareness you touched on in previous chapters. We will ask many more questions about how to evolve, and we will discover where the templates and real blueprints exist.

Of course, we also need to dig deep and discover where you have been suppressed. Surprisingly enough, you may find that much has been done already without consulting you. You may even find hidden agendas of others, which have suppressed you for millennia.

Earlier on, in what I call my unraveling stage, the largest obstacle I found was me. Actually, I hit on this subject a little before, but it is worth remembering. Some of your biggest discoveries will be right under that nose of yours, staring you right in the eyes. That's why you've never found them. You are welcome to prove me wrong. Everybody's contribution is gratefully received, and we all have our own part to decipher.

I was expanding on all that sat under my nose, and what happened years ago is still relative today. In guided self-meditations, I was more or less re-exploring consciousness that I used to connect to when I was around seven or eight.

This is an aspect that I found most indigos connect to. After stilling myself on my bed, my extended, conscious spirit was connecting in a physical manner. This consciousness was re-exploring my body through my hands, and it soon reacquainted itself with the energy around me. The light about me intensified until the large energy cores about me had my attention.

I could see myself receiving what looked like cylinders of light. Some went into me, and others were just stacked about me until they unfolded. I admit that I was hesitant to share certain parts of my self-opening with others, but apparently this is relevant.

T'sarisis, my guide this night, was expanding on certain virtues that I had stayed connected to.

"So, this is where I am heading in the future?" was my question.

"Not at all," was the answer. "What have you received, David?"

I casually replied that I had received the missing keys and codes of me. You see, I was very aware that this was great event, but I didn't get too carried away. This was a bit strange. One part of me was over the moon; the other part was saying, *Well, so what? Now you know what* they *do. What's the big deal?*

The awareness, I quickly figured out, was, "Don't get too carried away. Come back to reality, David. Sense."

This was a damn weird, acute feeling, to say the least.

"Yes, David, you will soon be aware and understand." And many guides came around me, and the keys and codes began to activate.

You might be wondering why I am exploring this chapter now instead of earlier in the book. It's because you would never have found the relevance in what is to be shared with you here. In each previous chapter, there was some personal ability for you to unlock.

The next sensation was like being shot through a cannon back into myself. It was not the usual gradual regrounding. It was a bit too late at night to ring anyone to share this experience, so I had plenty of time to adjust to it.

I did remember during the night how vital these keys and codes were and how they linked activations together. My solutions was, "Ah, well, I'd better sleep on it."

Later, I woke up more conscious than ever of all the energies in and about my body. I was aware of—or had better insight into—what was going on. I had no weird feelings about how I knew all of this.

I do remember saying, "I need a lot of help here to comprehend all of this." After relaying this to Julie, I let her sense what I had connected to and what it apparently meant.

The next installment was that I needed to grab some large sketch pads and crayons to replicate what I was sensing and seeing. I did pick up felt-tip markers and was told, yes, you will need them, but you need crayons at the moment.

So I had a coffee and went to work on interpreting keys and codes. Now I understood the crayon part, as many of the colours needed to be dragged together or blended. They did represent old-time texts, but I was told that they were not on earth as I know it.

Like a man possessed, I had about a hundred and twenty drawings to finish. Some, I had to admit, looked pretty, but what use does that serve?

Then I started to write down what each sketch meant. I was still a little oblivious to where this was heading, but each morning the self-awareness grew, with many new activations of energy presenting themselves.

Next, I made lots of cards—like guidance cards—using symbols of different colour and configuration. After this, I had to decipher a meaning for each and every card.

I was then told to hold my hand over each card corresponding to the sketch pad paper that had been interpreted. The vibrational frequencies that began to unfold led to a mass of instant knowing. After quite a long conversation with my guides, I was able to assemble the knowing of what was unfolding.

I hopped onto my healing table that night to do a little more exploring by myself. I was told, "David, you have misconstrued some of the interpretation. Look back at all that you have received, and let us guide you. David, you perceived that these are old-time knowing, yes? Well, they are not."

"So they are of the future then?" I asked.

"Yes and no. They are of a present moment where your consciousness is at this present time. David, you are free to explore all that will unlock your freedoms."

*What sort of a clue is this?* I thought. It was pretty ambiguous. I needed a more definite direction.

"David, your awareness is correct."

When I had stilled myself, I seemed to sink, not just into my levels of conscious awareness but also into unaware consciousness. As I reconnected to each conscious activation, I instantly knew what each energy was for, why it was doing what it did, where it was going, and, most importantly, the final response to this activation or final reaction.

Now I was able to appreciate for the first time the enormity of the keys and codes. This was more than a "wow" moment. Containing my excitement was a little hard. Then, all of a sudden, it dawned on me: Why did I comprehend this?

With all this recognition, the fact unfolded to me that all keys and codes were just light—nothing but light.

"So, they told me how to connect with the light source?" was my question.

"Yes, David, but they do so much more, do they not?"

This may seem like a play on words, because keys and codes are different forms, functions, flows, fluidities, balances, harmonics, and gravities that enlighten.

"So they give direction and guide the way," I said.

"David, you need to focus on each individual moment and decipher if you are present or separate in every self-form, yes. Then, my friend, when you are sure this is correct, you can ensure that every function is a free and natural flow of energy, yes?"

A free and natural flow of self-energy was worth considering. So was a response that was free to interpret what was actually sensed in a responsible manner.

Then it dawned on me that these are the foundational senses necessary to become a real sensory self, able to interpret in this same manner.

Then, and only then, will the true function of each and every flow of real energy align and balance. Why? Simply because it is free—free to reflect all that is of a free intention or desire.

This free energy will be of an efficient and natural flow, enabling every true, functioning energy to connect. Why? Put simply, you are freeing every self-resource to be actively free to receive, yes.

At this moment, I was feeling a little overwhelmed, which was rather strange. Then I realized that I was sensing appreciation and gratitude with source compassion, and I was able to comprehend the "why-I-was" factor.

I do appreciate that perhaps some of you don't have a clue what this last paragraph adds up to, so let's disassemble this and put it in layman's terms.

In the last chapter, we started to talk about lines of gravity and how some of them were a little skewed, not helping to direct energy where it needed to flow. So, if I was to decipher the skew and not connect to lateral thought, then there was going to be a 99 percent possibility that the thought was from an interfering source.

This means in energy terms that the energy is really a de-activating cycle of energy that is not desired.

The annoying part is that I have found so many of these, and emotions and feelings don't always indicate which is which, if ever.

There was an immense directional clue before, so I will return to how this all ties together.

The phrase "actively free" is a term referring to real energy. Let's decipher spirit language in an "actively free" manner. That way you are free to create with real consciousness and absolutely no interfering power that desires to enslave your thoughts, feelings, or emotions.

Why? If the interfering energy is able to release a conscious factor from your desiring thoughts, feelings, and emotions, then you are easily controlled. This means that you have lost all connective-consciousness with your awareness.

If you are unaware, it is impossible to have a logical and secure thought that gives you a secure direction.

This means that, in order to create reasons or lateral thought, you would use many thoughts you used for reasoning in the past. Remember, very few are ever going to experience this. It is an extreme situation, except when some major form of intoxication is present.

However, this outline is still a relevant indicator for breaking down certain patterns or parts of patterns.

Every time you become insecure, what is going to happen? You are going to process every thought you used in the past to resolve a certain problem. Yes, this is processing or consuming processed unconsciousness.

Yes, I am being direct. Awareness isn't created by saying one day that you will comprehend what was outlined. Everything must be direct and as concise as possible without being too conflicting.

This is also why so many parts are repeated—to ensure that each relevant consciousness is in fact reactivated, not left to figure out why you feel abandoned.

What is this scenario creating? A fear instinct.

Finding a solution to a problem without any conscious connection or the strength of a lateral conscious thought requires that the whole scenario change. Many more solutions from the past will be added to try and find some type of resolution, yes.

So, now you have a situation with millions of solutions to one small problem—millions of solutions going through your head for what may be a trivial problem. Mind-chatter is just one of the ways this comes about. Another is that many people are just used to the mind-chatter; the interference seems a normal and relevant part of their makeup.

When mind-chatter seems normal, the mind is going a million miles an hour, accomplishing nothing. To a person in this routine, it is a daily battle.

This is a major point of awareness to be alerted to. The effects are varied, except for what always follows this pattern.

Repeatedly and continuously revisiting the past is a constant debilitator in many areas of our life, so not all recycling is an ecologically sound practice. The reasoning for this statement is that we also end up recycling emotions and feelings that are often confused with thoughts.

Please consider this last sentence carefully. If we desire to diagnose conflicting emotions or feelings, how do we even know which emotions are real and not a made-up situation from the past?

Perhaps you could reason that inhumanity is only controlling restriction or constriction of energy, thus cutting off the real connection to our self-humanity or source-collective-consciousness. Releasing and freeing the parts that are controlled, restricted, and constricted, comes from our own self-connective consciousness, the forgotten spirit-connection.

In a way, this is the real secret of the new millennium. Where else is this passed on and shared, not controlled, freely tithed for all to find and use.

This is not so much my own work. It is the ideas passed on by the source that I have found to be correct through different circumstances I have worked through.

This really is opening up spirit ethics. These are foundational in all that frees our self-personal thoughts and past resentment-processing—the feeling that life-worth seems to have been stolen from you.

The effects of this, while debilitating and confusing for the affected person, can be also frustrating for loved ones, as this person's reasoning is quite unfathomable.

While you are aware of so many points of suppressed limitations, perhaps this would be a relevant time to reflect on a couple of foundational principles that you are more aware of now.

Remember that to have a free-flowing lateral thought, you need a strong spirit-connection. Otherwise, all sorts of interferences from in-consciousness and out-of-consciousness create illusional barriers. These illusional barriers are a diversion from seeking our innermost self-strength, which guides all self-energy to a true connection.

This true connection is the vital connective consciousness, which is only able to be created with the true strength of joining your spirit-consciousness and physical consciousness together. This we discussed before with the awareness of integrating real self-strengths together.

I may seem to remind you often about certain awarenesses, but this is to also strengthen you, not to annoy you. There is another reason for repeating certain aspects. As you become more aware, your self wants to link all these different awarenesses together and make use of them, perhaps in a subconscious manner.

This opens up a whole new train of thought that, until now, we have side-stepped.

In the past, many of us—and I was no different—linked unconsciousness and sub-consciousness together or thought they were exactly the same energy.

We all take certain things as being so, which is why the source told us to question everything and not take anything for granted. Yes, I know I harped on about this, and I'm becoming a real nagger.

I have to remind myself and you that when we are used to a certain scenario we may forget whether we questioned this subject to be correct or not. As you question a part of you, you heal this aspect of yourself.

This questioning finds the relevant freeing mechanism that exists within your self-purpose. This is your own personal response that has to be opened by you and only you. Do you realize this?

Yes, we help facilitate the opening by making you aware of certain blockages or separations. Yes, we help connect you to that very personal self-aspect where it resides. But it is your conscious connection that needs to initiate the connection.

Remember, what is being outlined is for your benefit—not mine or anyone other than yourself—so you are responsible for your reactions to your own responses and self-reasoning. Being responsible for yourself ensures that you miss out on nothing. You can't blame another for your lack of response to all conscious energies that exist in you.

With certain awarenesses, your whole strength changes vastly. Then, all of a sudden, many aspects will begin to unfold at once.

This may be great, but we also need to be open, ready to capitalize on any opportunity that should arise with a greater flow of synchronicity.

I don't know about you, but I'm a great fan of receiving, when synchronicity is perfect. This means we don't have to ask time and time again for even the tiny things in life.

This once again reminds me of what I tell everybody I have ever helped: take notice of all the smallest changes, even the recognition of a minute awareness is worth recognizing.

Why? Every change makes you stronger, and they combine to open levels in your sub-conscious that have not been accessible before. They help to open many levels of this sub-conscious that are not, at the moment, of a permanent presence.

Personal conscious responses—and using them in a responsible manner—are for your benefit, to help you connect using your own very personal consciousness.

Your real and true consciousness is only going to respond to your own vibration and frequency, not to any others, so you need to become more aware of working with your own responses.

Yes, this is not a normal speech pattern, so of course we know that a little unfolding is required, with some new awareness.

We need to consider which energy is connected to help create this new strength through the sub-conscious. Different terms of consciousness also need totally different comprehensions.

The first thing I guess we need to get used to is how to access this consciousness, which at present is like a caged animal waiting to be unleashed. Some people will think I'm overexaggerating in terms of its potential, but we need to reexamine this "caged animal" and where this consciousness sits.

Because of past separations, the energy or suppressed capacity of the subconscious sits within the unconscious. Sometimes it is hard to fathom how such a strong element of our self could have been suppressed, until you remember how the connective-consciousness of so many relevant working parts of us has been cut off and disconnected.

This consciousness is the vehicle that unlocks many physical elements. You are going to be able to use this vehicle to unlock a few more automatic connections to certain repressed desires. Perhaps you didn't realize these existed.

The strange thing is that some people can manifest large things, while small things elude them. Normally, we think we've got the little things okay, and the larger ones get away.

Next is the largest category of the lot, which we are unable to recognise. This category is the one we recognise in others but, sadly, not in our selves. This is why magazines sell so consistently.

On the higher end of the spectrum, people exist in what seems an easy life of immense material wealth. It looks like a constantly exciting life with exciting people around. Why is it, then, that so many want to escape it?

While we will be discussing a few of these dilemmas later on, we also need to concentrate on unlocking this caged animal and using the untapped potentials within.

The sub-consciousness should also be viewed with one understanding. It is a vast body, and we will only be scratching the surface; but we are making contact, and that is significant.

Why? Apparently, according to the source, we often misdiagnose which consciousness we are actually working with. We have often thought that we were in the sub-conscious, when if fact we were not even close.

This has occurred because of some mix-ups in our connections, which source is about to identify. This is why I use the source as my GPS unit. I don't like getting lost anymore, so I follow the source questions to my preparations.

The questions we've asked remind our sub-conscious that a preparation is imminent. To engage our lateral-thought awareness, please consider a couple of everyday terms: *extension* and *expansion*. In speech, these two words are anything but dynamic. But apply these two words to energy, and they represent vast fields of suppressed energy with immense potential.

The other surprising factor is that they describe two foundational movements of energy. Add to this that they both work in an exact and similar manner if unsuppressed.

This is one area of energy I love showing to people. Once we have reconnected vast amounts of consciousness that have been sitting separate, then it becomes possible to show people some amazing aspects of themselves that are not apparent.

This self-energy is vast, so I guess it comes as no surprise that it equals conscious mind and memory, which exist here also.

The surprise that shows on people's faces amounts to all that they connect to. When I take them on a little exploration of themselves, self-expression says it all—especially when I remind them that this is a part of them that they have been missing out on.

Remember, this is your own personal energy, where your real personality comes from, and we are also unlocking it.

I look forward to intimately sharing this understanding and experience in person with everybody in a personal presence of activation. There is so much to explore in our own selves that is untapped and desiring our attention.

Let's return to our conversation where the source was describing the dynamics of physical bodies of spirit energy.

Does this sound confusing? Well, just because energy is of a spirit nature doesn't mean that it isn't actively moving or doing stuff. At the core of every movement of physical energy is an energy scientists can't explain. However, many people are now able to see it vividly and understand it.

Up until now, we have really been connecting to vast areas of spirit-conscious that help guide our intuition each and every day with awareness.

Then we moved on, in a limited manner, to how these foundational spirit-energies helped create strength of a more real self.

Having consolidated what was desirable and then neutralizing many forms of interference, we connected this in a physical spirit-form through the physical consciousness of our physical bodies.

How this was achieved we will soon discuss, but all of this was only possible with the use of one immense vehicle: the connective consciousness.

Simply, we have been able to knock down many debilitating structures that have suppressed and locked up our self-potentials for millennia.

I would like you to consider this statement then.

New awarenesses have been unlocked with a new approach to unlocking vast bodies of potential. Does it surprise you, then, that freeing your questions actually opens so many different parameters that have sat stagnant for an equal amount of time in your life thus far?

What has actually been exposed is only the tip of the iceberg, so to speak. Does this then prompt you to discover what else has been sitting around in the potential-cupboard waiting to be unearthed?

The point that the source is pointing to here is this. As we become stronger, we become aware. At this point of awareness, we discover that perhaps something is missing to connect us to what we are now ready to comprehend and unlock.

The source also desires you to comprehend that perhaps looking to past emotions and feeling did not automatically unlock self-potentials. However, having said this, they can often give a clue to where we have been suppressed, constricted, or restricted from connecting to these vast potentials.

Remembering how we needed to relearn to receive, connect this in a tithing manner with a connective consciousness to ensure that it is now actually possible to ask while in a stilled consciousness.

Our messages that once got lost now have a chance of connecting to our own self-connective consciousness, yes, which then connects and communicates with the whole, real, source-collective-consciousness that exists.

Are we all on the same page now, yes?

You see, we need to redefine where we are at this present moment and remind you of the direction we have traveled. Why?

Well, we need all that strength you have connected to in order to ensure that nothing is interfering with you. Does this make sense?

What has actually been going on is this. The parts that we have connected to need a little something extra to soup them up a bit. This vehicle of yours needs turbo-charging.

In most instances, interferences make us hesitate to attempt something. We may consider that we don't have the expertise, the necessary funds, or family stability. The time isn't right.

In my case, I hesitated to actually type this out myself and not rely on others, as I needed to sense every vibration and frequency, making sure that it responded exactly the same as on paper.

You would think the two would be exactly the same, wouldn't you? Well, they weren't, and I wasn't able to pass on the same frequencies. This is something I just wasn't aware of, but I needed to be.

Perhaps by the end of this book, you too will understand that this is passed on as you read.

There is a whole myriad of things you believe you can't proceed with unless you have the correct resources, but a large part of you desires to do them. The spectrum of this interference ranges from, "Should I ask that person out?" or "Is now the time to purchase something I need?" to "Is this the time to pursue some lifetime ambition?"

There is the flip side to this as well, as interference may be pushing you to continually step outside your comfort zone on things you think will make you happy.

There is one element that joins both sentences together: joy. Real joy comes from something you have created and is not a fleeting sense.

On the other hand, illusional joy evaporates as quickly as it was purchased. Why is this so? Well, in the first sentence, you helped create the joy, so you would have appreciation for how it can enrich your life. You would also have given appreciation to where certain things in your life may head now, as your creation has opened the door to new possibilities.

The complete opposite of this would involve being coerced into thinking that something is mandatory to your future happiness. Once achieved, it leaves a hollow feeling with no real appreciation that it was achieved.

Naturally, you need to progress to knowing which is which. The emotions to receive both could be similar, just as the feelings not to go ahead would be.

The disconcerting point is that in a still consciousness, it may be possible to achieve real self-direction; but because we are discussing external energies from within the self, so many other parameters need consideration. The great part is that now we have a basic comprehension of how these interfering energies work.

Next, we need to remember that new indicators of awareness mean we will not be focusing in such a blind manner as before. However, we aren't under any illusion that we are like Teflon and that nothing ever sticks.

While there are some areas of this book that may seem quite different, other areas of understanding have stayed much the same or completely unchanged.

The source is about to vary this a little now and connect to how we and many others have been working for ages.

Before exploring all that exists—or is of an existence—around us, I need to clarify one enormous point that I have been directed to observe closely before making any opinion on the subject.

Consider some of our case history. We have identified many parts of us that have been separate from ourselves as a whole, yes.

We have discovered why so many self-areas haven't touched all areas of our potential.

We are also discovering varied ways to interpret quite a few elements in our lives that have been misrepresented.

Consider that there are many areas of our self that, in the past, we considered unquestionable and sacred. With this unquestioning energy, we are unable to efficiently reach awareness of any of the real self-potentials, desires, or intents.

Perhaps it is time to question many beliefs and faiths in ourselves that we thought were absolutely pure. Don't get yourself in a twist. We are not challenging our soul or heart, just a few bits that hang around us.

As I indicated earlier, I observed this area with very little interest for most of my life. There had to be a reason. So I asked the question, didn't I? The answer I received was, "What have you named the place where you work, David?"

You see, I called the place where I work "The Reflective Healing Centre." But what did that have to do with what I was asking?

"Well, you reflect on every aspect of your life constantly, yes?"

"Yes," I replied.

"Well, what do you consider to be this reflection—truth or parts of truth? And has your reflection changed somewhat?"

I then said, "I really haven't a clue, as I really never focus on this element of my life."

"Why not?"

"Well," I answered, "I guess I concentrate on the parts of me I know are correct and without separation—those that have real collective-consciousness strength."

"So, David, you are saying that this area you are questioning is also reflecting separation, suppressed energies, and elements of not-real truth, yes? Then you have a dilemma, David, yes."

"Why?" I asked.

"How are you going to explain this to people and to those you help?"

You probably don't see my dilemma. How could I indicate that the aura and chakra also have many elements of suppression, separation, and unreality in them when so many hold these parts as sacred.

I considered not discussing this subject at all, or only discussing it at forums and workshops. Before you check on this, can I add a couple of extra considerations?

If I had told you straight out that you needed to look at your chakra because it represented many real and illusional aspects, would you have taken this conversation seriously?

You can appreciate why I didn't desire to discuss this with so many who hold these areas of the spirit-body as absolutely sacred.

However, the source desired that we consider certain debilitating aspects. We are considering this from a logical perspective rather than a blind-faith perspective of what we have been told is true.

I have no doubt that at one point in time this may have been correct, but how can this be correct now in this distorted reflection?

Please check this with all that is of a sacred truth and causes you to be always present in a synchronized manner.

If I did not share in a tithing manner that releases so many suppressed energies, I would not be sharing—in the source's view—from my natural virtue or ethics.

Because this is something I consider so important for so many reasons, I can't digress from a natural flow, which is meant to facilitate change or to be whole again.

We all hate change, but remember that we are here at this time to participate, not to bury our heads in the sand. If you aren't comfortable with change, the alternative is to simply pretend that nothing around us is changing. This is the desired awareness of many people.

What do I mean when I say that forms of intoxication have never been so rampant? Whether alcohol or stronger drugs, has their abuse ever been so high? How many people choose them in order to avoid what is going on outside their door—those things they are becoming aware of?

This has led to many people being unaware of their self-environment, the self-energy system that is far more representative of what is really available. This is why we question everything.

Eventually this enables us to sense and be aware of the greater environment about us. I and the source really mean a *new* type of self-environment.

There really are so many great energies about us that nobody takes seriously or cares about. Why?

Well, how can you appreciate something if you aren't aware it even exists? You feel strange, different, or sort of confused about how you feel as a result of the energy changes about us.

Earlier on, we were talking about essences and elements and how much they contribute to our energy systems.

I would have loved to keep this conversation going before, but there were many different aspects or foundations of yourself to discover before we talked about different energy systems.

Everything else we have talked about, figuring out what was relative and useful, was so important.

Speaking of importance, let me recap on something I mentioned at the start of the book. I hope it is something you questioned. I'm talking about how so many people move through past lives, thinking that they are going through dimensions.

As with every other part of this book, awareness of different aspects needs to be grasped without complications. However, it would be reprehensible of me to assume that every little area we have covered has been immediately retained on a conscious level. Fortunately, though, anything you have bothered to read has been retained in one area of consciousness, even if you think it has not been.

Now that you have quite a different understanding of the many spirit-parts of yourself, we are going to work on a few physical parts. We can visit this area, now that you are able to grasp that not everything you reflected was real and vital.

If this was one of your main focuses, it would have severely hampered any new insight in the future. It also would have interfered with any physical rejuvenation, regeneration, and revitalization.

Every step we have taken has been connected to some form of consciousness, and we aren't about to change that format now.

There are some rather large physical consciousnesses in the physical body that don't involve the brain.

The first time I experienced this was when I was looking at a person's body and wondering why their lymph and gland areas were lighting up. I was quickly told that this was where the main physical consciousness sits in the body.

I said to my guides, "So this is how I can easily help heal the body," and I have to admit I was a little excited.

"Yes and no, David. You need to comprehend this a little differently." Also remember that this was ages ago when I really had a totally different energy helping me, and it wasn't nearly as strong.

This is something not everybody comprehends, or if they do, they forget about it.

What am I prattling on about is this. People just weren't as open to spirituality years ago, and in fact they were so closed off about it that you couldn't really discuss it openly without ridicule. Ask any of those people brave enough to write a spiritual message book years ago. It was sort of camouflaged as a self-help book.

So, how does all this relate to seeing a conscious presence in the physical?

Well, the energy that you create in a conscious manner each and every day contributes to everybody on a mass level of consciousness. You are aware of this, aren't you?

No matter how small or insignificant in the scheme of things you may think you are, you are wrong. Your energy is significant. Not only does it help you, it helps everybody. Please be constantly awareness of this: your contribution is vital.

This is an area I also wish to discuss later, and it ties in with physical conscious-energy in our self. These physical conscious-energies relate to spirit activations, and they integrate to eventually become physical activations.

The conscious energy of yourself helps awaken others to become aware, and it helps your energy move around this world.

How this happens in a conscious manner is what I would like to discuss. Why? Because then you won't feel isolated and alone.

This feeling of being alone and isolated is very common. When you embark on new endeavours of self-discovery, your body is not used to experiencing this new energy in a more constant flow. Perhaps you can spare a thought about how it was for very aware people ages ago.

You may think I am overexaggerating, but I'm not. The ridicule from people was debilitating, so I never openly discussed channeling with anybody for ages—not even with my ex-wife. People who did that were branded *looney*.

If you know people's perspective, you don't discuss certain subjects out loud. Why? Because their energy told you if they were open or not.

It seems ridiculous now that I could have married such a person, but I followed my physical self then, and I suppressed my spirit-self.

Don't let others suppress you innermost self-guidance.

While this is perhaps easier at home, it can be a little harder in a work situation—whether you're the boss or the employee.

In this chapter, we are heading into how spirit and physical consciousness are able to integrate into one and to become a source of self-strength. This means that you are able to follow the spirit-consciousness without being suppressed, and you can open many different awarenesses that are reflected through this whole world's consciousness.

Don't think for a moment that this is going to make you want to get rid of your partner—just in case that was in the back of your mind.

I have described opening your self-awareness to real consciousness as an onion with many layers—except that we seem to have millions more layers.

In this self makeup, we have some parts that are truly real; some are real but suppressed; and some are not even vaguely real. Some shouldn't even be in the equation at all, as they don't belong in this self.

The next equation we need to consider is this. Imagine onion layers as conscious energy that contributes real energy with the same dimensions as earth. They are the good thoughts and actions in spirit and in physical consciousness. These are the same good thoughts from conscious, spirit-energy strength that sits within all of us.

All this good energy is being shared with all the parts of you that are aware that this energy actually exists, no matter what state of consciousness it exists in. Remember that only the bits and pieces of you that are connected to a real consciousness will be able to share this good energy.

If we were then able to receive this good energy, we could face a couple of other dilemmas, because we are actually open to receiving this beautiful energy.

Yes, we are, because we opened our self to this potential, and we have learned appreciation, gratitude, and compassion. We have opened our self to receive this love in an energy form and activation.

The next dilemma is to identify the energy we are thinking of connecting to. Is it real or crap or suppressed antimatter?

Well, thank heavens, we have a lot of this energy already sorted out, but some still seems real and some still doesn't feel great.

Why? We are moving into some very physical areas of energy, so we need to be able to distinguish these physical forms of elements and essences first. To put this into our language, this is how spirit and physical elements or essences become one and the same as an integrated energy.

Next, we need to contemplate how to use this integrated energy. To do this, we need to be aware of how to connect source energy, which is complete and already knows what to do.

To comprehend this re-connection, remember one thing: we nearly have this already completed and figured out. How come?

Well, this is the how, what, where, when, and why we have been defining—the differences between all those different consciousnesses we have been discussing.

Once again, we have been doing the preliminary work or source-direction with the many different foundational understandings we need to comprehend real foundations of awareness.

I have been reminded to outline how integration of the spirit and physical bodies actually happen. I guess a more real scenario is needed in order to understand this. Imagine a person with mind-chatter so bad that he is unable to think or function.

His emotions are shot to pieces and, in real terms, he is not even sure what is real because of the constant confusion that is traveling through his mind. The whole scenario is not one I wish on any person, yet it is a common one because of separated senses.

How common is this? Well, I have never met a person without some form of this intrusion yet.

You may remember how we discussed that this person's spirit-consciousness had separated, leaving a confused state in the physical body, yes. Also, remember how we were able to create a new strength in this person by reconnecting this conscious spirit, thus giving strength and then direction for all other main consciousnesses to follow, yes.

Add to this equation that you now understand that there is a profusion of physical consciousness in the lymph and gland areas. Therefore, this is where the whole spirit-consciousness needs to travel through, not just any brain area.

Did you connect this thought when you were told that all lymph and glands areas held the physical mass of spirit-consciousness? They light up to indicate physical points where spirit-consciousness is able to stabilize oversensitive emotions. How?

If you are not receiving the correct directions, you create or make the wrong stuff in the wrong proportion. This is then passed on to the chemical response or reaction.

If your endocrine system is following this lead, then the rest of the body will always be out of whack. It is a foundational stabilizing point of your whole body.

This is just one of many ways that the spirit and physical energies integrate to stabilize or help the physical body to work efficiently. It also shows how spirit and science combine for an outcome that medicine is unable to fathom.

The main point of this conversation is this. If our minds are stable—not just the ones in the head, as many scientists now endorse, but minds in the whole of the body—then one common denominator is missing. They are not reacting or responding in a conscious manner.

What we are really talking about is responses to the spirit-mind and memory, a spreading-out of responses to the first point of every response.

By being aware that not all consciousness is confined to the brain area, we are able to greatly strengthen the self as a whole, whether we have mind-chatter or not.

Another point of this reflection is this. If the mind is able to chatter without this strength of conscious, connective spirit, then what reactions happen to the rest of the physical body?

Perhaps it is easier to comprehend why certain chemical imbalances occur in the body as a whole, yes.

Now I would like to throw a cat amongst the pigeons, so to speak, and ask you to do a little thinking and contemplating about how to render this supply from the lymph or gland systems. You immediately thought to integrate the two consciousnesses—spirit and physical, yes?

Well, this is correct, but it's not quite that simple. Why?

The spirit-consciousness became separated in the first place, as it was not able to communicate with the physical consciousness, yes. Well, the same energy system that separated the two systems is still there, stopping the two from communicating efficiently. This produces underreactions or overreactions.

This scenario then adds up to over-response or no response at all. Does it now hit home why we are learning self-responsibility in a totally new way?

You can probably tell that quite an evolved source is guiding where this conversation heads. Yes, most of the time I am really just an interpreter.

If we understand how this system was created, we are able to fix not just this problem, but a whole myriad of spiritual and physical problems as well.

Why? Because there is a control issue between all physical consciousnesses. Some consciousnesses think they're more important than others or that they're worthy of receiving more current than the rest.

Because the aspects of understanding are in our head, we thought all consciousness sat in the head as well, didn't we?

Well, we all make the same mistake, don't we? I would never have picked this up myself, unless I had asked the right questions and been shown a very different sequence of questions to comprehend a very different outcome. This took some digesting.

You see, even after seeing the consciousness in different physical areas, it took a bit of prompting to decipher what this all really meant in spirit and, especially, in physical terms.

If we just look at the physical reflection, all currents are more appreciated in the head-consciousness region than in any other. We naturally have a headstrong self.

With a headstrong self, it is easy to ascertain that only a limited current is flowing to the rest of the body. This then means that with inconsistent energy fluctuations, the spirit is unable to help the physical consciousness throughout the whole body.

Without a constant energy supply, the lymph nodes and glands—the endocrine system—begin to produce irregular amounts of chemicals, which means irregular emotions pushed about by indifferent flows of hormones or secretions.

Reflecting straight back to the spirit-understanding, this energy interference and certain areas of energy receive more constant supplies.

We now comprehend that a stable spirit-consciousness contributes as a blueprint or template for all of our spirit and physical matter to follow—if we desire a balanced self in every real sense.

How does this work out in our language? It means that there is a spirit-blueprint that actually directs where lots of new energies can be unveiled.

We have many energies that are extensions and expansions of consciousness, but they have never been connected through our connective consciousness.

This is like the square root by the square root, in mathematical terms of where your energy is heading.

Once this energy begins to unfold, so too does your consciousness. You are probably wondering how consciousness suddenly expands by connecting to an energy, which is a very relevant point, don't you think?

Imagine yourself as a computer. You have the software and the hard drive but nothing to link everything together.

We're providing the power to fire up the computer first, then all the wiring to connect everything, so I guess we are like a mother board.

If you were to bundle together every conceivable subject we have discussed so far, and then look at where we or our energy seems limited, this is the area we are heading to.

Conscious responses are in every particle of our self. Automatic responses need to be balanced out and work as one, not as many separate energy systems, competing and not communicating. Perhaps you need to think a little longer on this.

With old energy systems, we essentially used our depth and ascension most of the time. We focused on the old saying, "As above, so below," which refers to the energy lines going through our head and out our feet.

What about all the other energy systems that travel freely through our bodies, are grounded in our bodies, and work so efficiently? Wouldn't it be prudent to acknowledge all these systems as well, and not just the depth and ascension?

The limited chakras, auras, and meridians we see in many charts represent limited energy, as there are so many more energies to be integrated and represented. The rest of our energy can end up resented and unused. Do you comprehend this?

Just focusing on the "as above, so below" or "depth and ascension" isn't totally correct. The energy doesn't just go straight up or down; it makes whole circuits in many directions similar to a star. Are you comprehending this fact?

If we apply this to a quantum circuitry system, all of a sudden it does so much more. Yes, we are definitely not thinking of energy just going in a limited circuit up and down our body. It's just not logical and is of limited potential.

At times I would like a computer that I could plug into my energy systems so I could share with you all that has been shared and that unlocks many different parts of us.

You see, it's exciting to find out what makes things easier and relevant and to get things happening, but unless everybody can use this and not just me, there is no point in discovery. Why?

The reason we are all using new consciousness is to become aware. This requires all who are aware to share—or desire to share—awareness. As the source points out, this is conscious tithing.

So, everybody is helping to make our earth a much better place. This is at the core of our purpose. It's not about getting handouts but about helping ourselves, which in turn helps others, yes?

The energy of others creates a strength of peace, harmony, grace, ease, synchronicity, and a contribution of energy in order that others become aware and we use our energy more efficiently. This is real peace, a moving presence of humanity, not a stagnant one, with awareness of all that exists.

To help you create this strength, the source and I desire this tithing to become a reality. To help facilitate this, there is an immense self-unlocking to be passed on.

Before we start, though, imagine an immense energy similar to a star that starts at your soul and heart and pours through your body. This energy is making a complete circuit back to your head to release limited activations, thus freeing a whole energy system.

Repeat this by starting at your soul and heart and using the whole star-energy, which is liberating in the same manner in the depth of yourself. This means many self-responses are also liberated from responding to limited activations.

We now need to connect to many different facets of your actual energy flow.

Whether or not you recognise the fact that your energy is capable of many different movements—which, at present, it is not connecting to—this is awareness worth opening.

Perhaps you have recognised the difference as your energy made complete loops. The energy wasn't simply going up and down but was moving with new potential. You see, with energy just moving up and down, it isn't going to connect to anything but limited potentials.

We are about unlocking and, most importantly, freeing self-potential so as to free up old mind-sets as well as energy. You may feel you need to expel an extra breath now.

Yes, you are consciously connecting to the real self-matter and all dematerialised connections of connective consciousness. This is the grounding sensation.

This also means that you are opening active responses to react in a harmonized manner—not in an over—or under-response. So, a balanced reaction to stabilize the self-energy circuitry is what your self-intention desires.

To help facilitate this, many keys and codes are opening within the self and are corresponding to real source keys and codes. This looks like many strobe lights joining.

To create this strength needed to open and reactivate all keys and codes, the self-affirmation to re-intend all creative purpose through all creative presence is now opening.

I am of this wealth of health within all reactive self-natures.

I am of a real reasoning in order to prepare all self-reactions for real, conscious reasoning, which relates to all self-harmonizing, bringing all soul-responses to be purposeful heart-responses.

I therefore reflect all true appreciation through restoration within all creative self-compassion.

All natural love is rejuvenated with real self-purpose through the real, connective-consciousness flow of real gratitude within all self-humanity.

I am simply of this presence.

This is a reactivation of many minds and memories, not of resentments or under—or over-reactions but of foundations of self. These in turn stabilize the self-foundations by connecting corresponding connections of current opened previously through corresponding circuitry preparations.

This means that you have received a strength of self that now ensures that you are able to tackle all that is never to be restored again.

These preparations mean the release of old-time, preconceived mind-sets. They are now all corralled into one self-cycle pattern that you are following at present.

Each and every mind-set cycle has become your own personalized schedule of limited potential. These schedules are a combination of your contributions, but you would also be surprised at how many are contributed by others, not simply through cellular memories or even past life.

Understanding this animal is to liken it to a box of octopuses with lots of little tentacles constricting your potentials. The constricting parts are where your energy isn't able to flow.

The constricting tentacle is the power of others who desire to restrict you from your source energy, the energy that gives you directions to what is available in your blueprint. This prevents you from receiving in a tithing manner because your synchronicity isn't able to connect.

So, we have the how, why, where, and when for why you aren't connected to immense potential and automatic knowing that desire to contribute to many facets of yourself that you are unaware of.

You are aware now of how incapacitated the ascension area of your self was when many areas weren't able to contribute. This means the whole flows weren't able to connect, yes?

Apply this same formula to the extension of yourself. This means an energy on the left-hand side of your self is sitting idle at the moment and would love to connect and contribute what it is meant to do.

Consider one other major point. When an area of our self is unable to contribute, its existence is meaningless.

Now multiply this by many areas that are in the same boat. You are unaware that this energy desires to exist or contribute.

If we consider how this energy feels irrelevant, this feeling could be passed on as a self-expression or feelings as well. This also means that these energies desire to contribute to the collective consciousness as a whole. You are able to receive all self-energy contributions, so you desire to complete the tithing cycle of current to make it relevant.

Does this explain a few feelings that seem to be going unanswered or unexplained? I guess I should explain that each restrained energy system restrains you personally.

The energy that unlocks comprehension, understanding, mental and physical healing, and potential exists.

This is also a foundational point in unlocking all that we manifest, all that is needed in our daily lives.

Yes, this is opened to awareness by simply adding our energy to real source-energy. Everybody becomes aware. If you can only do this in what you call a pristine environment, then do so, but don't forget to contribute to the environment as a whole.

What has just been outlined in you is complete, so let's get on with unlocking a real star-body hidden away deep within your soul.

P'saris is ready to help all who desire to bring completeness to the whole of their self-consciousness.

This has then helped us to open up suppressed spirit energy within us. We are now embarking on how energy affects all physical energy. There is a reason, and it is just so simple: the mass of each matter must balance out.

To start with, the energy might be of spirit, but the strength of the spirit will be matched with a physical matter, which of course creates a mass. Each and every self-mass of matter is to be realigned to a real, relative purpose. I am of this intention; therefore, each and every self-mass must matter.

I open all that is before me to enlighten every prospect of purpose to real intent with real essence flowing in every essential purpose, allowing unrestricted presence.

All enlightened presence creates all self-awareness to all present future. Therefore, I am able to reflect this natural, essential element of love.

I'll describe how I saw this unfold for each and every one of you when you connected to this star body as a mass of star energy unfolded.

This is when you transformed to look star-like. You were then guided to many receptacles where this energy was suppressed and quickly unfolded. Thus, masses of energy bodies were unveiled.

You are, of course, aware that no exercises were examined nor connected to. If you desire and are ready, this is really a preparation that will automatically link if your consciousness is strong enough.

Parts of this consciousness will begin to unfold, but this is an energy that can never be hurried. Much of you first needs to be more aware. However, it is easy to ascertain how unfolding all this potential is going to enhance so many spectrums of understanding that are to be unfolding daily.

I'm no Einstein, but it made sense to me, and I see it working with relative ease. When all is sensed, then all harmony balances.

This same theory is reflected by many guides in many different levels of quantum movements that flow into each other easily.

If you can find out why this activation isn't free to move in a free manner, form, and function in a free and synchronistic way, then you can figure out the cause. Then this energy is designed to fix itself automatically.

I have been shown this equation, which is a basic equation of real humanity in a relationship that I could understand. The relationship is that with miles of preparations, you don't need to go through the hard work of finding every relative aspect that is easy to miss—or experience the side effects of reconnecting.

For this reason, please remember to have a lemon bath after reading this chapter, and don't forget how much of your self is changing daily, thus releasing old emotions.

Please have a break of at least an hour before resuming reading.

Also, write yourself a memo that taking a lemon bath is important.

# 14

## A NEW-TIME RELATIVE PURPOSE

As we discussed, there is a very definite need to find our natural harmony and synchronicity in many new or different manners, from past to future.

To help this flow a little easier, the source has provided an affirmation to help us on our way.

Each and every point of divine faith is opened to a divine point of intuition.

Every point of intuition, then, never lacks any reason to seek grace with an ever-present future of ever-present reality.

Every perfect picture of our creative future is graced with true presence of ease, capable of only greater senses of our own individual purpose.

Each purpose is as individual as the structures of snowflakes, complete yet individual, able to interlock and create a natural element with real purpose.

The purpose of this natural equation is to recreate a true harmony of evolved purpose in a true relationship of self-ease.

In each and every relationship lies a divine purpose, with divine intent and synchronicity.

This relationship creates a divine love, which links each and every divine reality of humanity.

This new-time presence of purpose can only evolve with real purpose to unite all humanity's purpose with a new-time, creative nature.

Purposeful natures created with all elements and essential essences are now abundant in every environment that exists within all self-love.

You may not relate to this affirmation straightaway, but the spirit-consciousness of your self was soaking it up.

The reason for this refined affirmation is to unlock your own abilities and to translate—or to be able to figure out for yourself—a direction you need to travel automatically.

Then, once again, you automatically connect to every abundant self-fortune that has never connected fully.

One of the greatest reasons for this is interference from other people's telepathy. You weren't expecting that were you?

You see, in the not-too-distant future, telepathy will become more of an asset than a liability. This is a strange comment that telepathy could ever be a liability, isn't it?

Just as you weren't aware of how much you channeled, so it goes with telepathy. Yes, this is also a vital piece of your intuition. Many people put channeling and telepathy in the same basket. This is a shame, as they both can contribute so much to intuition.

While this is correct, one can also block the other out completely or distort the other's meanings and mess up any intended message.

In many ways, we have de-evolved while evolving simultaneously.

How annoying is this then, or doesn't it worry you? If you are like the majority of humanity that is becoming more aware, "annoying" is a considerable understatement.

At least there are a couple of choices. You can take medication and keep yourself out of it so you stay unaware, or you can change the de-evolved aspects. The first scenario is a waste of precious life, but some believe it is fun or makes life tolerable to a point.

I guess finding life purpose is a bit harder, but both have frustrating elements to unravel with this mess of de-evolved bits and pieces.

My purpose is to share what I have been guided to and to make this easier and more relevant—with the source's help.

I know that you know this, but the vibrational harmony message interlocked in the sentence before is quite vital, as it links the affirmation to the future intention you are presently grounding.

This means that you are going to be responding to many consciousnesses that you were before unable to even acknowledge, let alone respond to. This also means that not all of your responses are simply from your head region; you now respond and want to be connected with responses from your whole body.

Please think about this a moment. You are using your consciousness in your whole body in a more efficient self-manner. This means that you desire to use your whole body to interpret many different languages that your body uses. Your body talks to others but not just through your mouth. You do realize this is going on, don't you?

This is why you desire to talk to some people or cut some others off. Instead of just relying on a limited intuition, perhaps it is time to talk to others through many senses that you have been blessed with.

This also answers a conversation broached earlier in the book, where I was giving an observation how people of a certain vibration stick together. This is an extension of that.

In this conversation we are unlocking how, if we are not using these same senses to talk to each other in a different manner, we stifle our self-potential.

In much the same way that you are able to decipher what another is saying through their body, there are many messages flowing around in the matrix that surrounds you. I contains many potentials that perhaps you should explore.

You see, this is about using your whole body to explore what you are asking for but not connecting to.

Many people come to see me for this reason. It's like they have all the resources but are unable to connect. The simple reason is that they are not vibrating at the correct level to connect to what they are really asking for, not what they *think* they are asking for. What they think they are asking for is obviously not of a frequency in the environment where they sit at this moment.

This means that the vibration of their self and the frequency of their own environment are not on the same level or harmonizing. Thus, the self-harmony of all that is being asked for is unable to materialize. Does this make sense?

I have just shared what is obvious in an energy sense—not just a spirit or emotional sense. I have reflected where the self-belief, self-desire, spirit, and physical self-matter aren't communicating. Are you grasping this scenario?

Our guides are unlocking a different way to see different scenarios that have played out in ourselves without our being aware that we want to change them.

On behalf of myself, I would like to contribute this: Every time your self is able to raise its vibration to match a frequency that is in your new self-environment, it takes a couple of days to adjust. Remember, this isn't familiar to your body energy and might seem rather strange to you.

This is another reason I have asked you not to hurry. Don't be afraid of stepping out of the frequencies that are reflecting from those about you. Think and learn to sense outside the square.

The fact that this new and different manner of translating messages is possible means that you are beginning to raise the vibrations to a new frequency that modulates to new possibilities. As corny as it might sound, this also relates to new abilities that sit within the new possibilities.

Some of you might sense a swirling effect within and then about you. It means that you are releasing the effects of being surrounded by energies that are holding your vibrations down. This is not due to those you are living with but to some people who reside around you. You may not even know them.

The fact that a ten-kilometre radius is about the area within which you are affected is probably news to you. When you take into account where you work, play, or go shopping, is it any wonder that it is sometimes hard to keep our vibrations at a more constant level? Simply, our guides are opening our eyes to the facts of how and where we are experiencing energy drains in our self, and they desire to change this immediately before exposing you to how this has affected your self-energy systems.

Before reading these next sentences, please keep your eyes open until you are asked to participate.

This next exercise is to open your own self-belief and self-faith that exist within your original soul through all origins of your heart. Where there has been suppression of these aspects or foundations of self, this self-body will be able to eventually contribute and be present. Before, this element and essence of all aspects of yourself was frozen out from contributing.

This is only able to happen as the whole self responds with self-knowing that unlocks new responses to knowledge. This knowledge has been suppressed for quite some time, not just in this life but in many previous ones. Your guides remind you that this is hundreds of lifetimes, not just a couple.

Please don't do any connecting yet. Keep those eyes open until all that you are to connect to has been outlined.

A self-purpose of all that has been outlined is, and has been, moving through you, unlocking. This is why we asked you not to view all that was unlocking, as it might deter you from releasing and connecting in a new manner.

The grounding you are sensing is the release of many self-consciousnesses that have been impacted by denser environments about you. A new self-environment is opening. This may become apparent by the restless feeling in your back area. This will be joined by the suppressed element in your arms releasing, which is where communications have been stifled and unable to convert reactions of real essences and elements to the purpose they were intended for.

Next, this will be repeated in the leg regions. This is unlocking many minds and memories that respond to every particle of matter that resides within any suppressed matter, spirit or physical. Both need unlocking from impounding and suppressing matters.

These suppressing matters of others' environments use overpowering elements and essences. Overly sensitive power has been used to suppress your self-faith and self-belief; thus, they are unable to respond to what all senses are reflecting in your whole body, and self-purpose is suppressed. Do you understand this?

Once again, if self-purpose is unable to respond, then how is your own faith and belief able to respond? It is suppressed before taking another step. Please understand how much of your self was consuming others' faith and self-belief, as you are unable to respond to self-reasoning and self-purpose.

The whole reason for writing this book in this manner is so that all of your self-guides are able to communicate with your whole body. Otherwise, how is it possible for you to reason or connect in a connective and conscious manner with your whole body, not just with what resides in your head region? Are you understanding this in a whole self-manner? See, your eyes are still open, and you are able to sense a change in your makeup, yes?

Now, perhaps you are able to identify that every word has been channeled and you can identify where your whole self has been a little limited, yes.

The whole of your conscious self hasn't mattered, in a way, and there has been a lack of response, as there was no reason to respond. There was no question vibrating to the frequency of answers to respond to.

I know that I have really gone way over in reasoning, but this is because unconscious and suppressed parts of yourself sometimes take time to respond to a different purpose in your whole body, not just the consciousness in your head.

You might notice that you are feeling restless in all regions of your back, so now the whole activation is to be shared with you. Then you can close those eyes and experience the shifts in many parts of your body if you choose to. The choice is always yours.

Being grounded, you identified that this suppressed energy response needed shifting. This means that many parts of your whole unconscious self have been connecting and are now present and desire to respond. That draining and over-sensitive part in your body is unfolding, so hold the flat of your hand in the direction of the floor. Much of the rest of your body's vibration is reactivating and registering to a higher vibration.

A reaction may be sensed under your arms. This is denser energy, not of your own energy's purpose.

As this energy dissipates, an ascension energy might be sensed in your neck region, connecting to the whole of your body.

This means that an energy is about you. No, it's not your aura or meridians. A new-time environment is raising every energy form about yourself.

This is going to work like a buffer zone from many lower vibrations and frequencies. It is expanding quickly about you and looks like many shades of blue, then white, with vibrant colours in between. Now you can look. Some of you may be surprised that you can see this just as clearly with your eyes open.

The purpose of identifying with this new energy is to release many interfering energies that in the past you have been responding to when there was no reason to.

The next exercise is going to be similar. It involves lying on your back, then facing the palms of your hands toward the floor. Once again, many parts of your self are going to ground, only in a different manner.

What you are just sensing is another reason I'm writing this book. You are grounding to the environment, then to an atmosphere about yourself.

Remember, it was outlined that we have followed blind faith sometimes. This is an extension of this line of thought. The self-belief was unable to examine how the self-belief existed; thus, it was suppressed to a state of existence.

All that you are interpreting with the whole of your body is in fact integrating in a whole different manner.

Let's move on to the next exercise. Please hold the palm of the left hand above your navel, and place the right hand about a hands' width behind it. You may sense your soul being drawn throughout the whole of the body and extending to the self-environment and atmosphere.

This is like a reactivation of your new gravity. It also means that if your self is in harmony with all that surrounds it, then it is possible for certain things you are asking for in a real manner to gravitate to yourself. Do you suppose that this is worth experiencing in a purposeful manner?

Please change hands now, with the right hand in front of the left. Many consciousnesses of your self will be reacting once again in a different manner to synchronicities. You may now drop your hands. Thank you.

What you will eventually be sensing is the reaction of moving all higher vibrational matter together, then creating a new self-harmony, so the strength of your soul is harmonizing a strength of your heart. Thus, both are reacting to a peace between your soul and your heart, as both are interpreting each other as whole bodies of yourself, not just in your head region. Please understand this.

This then means that you are creating strength in the whole self. It is not a power struggle between the soul and heart. This is then interpreted as having no suppressed energy between all origins of yourself. Thus, there are no power struggles. You desire to send your own strength of love to enhance the self, and you are able to share all self-abilities and purpose with all humanity.

Do you comprehend now, in a present manner, why it is relevant for the self-energy to have self-strength? Otherwise, it is simply given away to unresponsive elements and essences of in-conscious matter with no spirit-direction, only the physical desires of others without respect to your intent, faith, or belief.

You see, the image of your self needs strength to resist all the consuming energies that desire to interfere in the strength of your own belief. Thus, there is the need for a new environment and atmosphere. We all are free to evolve in a free manner outside the consuming powers of others.

I was very tempted to leave this chapter until the next book because of the confrontational manner, but this would have been quite recalcitrant of me, as I would have been interfering in all that the source desires to share. No matter how confrontational this may be, some self-images need awareness and are not to be left in the dark with imposing dense matter. The choice is yours, though.

I say this because once awareness is opened, we usually desire to resolve any self-issue that isn't of any self-purpose, to remember any self-limits, and to limit all others.

This means that as you free yourself you are also able to help others free the many selves suppressed by the over-positive power of others that has never been converted to self-strength.

Remember, power used within the self is a wonderful energy; used against others it is debilitating. We need to be aware of how we actually use our own energy in a totally conscious manner, especially when so many simply live to sense this power. This is their version of joy, even if it is without consciousness.

I want to share a high-five with you, to give you a congratulatory hug. This means that you are really grasping a concept. Responding only to what is going on in your head is a limitation of your self-consciousness. This means that you desire to use in a real manner the whole of what you are capable of.

Check this. Sense yourself now grounding this energy. Perhaps you might also sense that many levels of consciousness are asking to be involved.

Here's another exercise to align and ground yourself. Point both hands toward your chest, please. The next feeling can be a rather strange sensation. Notice how it is almost as if your hands feel like disappearing into the chest area.

This actually means that you have a greater appreciation of many aspects of yourself than perhaps you realize. It also means that you are grounding this appreciation with full gratitude and compassion of what is now a present, whole self-consciousness, and you are actively using this for its intended purpose.

So clasp your hands, please. Now, sense that more of your self is to be registered as a whole body, more alive with active energy. You may drop your hands, now. Thank you.

Another reaction that might surprise you is that you are also registering in many new ways. For some, this will be immediate, and for others, it will happen as you relax and many new guides are helping. I will expand on this in a moment.

Remember, the lungs hold many different aspects of appreciation—spiritually, physically, and in many different bodies that you will learn about as you are ready.

This is a good enough reason not to smoke in any manner, and why many desire to teach breath-work or to sense the breath.

Why is this so desirable? Earlier on, I was identifying many different elements that exist naturally about you in many different grids. You are connecting to this foundational self-grid in order to connect to the complete, collective-consciousness matrix or the divine matrix.

These flow naturally, even through buildings, if the energy inside doesn't hold too dense a consciousness. You see, the energy you emit is always going to affect the matter or particles that sit about you.

This means that there is a region about you that perhaps you are totally unaware of, and I do most certainly not mean anything relating to your aura or chakra or new-time meridians. Perhaps this area is really more of a self-environment with real purpose—yes, another environment.

Please let me explain as best I can. I am describing an energy that uses the energy of your whole body as one energy mass. You might think this is such a simple thing to use the mass of yourself as one. Well, it is much easier if you are able to appreciate every part of you that exists, which is why we have been reflecting on the foundational aspects of this area.

Once again, it is harder if you are unaware of so many existing bodies, but you have no awareness that they actually exist, so I guess you understand where this conversation is going.

Well, to make things simpler, our guides are showing us a way to use our bodies more as one without finding the many bodies that we are unaware of. This means that we are going to create a neutral zone. This is a zone where you can grow and find many areas of yourself without the side effects of rebounding and, most importantly, impounding energies.

There is one very important purpose for this energy, which will become more apparent in the years to come. Please view this energy as an almost-sacred sharing of the source.

Notice that I said "almost." When your consciousness accepts the reality of this tithing, then and only then is it possible to become a sacred body of the source. This allows you to grow in a free manner: to experience new understandings, consciousness realities, activations, gravities, harmonies, harmonics, resonances, grids, matrices, lay lines, essences, elements, body makeups, celestial balances, and a myriad of new aspects.

You see, if you think you are missing out on something, it can become consuming. This is an extension of all understandings expressed before.

The same thing happens with the release of new technologies. Some people just have to be the first to have something new in order to feel complete.

It is the same when you are on a voyage, rediscovering who you are and what is it that you have been separated from in this or any other lifetime. You might remember when I conveyed early on that we need to learn. We desire to protect not only ourselves but others from our vibration.

A time comes when simply asking to protect ourselves isn't enough. This is a space that your soul and heart are asking for, a place where you are able to sit with ease, grace, and sequences of synchronicity. All of these are present at this moment of self-collective consciousness and relate to all that is of a complete, collective consciousness.

This means using all areas that have been reconnected in a conscious manner to communicate with real collective conscious in a neutral manner without interferences of any kind.

No unconscious power is to be present. The source describes all self-capacity of current as a real *empowerment* of conscious self-strength. Thus, you are able to interact and respond with purpose with all conscious matter. Remember, you do not desire to use any power on any other person as you relearn how to use self-strength in an efficient manner.

This environment is an extension and expansion of self-energy and must be treated as such, meaning that you are asking to bring more purpose to the how and why. You activate a response, then decided where and when this response is to be beneficial or valuable.

In our language, this energy puts a whole neutral barrier—in reality, many layers—around our self. It allows us to detect if some energy is pushing our buttons without us knowing. This then lets us know where this is coming from and how in the past it affected us.

You see, some bodies' dispositions don't always signify how they use energy. Strange as it might seem, some louder peoples' energy just sort of tippy-toes up to you to judge a reaction to their energy. Some people who seem meek and mild and openly loving want to control every speck of energy in you. This is only an example, not the normal pattern, as there isn't one.

To explain this a little more efficiently, perhaps we should consider how certain flower essences are made.

This is to open your mind to the vibrations and frequencies that exist and that we respond to, although they are unseen by the naked eye or even under magnification.

This is a rather large area, and normal pharmaceuticals have no understanding of why they work.

If you were to hold your hand over any flower in your local area, you would find that it emits energy. Yes, any plant will vibrate, but ones that are native to your area will be more responsive.

Perhaps it is worth wandering into the garden to experience this firsthand, but before you go exploring, let's consider a few things.

Each flower is connected to many different grids of energy lines. These can be made to reflect energies that exist about you. They may also be connected to another plant on the opposite side of the world.

The other surprising aspect of this is that an arid plant may be linked to a tropical or even mild-tempered plant.

Why am I bothering to fill you in on these phenomena? Because the more you understand, the more you consciously become aware. The more consciously aware you become, the more you automatically use many natural abilities that you presently never use or use only in deep meditation for a few moments as a supplement.

Instead of using your consciousness in a limited capacity, you are able to use it more readily all of the time.

By using this conscious ability, you consciously conceive what is consciously desired. You are using many consciousnesses at one time, not just a few or in a limited manner or in a limited ability. Remember, you are in a "now" presence, using connective consciousness in a more automatic way. Really, this is meant to become a natural ability, isn't it?

What do you think? Is this desirable, something you want to use in a purposeful manner or make a part of your life?

This automatically connects through the integrated inception of your combined soul and heart to create the synchronicity needed to automatically connect the correct matters together.

This means that your consciousness is already connected to this matter. We create your whole consciousness by asking if this is possible.

If this desire is of your whole self and not interrupted by the interfering energy of others, then all guardian guides help make this relative and valuable in an appreciative manner.

This means, then, that this desire was needed. It was only of your own intention and not those of others. When you accomplish manifesting this matter, it is not a hollow accomplishment, as it will probably bring joy to many as you share it.

First, you learn to do this efficiently in a smaller manner. Next, you learn that something large is just as easily manifested.

When something is really manifested and comes through your source of collective consciousness, it then connects to the connective consciousness of all that exists.

The outcome of this resolution is that instead of feeling empty when you receive something you knew you desired, you will sense appreciation and gratitude with self-compassion.

You are not simply consuming what you think you want, as you were not responding to every conscious response of your whole self. Do you comprehend how we learned to be efficient consumers with limited contribution to self-happiness or joy?

When you desire to connect to what you consciously and really desire with the whole of your self-consciousness—and not what you *thought* you desired—then this is the desired outcome of this chapter. Surprisingly, this can even help in what you sense you need to eat, rather than what you feel you're missing out on.

This may help those of you who repeat tense or disastrous relationships yet only feel happy when you are in a relationship. This also applies to the work choices we make.

Some of us have a mind that works constantly at a million miles an hour and never shuts off. This scenario we have touched on already, but it is very much a contributor to this chapter as well.

The thought pattern is easily the one common denominator that denotes the state of your personal mind. It is one of the least thought-about states and determines how we are going to function each day.

When was the last time you just stopped everything going on in that mind of yours or were able to actually switch it off?

Perhaps it is worth considering the different lines of thought that consume, say, two minutes of your day—but not consciously. You see, if you are quite conscious of this fact, the mind will almost stop. Give it free rein, and off it goes again. Go on; give it a try.

It's quite amazing how many thoughts go through our heads each and every moment. Have you considered the amount of energy required to keep this activity going?

Now, I would like to share one immense secret the source shared with me. If we are to spread the mass of our consciousness throughout our entire self, the rapid and often useless thoughts quickly diminish. Why?

We are about to use the self-consciousness and apply it to a different self-purpose.

Consider the image of yourself. Are you looking at it? Now have a look at your mind and consider how it is working. You're trying to look deeper into your brain, aren't you? Is it doing much, or are you able to ascertain that it in fact feels a little soggy if you use your new senses?

This depends on whether you are asking in a free manner. To help sense this, clasp your hands and put them on top of your head. For some of you, this will be a complete surprise: it might feel like liquid coming down the side of your head or face.

The purpose of this exercise is this: the spirit of your self desires to be more efficiently connected with connective consciousness to your mind—or minds.

Have you ever had a conversation with your mind?

As soon as I mentioned have a conversation yourself, immediately you thought of talking with your mouth. You do communicate and have conversations all the time with other whole, conscious-matter parts of yourself.

Okay, let's imagine a very appealing image of a person you desire. This person will probably be dressed in a certain manner, but have you considered how they smell? Go on, give it a shot. I hope you picked the right person, as it might come as a shock to some of you that this person doesn't smell right.

Let's say that this person was pleasing to smell. Notice how this person's energy sort of wraps you up. Do you sense that this person is vulnerable or asking for help? Does he or she feel independent, strong, or wanting? If you desire to ask the questions, you can sense these things and a whole lot more from this person or the person standing next to them.

You thought this was going to be easy, didn't you? See? You are not using all you abilities in a purposeful manner. Let's learn how to do so. We don't want to be led on by the wrong person, do we?

Consider that earlier we discussed telepathy. Everybody thinks we use our heads for telepathy. Remember, when we look at a person to decipher whether or not they are telling the truth, a certain body language is used. If I said to look at the body language of some politician, you would have taken an action as a real response, when in fact it might have been something this person solidly believed in.

Perhaps, then, we should consider the mind capacity in the body as well as the memory. All minds need memory. If we hold our hands to our shoulders with the flat of the hand facing the ceiling, it's almost as though you had a "shot put" in each hand. It's not too heavy, though. We don't want to be weighed down.

The left hand would represent the body mass of mind and the right hand the head mass of mind. Which one is the heaviest? The body wins hands-down, of course. This represents conscious mass. Did you fall over to the right side? What does this tell you?

You were expecting this to be present, weren't you? Let's consider whether all of the mind-mass of your self was evenly displaced throughout your whole body. Yes, it would be conscious, but did you consider that the mind would be present where it was meant to be, and not separate?

Presence holds a load of strength, doesn't it? Perhaps this is a strength that needs to be utilized with a full purpose to ensure that all minds are present and able to be utilized, not separated from the functions they were designed for.

The mind will stay at home and not go roaming about. More importantly, it will not succumb to sensing just in the head but in the whole body. Only sensing in the head does not limit its worth, because it is done in an unconscious way. It is what was told to the poor, old minds of your whole energy.

With all this mind-matter flowing into the head only, it would be rather cluttered or even painful, trying to squeeze all this energy into one area. Perhaps you might understand migraines or simple headaches now.

The real scenario I wanted to discuss, though, is this. If all this mind action is in one place, sending out currents into one area, its going to be confusing, as each mind is asking for a response.

This is simply another reason for mind-chatter or, if you like, unconscious matter contributing to how we live.

If, on the other hand, we add connective consciousness to all this matter and it automatically desires to return home, it does not contribute to energy that it has no response to. Does this work for you? We all like our responses to be appreciated, don't we?

Did you just respond automatically to the last sentence, or did you miss the significance or purpose of what was outlined for you?

You see, we have a type of spirit energy that distributes energy in the spirit-body, which is then reflected in the physical. It is an integrated blueprint.

Instead of having a thousand thoughts a minute, you concentrate on a few. This doesn't mean you accomplish less; you actually accomplish more, don't you? You are having real thoughts that link together in a synchronistic manner. This can also be interpreted as having the right thoughts but without constant interferences.

Avoiding constant interference is the whole point of our objective direction. I don't know about you, but I really dislike constant interruptions all the time.

It's such a simple thing, wanting to think without interruption so we can concentrate on what is necessary and needs to be accomplished and created.

Interference certainly isn't a trivial matter; the ramifications are more far-reaching than you might first consider. When I stumbled on this years ago, I took it with a grain of salt, so to speak. I definitely never considered the havoc being inflicted on me, and I don't desire you to make this same mistake.

You see, in a way I pretended that this interference wasn't important, and I tried to dismiss the effects—until a time came when my obstinacy was costing me dearly. All synchronicities were far out, and the annoyance of this does a sensitive head in.

Please don't think that I am chasing overly negative or overly positive matter or energy. This isn't the case. I simply follow a direction to where I am guided to sense why a real activation is limited. This means finding many types of currents that don't fulfill their full purpose or ability in a conscious manner to ensure that only conscious matter is reflected.

I just needed to get this off my chest. Some people think that because you don't follow an old-time schedule or thought patterns you are a bit strange. They think it odd that you think outside the square and don't conform, that you ask to be free of old-time constraints. Hence, there is a need for a new millennium or new conscious purposes linked to abilities that have gone unused for such a long time.

With this off my chest, I can continue.

I have discussed that in the endocrine system we have what is like a major conscious area. These parts just light up. The amount they light up depends on the current they are receiving.

I suppose you want to have a look, don't you? Do you mind if the source clears the way or opens your consciousness to a conscious image?

Remember that we use the head area for our cognizance, comprehension, and understanding, meaning that the head area is always going to have quite a bit of our attention. Sorry, I know I'm nagging, but this leads to a different line of thought.

This attention means that the lymph and gland area in our head region sort of hog the spirit-consciousness and physical responses.

This spirit-consciousness responds to energy and then directs the physical, meaning that the head area ends up controlling a lot of energy. How did this come about?

You see, this is how we all think things are meant to pan out, with the brain telling the rest of the body what is going to happen, like it or not.

If the mind area, the head, is receiving an enormous amount of energy, then it is going to be working overtime and doing extra work. Keep this on the back burner: your head is overworked in some areas and doing nothing in other areas.

This we talked about in the last chapters. Now my guides would like to add a few different thoughts that need attention.

In our spirit and physical bodies, we have large amounts of mind and memory energy—if we allow this to be connected and to contribute.

The endocrine system has large amounts of mind-matter that works like the brain, which then relates to every particle of our matter. These areas are major consciousness sources that affect how we are able to interpret elements and essences that contribute to our well-being. What a pity that most of us have no idea that this source or service of energy is actually contributing to our daily well-being.

Inactivity or inability to contribute as a vital component of energy means that this energy will regress or become insular. Therefore, many conscious areas become unconscious.

If we apply this to a whole region, then this suppressed self-region draws in many energies like a magnet. Remember, we are designed to reflect who and what we are.

I would like to apply this suppression in a physical way—how it relates to us or how we are unable to respond—as this area is unable to communicate. Some areas then become understimulated or overstimulated. When you limit the connective consciousness, this is reflected automatically in all energy regions.

We could then over-respond in one area or not respond at all where energy is needed, as this area is suppressed from being vital. If this current becomes chemical, then some glands produce extra and others next-to-nothing. Remember, this all started in the spirit-body.

Over time, this situation is then reflected throughout the rest of the body. Many extra chemicals are created, and with extra energy happening, it is also harder to switch off. It is much harder to reverse this process, as the current needed to respond is now suppressed.

The surprising thing is that so many are unaware or simply have not thought about how active their minds are. This is why I asked you to review what is really going on in your head.

After relating to the head area's overactivity, we can easily comprehend that the rest of the body's energy is going to be a little debilitated. Perhaps it is worth asking if you are skimming rather than reflecting on what you're reading.

There is a reason that I'm reviewing. We aren't simply talking spirit here; we are relating more at this moment to physical matter. If something is happening in the spirit-body, it is most certainly going to be mirrored in the physical. This means that artificial supplements are only going to mask a deeper problem.

Natural supplements can stimulate certain points of consciousness to send out electrical impulses or to stimulate connections.

At this relevant point in time, our guides would like to contribute in a direct manner to this conversation, which has been essentially guided throughout every conversation.

If, my friends, you were to discover that a massive part of your self was underutilised, this could make you envious that someone else is using this element of life in a more efficient and purposeful manner than you are. It is also conceivable that this person is using your own inability for his own efficiency, adding part of your power to enhance his own ability.

This is then interpreted as his using your unwanted energy to amass a greater self-mass at the expense of your own awareness. You are then unable to sense all that is of a vital component to your own makeup. This leaves the self debilitated and unable to sense all self-gratitude and compassion. The self is unable to restore all real self-faith and belief.

My friends, faith and belief are a response of the present in a conscious manner to every efficient manner and to all of your whole, conscious self-matter.

It is vital to be present in every conscious presence of capacity, in every self-component that relates to every fully conscious response. We are conscious of a conscious makeup, which is therefore a self-conscious responsibility.

Remember, my friends, it your choice to be of this freeing nature, this freeing environment, this freeing atmosphere. Your self is free to engage in each and every self-freedom that relates to you and only you.

Do you comprehend that you are free not to suppress all past, self-unconscious actions of a separate nature, environment, or atmosphere? Do you also know that you are not responsible for freeing all of these irresponsible reactions of past relatives?

As you release these unreasonable reactions of deactivated responses in the self-past, you also free the irresponsible responses of all selves and relatives of past life or life-after-life, which in truth you were unaware of.

To follow this line of thought, we can reflect on our conversation about major points of consciousness in the endocrine system. Perhaps it is time to reflect on the parts that aren't receiving this energy in a balanced manner.

You see, there is almost a fight going on for the rest of the remaining energy. That's a bit of a surprise, isn't it? We need to think about this energy grabbed by the body and consider the consequences this creates.

There are still messages going out, saying that the energy needs to be evened out, so messages get redirected to the next lymph or gland, saying, *I need extra energy,* or *I'm getting swamped with energy that doesn't relate to me.*

This lack of current creates a question that creates constrictions. A restriction is needed because I'm receiving too much energy, first in the spirit-body and then in the physical. The extra questions create extra thoughts that flood the mind as we try to think. There are quite a few of them, aren't there?

To put this in a different perspective, imagine that the messages meant for some localized mind and memory are not being received. Where do the questions end up? In the head. Please think about this a little bit longer.

These messages are really questions like: *Why am I receiving too much energy? Why am I receiving the wrong energy? Why am I not getting any current?* The vast array of questions grows to clog the mind in the head region. This is simply a consequence of the lack of communication between conscious minds and spirit or physical matter.

This then highlights the importance of connective consciousness or all self-matters responding to a self-spirit consciousness's message. Remember that this is how sequences—or parts you desire to connect to—are created.

This sequence will automatically be highlighted, meaning that there is probably a vehicle that is a special self-resource that needs to be followed in order to connect many aspects of your life to your own real purpose.

There is a special "you" within the depths of your own resources, suppressed and unable to respond. This is going to be your personal contribution to strengthening the self and reflecting its relevance to all humanity. It is something you have innate understanding about, so you were born with a special awareness to this subject or life potential.

This innate potential is locked away within your self-energy system. Using this potential is going to bring immense joy to you, because you are connecting to self-purpose. This joy and purpose means that you are not waiting for others to direct you. Your intuition is presently using every particle of intuition stored in every self-particle of your body, not just your head region.

Using whole-body senses means that your whole body is learning to react to many different elements and essences that exist naturally about you but that you haven't been using. You are listening for the first time through your whole body in a conscious manner. What is unfolding is what many self-senses have been saying all along—that you were never clued in to the language they were speaking.

This new dynamic of interpreting many different languages means that you suddenly become aware of many energies that have always existed; you just forgot how to communicate with them.

In a way, we let others do this for us. We have suppressed and undervalued all that our self is able to interpret. We have been sensing or listening to a vast array of messages that have gone unanswered for so long. It is not so much questioning as it is intuitive, automatic understanding.

If you are not listening to this automatic understanding, perhaps there is a whole new self-purpose that is undiscovered.

Getting in touch with this self-language is also a core component of this book. If you are not having a conversation with your own soul, how can you really know what exists in your heart? Remember, your soul is the foundation on which you are created, and this is worth considering.

There is, in fact, a language just like channeling that isn't used with much purpose. It is another core self-language with a spirit-based foundation.

We made another point at the beginning of this conversation, and the subject needs a little clarity: telepathy. This is how we communicate in a spirit-sense to help each other work more efficiently.

Essences or elements that are a natural way of receiving what our bodies need point to areas of natural understanding. But if these areas are unable to contribute, then what is going to happen? Non-corresponding areas will respond or interfere with an area from which our self-resources are asking for a real response.

These interfering thoughts like to contribute, so if they are unable to contribute in the head region, they may also see if they can contribute in the body.

Questions and answers that we are unable to receive can easily be made up, but we cannot respond to them, so there is no comprehension or understanding of the direction needed to rectify the lack of current.

We now have a vital area of consciousness that is not receiving equal energy to respond to a real, conscious purpose.

As these unequal energies interfere in this most vital area, many imbalances begin to take shape, but not in a desired manner.

Remember, this is only a representation of awareness. We only desire to show how a limited energy source influences first the spirit and then the physical matter.

This total scenario is the reason we need a new understanding. We need to know how the relationship of every energy-body influences every effect on our relative self—or, most importantly, how this energy inefficiency came to be present and reflected on life after life.

You see, presence is the perfect balance of each and every self-body that contributes energy to our selves. Remember, each of these bodies needs to work as one and not be in competition with the others.

What I just wrote was not just my understanding but that of so many guides. Think long and hard about all of our self-bodies working in competition with each other. Think of the ramifications.

Now, I would like to throw a cat amongst the pigeons and ask you what is the outcome of this. Got any ideas? Well, there's *disharmony*, where all energies are in disarray, or *discomfort* where there is no ease of communication between all bodies. So, what have you got? Disease. Yes, disease. Are we hitting the nail on the head now?

If you were speed-reading, you were going to miss this and all the keys and codes that cover you. If you were speed-reading, the vibration frequency you received would be different—not activated, not moving.

You see, some parts are only tedious when your self isn't able to grasp the extra language that is written into this book.

Most of you will sense gratitude and compassion for this energy that is connected to real self-humanity, saving you from the inhumanity that you have encountered thus far in all of your lives—yes, inhumanity that you were totally unaware of.

Perhaps you can understand now that the time for affirming is present. This does not mean *later* or *sometime*. The time to be firm in your intent is *now*. Let it be in a present nature, not a past life.

Yes, our guides are saying that this is the purpose of the new millennia. All must consciously be firm in their real connections to real self-consciousness; the time of indecision is over.

Now is the time for all to learn that there is more to the self than just a physical body. There is more reasoning, more response to what, how, why, where, and when all is relevant. Now it is time to realize that there are more perspectives to every relevant particle of ourselves in an aware manner.

The time to postulate is over—no more sitting on the sidelines. Now we move into a time where all must participate in a real manner with a conscious outcome.

As you have probably already figured out, this is channeled through all that has been affirmed through this self-soul and self-heart and through so many bodies. It is what all guides desire to pass on to all humanity in an absolute, conscious manner.

Perhaps it is time to return to our conversation, remembering that everybody contributes energy to our self or to our balance or self-purpose. We actually have quite a few bodies that are in our relative makeup. This is why the source directs us to follow our energy makeup to tell us what is really going on—and what isn't.

What is interfering with our energy without our awareness? Remember what was outlined in the previous sentence: everybody is presently contributing to your body.

The annoying part is that this is happening at all. Remember that we found this same relationship in the way that you were unconsciously channeling, yes. We found many portals in many different areas that allowed energy in or out without our consent.

Telepathy works in much the same way, but instead of the endocrine system being targeted, we look at all of our major sensory points. This also means that we are targeting the nervous system. Remember your acute feeling? Perhaps this hits a nerve, yes, a very tender one.

This also means that we automatically understand many implications and the reasons we become agitated without provocation. This can happen instantly when we meet some people. Even if they are being polite, they may instantly rile us. This also happens when some people use their energy system like a weapon.

The interesting outcome of this is that the majority of people are unaware that they consciously use energy this way without purpose.

Is the source hitting home some relative insight?

Those who consciously use power as a tool are rare, but believe me, they most certainly exist. The most surprising realization is their blatant openness in expecting everything to come to them as if they are in command. These are people who enjoy a power struggle and who enjoy using fear and intimidation.

We definitely are not going to focus on this set of people.

Everybody senses or sees differently, but just in case you are wondering what this energy would look like, I will give you a simile. It was shown to me as a large sphere with lots of holes in it. In fact, it looked like the moon with very large holes.

People I have healed seemed to see this before me sometimes, and I have used the source's description to see or identify this interfering energy. This energy is also related to how we have felt guilt in a past life or how we have released what some people would call *karma*.

Actually, we are now going to rewrite the history books somewhat—not according to my judgment but by an interpretation from my guides. I'm not asking you to agree with this synopsis, just to keep an open mind to what the source is endeavouring to pass on. Then you can decide if I have misinterpreted this segment or not.

After this segment has been *unfolded*, to use a source term, we will be showing how telepathy, the ego, and karma are interrelated and rebound on our daily lives to disrupt the purpose of our abilities.

I was having a difficult time comprehending ego and karma ages ago, as something in my intuition just didn't add up. I guess I was guided to explore this segment of energy and not take old explanations into the equation.

This is a source translation of how ego and karma came to be part of our existence.

In discussing many areas of life, we have reflected back to where we got a few things wrong ages ago but have held onto those beliefs.

The source is endeavouring to highlight a few alternative outcomes.

To start with, I was shown that where the soul and heart have separated in certain elements and essences, so have aspects of our life. Imagine the energy that was created by the separated soul. This then became karma, and the energy created by the separated heart became ego.

You can also think of this creation as a direct relationship with our harmony or harmonic balance. The harmony is an indicator that ensures that all is correct, a true and balanced current with the capacity to tell us when all is not correct.

This is what our ego and karma did when linked to our soul and heart. According to the source, they were never meant to be separate identities. This was news to me at the time. Perhaps you are viewing this in the same light. This is why I have highlighted this scenario.

I needed many new, plausible answers as to what had happened and how this monster was able to grow at such an exasperating rate without dissipating over lifetimes. It's one small sentence with many outcomes that we all need clarity on. It reverberates as self-disagreements that we all seem to hold on to so efficiently, yes.

Now, please check to see if this adds up and is correct; then we can move on. To check efficiently, ask to free all preconceived thoughts, memories, and conclusions of past-time where the self was never fully present.

Now you can ask in a correct manner.

Have you ever contemplated that ego and karma started out as a harmonic balancer of our soul and heart? If this is correct, then in the parts of us that have never experienced separation, the ego and karma must exist as they were meant to be, yes? Exactly. There are still many balanced aspects of our selves in perfect harmony.

The good news is that there are many aspects of ourselves that have never experienced separation. They have only been unable to receive all the information required to operate in a completely uninterrupted manner.

I asked for a very clear and definitive set of questions and answers to understand this problem. First, I was told to think of the separated ego and karma in terms of energy. Next, I was to think about what happens when a current is loaded with either too many negative or positive points; either way, it is going to set us off a little.

Next, I was to imagine that the ego was trying to balance an energy problem that was a result of over-positive and over-negative energies initially trying to balance themselves up. This meant that the ego needed to communicate with the karma to find a solution. It was like they were in a stream of energy, trying to find a destination. The ego was then unable to communicate with the karma due to a breakdown.

Are you figuring out why connective consciousness is a vital link that we have been searching for? Do you have a different appreciation for how vital this currency is in connecting everything together? Energy of this consciousness, if broken, causes the easy separation of any main mass of conscious matter and is therefore plausible.

What a downer this is, you may think. But if we know how something was broken, then we can fix it.

How you can fix what you don't know exists? This is like having many needles in the middle of a giant haystack that you don't even know exists.

This is another reason we follow the energy—to enlighten us to areas of energy that we are unaware of.

Following emotions doesn't always define all problems, but it does give a very good clue that they exist or that they presently sit in a state of existence. This state of existence basically means that the energy is separated from the conscious matter. It is not balanced, and it is certainly not receiving the correct capacity of current.

There is quite a large picture forming, but there is probably one scenario that you have missed entirely.

In this conversation I mentioned over-positive and over-negative currents, and the connotations of this energy rebound beyond all comprehension.

First, I would like you to think of over-negative or over-positive energy and figure out how they came to exist. I would also like you to think about how many places this energy has been rebounding inside of us, undetected for millennia, just having a merry old time of it, almost uninhibited and unchallenged.

The source basically wanted you to comprehend the immensity of this spreading energy and to think of the ramifications if left unheeded—not in a frightening or fearful way, as all is about to be reversed. Simply, they ask you to be aware that many areas of your energy need your total awareness and that some different lines of thought may be required.

Remind yourself that we have been discussing a major contributor to the separation of telepathy, but a couple of other elements of understanding should be opened before tackling that monster.

Let's follow up on with the story we started earlier, with our ego out of balance and wondering what to do with all this built-up or out-of-balance energy. What happens next? Well, it just holds on to this energy until it can work out this problem of an unbalanced mass with the karma.

Exactly the same scenario is going on with the karma, and now both are creating large masses of energy and not knowing what to do with them. Imagine these large masses of energy growing larger by the day and competing for current.

The two separated masses are now stagnant, and they begin to take on an entity, the many aspects of which are trying to solve some imbalance. They get sort of clogged or stuck, so many aspects of energy are added to this ever-growing entity.

Instead of blaming ourselves for bad decisions, perhaps we should take into account that perhaps we made many decisions simply because the ego and karma were unable to communicate. This was because aspects of the soul and heart of our source indicated that we had made the best decisions possible with the information available to us at the time.

This then means that perhaps it is time to release a lot of self-guilt for decisions we have made in the past.

Don't put this sentence off too lightly, as it has reverberated through us for millennia. Perhaps it is time to release this guilt that we haven't done everything perfectly all the time.

This we will revisit in a moment, but there are still a few other issues to chew on.

As we were discussing, this puts a rather different twist on how we view the ego and karma, as they came to take on different roles than what they were intended for. We need to reexamine the masses of unbalanced energy creating more unbalanced energy, which unconsciousness.

All dysfunctional balances are totally different from and independent of each other. They are non-corresponding, being of different gravities and energy systems.

Unbalanced energy needed to go somewhere, so it ended up hanging on to the mind and memory in either the spirit or physical. This resulted in large areas of stagnation for these areas as well. The unbalanced energy of the mass ended up hanging on to the consciousness we discussed, but all these points of stagnant energy created blockages and, eventually, dense matter.

This adds another thought to our discussion. Do you realize now how vital it is that all energy keep moving? As soon as energy stops, we want to know why, and the spirit picks this up immediately. It is then interpreted by our physical self as fright, anxiety, or pain, depending on the circumstances at the time.

The next reaction, of course, is an emotion. Why? Because the full current is incapable of creating a full circuit. The inability to create a full circuit then triggers the closest consciousness, which fixes this imbalance by the only means it knows—creating more energy.

This consciousness will be the closest point of consciousness—the endocrine system. These are the glowing bits of consciousness we are able to see so often.

I interpret this as seeing lots of very bright balls of matter that are totally different from orbs. They have always looked like white light and are very intense.

For those who desire a clearer view and are able to see these already, touch your forehead on the hairline and rub across this area. This will often free your deeper insight.

For those unable to see or sense these points of consciousness, hold your arms outstretched. Most of you will feel that energy balls are falling out of your arms. You may see some orb-like balls of consciousness throughout your body.

To enhance this, open and close your hands into fists. Now extra consciousness will light up. Some you may not be meant to see this image straightaway. You might be clearing this limitation; then, when you least expect to see or sense, this image may appear.

Let's focus back on the conversation of what happens next, as there is limited energy moving, and the separated consciousness is becoming frustrated.

The inevitable reaction to this frustration is then sent to the physical, which results in extra chemicals being produced by the extra current. The extra chemicals are another unbalanced reaction, which causes impulsive reactions or emotions.

Do you comprehend why the source desires us to focus on the energy of ourselves and not just the end reaction of the emotion? The greatest reason for this is that the emotion may not even relate to the reaction but is just a reaction to some energy blockage.

Everything is not always what it seems to be. This is a reaction I have seen many times, so please let me unfold this in our language and terms.

The greatest understanding that needs to be comprehended is why, where, when, and how this was able to take place, but you also need to comprehend the overall implications.

The next scenario that needs an equation involves how the imbalance of a greater mass of ego or karma occur. You may identify this with something that was discussed earlier in the book when we held a mass of correct energy in one hand and unbalanced or dense matter in the other, yes.

This related to an unbalanced or unconscious mass of matter that, over time, became a dense mass, yes. If we follow this pattern through many different dilemmas or repeat it life after life, we end up with quite a few of these dense masses throughout various parts of our spirit and physical bodies, Have you factored this in?

The next logical step would be to look at the imbalances that have devolved in a similar manner, remembering that they are connected to the mind and memory. Remember that memory is not just in the brain but in the membrane of every particle in the spirit and the physical.

In the end, we have two self-akashic records of many different scenarios or cycles of imbalances we have been unable to balance out. Luckily, we also have the original, complete record, and how we use our energy depends on which one we connect to.

The energy we use is also connected to our own faith and belief. In real terms, the strength is reflected in the original soul through the original heart, through the soul of this life, through the heart of this life, using this as one whole body mass.

I hope that I have not just confused you and that you are integrating as you read. If you rely only on feeling, then not too much will be felt. If, on the other hand, you use conscious feelings, this becomes a sense or a real ability to consciously interpret the whole mass of your body as one.

This being the case, we desire to be at one with an evolving energy, or to experience an integrating sense. You are also having a conversation with your guides to bring new meaning to all that you will sense in the future.

This means that as you relate to this new sensing, new awareness will flow throughout your body. It doesn't matter if this is instantaneous or not; it needs to grow, layer upon layer, so it doesn't disrupt or become overly sensitive or overly aware.

If all of a sudden you are aware of too many new senses, this might become daunting and overpowering or unbalanced. We are all a little impatient, but we are only able to respond to one source of energy, when we are, in fact, used to a few. Think about this, please, as we desire to use no external source of energy, only your own. This might be or seem strange, because we receive outside energy when we are healed or receive from our guides.

If a healer is healing properly, he is not using his own power. He is only showing you how to reconnect to your own power and convert it to self-strength. The same goes for your guides. Yes, they may let you sense their energy to remind you how to reconnect, but this is always your own energy, always.

Why? Because you would become dependent on their energy or their power. This does not empower any self. Rather, it debilitates the self, taking away self-worth, ability, purpose, appreciation, gratitude, compassion, and a sense of living life or a love of living. Then you would be consuming only another's faith and belief, and you would then respond to their version of love, not your own.

This is another reason this book has taken so long to write: to ensure that no self-power was ever used or that of any other sources. This is worth thinking about a little longer, isn't it?

Perhaps we can recap how consciousness that was sitting in a separated state was easily interfered with. The same goes for the mind and memory. So does all that you have been exposed to when it suddenly comes flooding back. This is your real consciousness, which has not been interfered with by others' consciousness.

Don't get too excited if this recap seems to be rather extensive. Your real memory was reconnecting to this in a conscious manner as you read.

You are going to read about the changes your original spirit desires to have present in yourself as one whole self. The changes are the response to your whole self asking to be given real purpose. This is like an energy response to real self-purpose. The choice is always yours, though.

This is a scenario from the source concerning what happens next. As the spirit and physical membranes were created without correct current and capacity, they create artificial membranes and a mass of different events.

This then creates an even greater mass, as greater miscommunication creates rifts or separation. This is how the spirit and the physical have grown apart over an immense mass of matter. In a way, the matter with the greatest mass will blame the other for not communicating with the other.

This may not be the easiest scenario to follow, but it breaks down to this. If the heart and soul are not able to communicate and create a stronger bond, then the ego and karma get stronger and create more separation. This then means that the whole of your focus is on the separated mass of the ego and Karma, not on the soul and heart.

Please think about this scenario for a moment and consider how it reflects on you. Think of this separation as lots of interference from dense matter, interrupting all of our decisions or correct intuition.

We are going to recap what was just said; it is just so important. If the communication between the soul and heart breaks down, then instead of the soul and heart becoming stronger, the ego and karma receive this strength—not as strength but as power. Does this explain a lot?

When two powers face off in a power struggle, holes in the self-energy system are created or the self-energy system devolves. This was outlined in many formats.

Perhaps now you also understand why I was guided to study interference, which creates separation so we are not able to be at one with our self—as many different texts relate.

While you are reading, many parts of yourself are responding in a purposeful manner, but only if your real self desires to be restored from devolved matter to evolved matter.

Now you are able to proceed in a purposeful manner and be present with all self-presence, with real desire and intention. These are not my words, but they are to be interpreted as self-love, guided by the real source.

The next image to be contemplated is this. If we cut off the energy that is keeping this dense mass alive, then it will simply cease to exist. Believe me, this works.

You are learning to neutralize power that is not of yourself. Does this explanation work for you? This means the power will cease to exist and will not be transferred to others. How?

When you are guided, please consider that I said that all consciousness that exists in our bodies is unable to properly contribute and communicate, yes. Please remember also how it was outlined that if the body was not of conscious matter, it would cease to exist. I kind of like mine as it is, as this is who I am.

If this matter was not made of conscious matter, it would be impossible to exist, yes. If this energy is not of yourself, cut off the non-self-consciousness, and it ceases to exist.

Next, consider the extent of this energy release. The interfering energy is instantly gone. It ceases to exist. Thus, it prevents the interfering or separate matter from keeping the real self-consciousness from being separate or in a state of existence.

You might need to read this a couple of times to get your head around it, but I pray that this is easily comprehended, as it has a real purpose.

You might think it's possible to neutralize parts of your own matter, consciousness, mind, or memory. This is impossible, because your own self knows its own real consciousness.

We don't need to know the emotion or feeling that created this imbalance. To be perfectly honest, it isn't necessary, as it was made with non-corresponding vibrations or frequencies, completely without harmony. So, why reflect on its outcome?

This is why, when we heal through any regressive area, we never, ever, ever focus on the illusional feeling or emotion. It was created by unbalanced energy, so why focus on this? You would be sending power to this unbalanced energy. You do comprehend this, I hope, so that no energy is ever sent to energy that we don't desire to focus on.

Using this equation, we are able move vast amounts of interference on many levels at once instead of a layer at a time. Does this interest you? This means a quicker release, period. Consider then that a greater ease of release is accomplished, as the energy isn't rebounding with such an impact.

If this impact is unable to rebound, you never gave the unbalanced energy a connection to recreate interference. This is important.

The reason this is accomplished is because we hold so dearly to our mistakes. I repeat, we hold dearly to our mistakes, and we have unconsciously sent continuous power to the same scenario that existed in a past-life mistake, and this keeps recreating in life after life. Can you see the image of this pattern?

Please heed this next part, as it is vital.

If we reflect more on the records of what we have done wrong than what we have correctly achieved, then is it any surprise that this is what we receive? Please reflect on what has just been revealed to you.

If you focus on the past, then is it any surprise that it manifests more easily, more readily, more of the time and that it creates more interference, yes? Were you aware of this situation at all or how it was manifested?

We have repeated awareness, awareness, awareness—but awareness of what?

Now that you are aware of all that you do and do not desire, you are aware of the extremes of living in a harmonious state—a natural and fulfilling manner in which to live. Perhaps, then, a couple of the chapter titles are reverberating a new awareness throughout your now-present self.

This was actually in the affirmation earlier about how a correct faith in self-strength attracts a neutral harmony. A neutral harmony then opens all of your abilities to flow in a creative nature. This opens a creative self-nature, which you constantly reflect upon to ensure that all is created with only neutral tones.

This ensures that only vibrations and frequencies that balance each other are used to create a harmonious creation. This creation is then able to be shared, as it will fit in with all humanity, even if this is primarily for your own use.

The point is, if it works cohesively with all, then it was meant to be created and reflects balanced self-respect. This balanced self-respect means that a neutral virtue ensures that all your self-energy reflects self-ethics that are your own desire, not anybody else's.

The reason for this is that you can only be responsible for yourself. You create something that may seem to be for you but, in truth, is more for another. This is so very important, because if this has been sensed to be a feature in past lives, then a lack of responsibility in certain elements of our past will be reflected in this life.

Why would this happen? Your sacred spirit would sense that you are creating without real direction or purpose, simply being true to yourself.

The source would say that we are responsible for being here at this true time to create a certain aspect in a form true to our real nature.

Therefore, we are not able to create what is not true to our self-nature, environment, or atmosphere, as this would be instantly sensed not to be our own response. In a way, you are reprogramming the self.

I received an instant affirmation to give you an idea of what has just been represented.

I open all true faith to all true reasons of self-response.

Each and every response is able to reverberate with true virtue in a true sense, only to be reflected in a resonance of all vital, natural nature.

I ask to consistently reflect each and every action in an image of self-peace, true tranquillity, and absolute harmony.

This balanced source harmony is only to be of a self-gravity, reflecting all collective, connective consciousness of all that is defined as true source love.

Perhaps then we could take a different view of what we have called reality in the past. This means that you would sense anything not true to yourself as not being responsible.

Our full consciousness is not fully connected or responsive to this unconscious creation, meaning that this would not be a conscious desire or intention. This lack of conscious responsibility causes stagnation in certain appreciations of the self. You would instantly sense this.

This results in an over—or under-abundance of negative or positive current, and this same efficiency is then related to devolving power in the same manner as the spirit and physical body. The most important point to be made at this moment is that the harmonious current is never of a controlling nature.

Throughout this chapter, we have made sure that there is a purpose to every step taken—before moving. This has ensured that our desires are correct and that other energies have not influenced or interfered with them.

To ensure that no controls from the past reflect on the future, please bring your clasped hands to your chin. You will immediately experience a draining sensation. You may notice that your head drops forward. Now you are free to continue.

All that you contribute your current to has a purpose: to create real joy for yourself. When you desire to buy something, it should be something that will bring you joy even after you purchase it. This negates that empty feeling of buying something and feeling hollow later, wondering why you bought it in the first place.

This is another reason for using the strength of your integrated soul and heart. It gives a direction to what you really desire to experience in a neutral manner. This desired experience then equates to freedom from hindrances or interferences—freedom to create in a balanced atmosphere.

Does this start you thinking about releasing many of those interferences that distort your daily thoughts?

You see, the affirmation that was shared with you earlier held many aspects to it. It has been preparing you for each step yet to be discussed, without your feeling over-anxious about what you have missed.

There is another name for this: rebounding energy. And rebounding is exactly what it does, in exactly the same way it works in a drug addict. Remember, your body will be used to working in an unbalanced manner, and no matter what you think, your body is used to using or working with this dense or interfering energy.

When the body suddenly experiences real or balanced energy, it can come as quite a shock. You don't have enough self-appreciation to allow yourself to experience real, balanced energy, as it has not been your natural environment. Perhaps now you will be more interested in your own welfare instead of what Paris Hilton or Brad Pitt are up to.

We now move to reflecting on preparations. We want to show you real outcomes and not gloss over them, because this would just simulate taking a pill—without you committing any energy to a real resolution.

Energy is committed to your soul, which communicates through your heart. Energy that has been contributed by external sources needs to be disconnected first. You see now that you are strong enough to move into new territory.

When all is said and done, energy contributed by external sources is interference. You need to disconnect outside interferences that have been keeping you from actively knowing what you are missing.

This does make sense to you, doesn't it? If not, perhaps you need to consider that interference adds up to the creation of dysfunctional beliefs.

Why? Look at how interfering energy is created: by looking to past, unconscious energy for answers. Once again, we only looked for the answers. We didn't question how this situation arose in the first place, because we just wanted the outcome fixed.

This would be like getting sacked for something that has nothing to do with you and then accepting the situation without question. You have done your job capably, and the termination has come as a shock. Why, then, don't you question the outcome?

Well, everything doesn't add up, and you go through your past experiences, trying to find a similar outcome that will help you make sense of this one. But even past situations don't make this one add up. You are confused, but you're not asking any questions about why it happened, so you don't say anything, and you don't reach any conclusions. Questioning through the past creates one rather large incapacity called *trialing*.

You may have noticed that when I am describing how something needs to be created, I often say "endeavour" instead of "try." The frequency of "I tried to do something" indicates that I'm busy digging up the past to find a resolution, most likely without results.

This trialing creates another scenario where you question resolutions in this life as well as many that go back for ages. How many questions do you think this would actually create—a hundred, a thousand, a million? In fact, you leave the door open to continually keep this question going, even after you think you have found an answer.

This can't be correct, can it? No, this has to be crap. This couldn't really happen . . . could it?

There is one element that keeps you in touch with the here-and-now and ensures that you don't keep going back and back continually. What would that be? Yes, of course: collective consciousness. It lets us know when we reach something that we sense to be correct.

Remember, this includes every aspect of you, not just a couple of consciousnesses.

Let me clarify. You have two sets of conscious matter, one in the spirit one in the physical. Collective consciousness needs to use both sets together as one whole body. We need to ensure that this is the only consciousness we use so that we are connecting to whatever is correct. This means that there is a soul and heart for the spirit and the physical.

There is a flip side to this. You may think that we instantly receive the truth as soon as we hit any type of conscious matter. This has been a huge problem in the past. We have sometimes been confused by the whole collective consciousness and separated aspects of consciousness; or a whole consciousness has been fractured, so some of our conclusions have been rather out of kilter. We have confused what was our own spirit with that of others. I need to repeat this: *we confused what was our own spirit with that of others.*

The dynamics of this are so immense, it is virtually indescribable. Every image of interference actually relates to this one problem.

Now, how can we know if we're checking this with a limited amount of consciousness and not a whole, integrated, collective consciousness at the moment? Damn. That makes things awkward, so we are only checking with a very limited amount of conscious ability.

There is another liability to this limited consciousness indicating what we need. If a power surge comes through, the whole process is going to be repeated.

Now we are about to tackle one process that has been at the forefront of my mind since starting this book. This process is one that has annoyed me for most of my adult life, and finding the offending elements, essences, currents, balances, gravities, and aspects has at times done my head in.

There is one thing I am grateful for: I have nearly always been aware of this symptom. But I have not always recognized the vast array of forms and functions it uses or how it debilitates myself and those around me.

My greatest fear was that I wouldn't be aware. This symptom can confuse the most sincere of us, those who have the greatest of intent and who endeavour to always do the correct thing.

As you can probably tell, I desire to create a picture of an energy that has been interfering in an uninhibited manner through generations, bastardising our abilities, awareness, and sensitivities, and generally stuffing up how we desire to live.

Before we tackle the indifferent interferences, we need a rock-solid indication that we are connected only to collective consciousness. This is then a direction we are able to follow.

This ensures that the disgruntled self that has been connecting to bits and pieces of separated physical consciousness isn't going to get a look inside, because we have a new awareness.

Perhaps now you can appreciate why the source is indicating that it is time to be firm. We are to identify with all that is really possible, not what others tell us we are incapable of achieving.

This self is then going to be cleansed by a neutral energy, which means that it doesn't come back to haunt us later or interfere in clear and decisive decisions.

To define this, and to connect to your real consciousness in a real and true manner, here is a new affirmation. It ensures that, in the future, this is the only manner in which you communicate within yourself.

The word *within* is the key here, meaning that you don't seek separated consciousness outside the whole self to give yourself directions to your next destination.

Gabriel is opening a new-time affirmation, creating a new awareness of yourself in a correct manner. This means that you are to seek only self-spirit and no other.

You see, guides are never just a separate consciousness; they are always of a true collective consciousness—so that Aunt Maud's separated consciousness isn't able to interfere in your life. If she were here to help, then she would be coming through with a collective consciousness.

This individual self-presence is now to be of a total reality with all of the conclusive self, complete in all collective matters.

I ask for all self-reality to now compile all new-time self-purpose. This absolute composition is complete in all real virtue, in all real, creative experiences, and in all creative influences of the source.

All resolution to true presence is now able to exist with real, evolved love, which creates only true purpose in an evolved time.

All creative purpose creates a gravity of a new, intuitive intent, through all new abilities, now sensed with a new, creative nature.

Love always,

Gabriel

The affirmation, as usual, is talking to your real, integrated, collective consciousness, which opens you to receive only real potential. While your real potential is open to receive, perhaps we can look at a few of the dilemmas that have come about without your realizing it.

Earlier in the book, I brought up the fact that I needed to re-contact a point of myself where I remembered strong links to my spirit, so my spirit and physical more or less worked as one. You see, I was able to sense that I had been strong at that time, as I hadn't been influenced by the energies around me as much.

When you sense that you are complete, you stay strong instead of being vulnerable to outside energy. Then outside energy doesn't interest you, and you don't wonder what it does.

In our terms, this means that our mind doesn't wander all over the place; we are able to actually concentrate on what is important. While this is happening, you are solid in your connection to intuition, so you are content in a harmonious or stable self-atmosphere.

Your energy is doing exactly what, where, when, and how it was meant to do in a very natural self-nature, so you are content. The whole trouble with this is that you are still a child. You don't know if you are actually doing everything correctly.

No matter what time frame we have been born into, the hard, physical realities eat away at our strong environment.

You were shown what is correct before any separation occurred. These are the parts that have never been tampered with. In a real sense, you have a template to work from.

You are able to ask the correct questions and answers to create a real conclusion. You are able to neutralize energy that you desire to use now and in the future. This energy is clean or clear and will open up conclusive understanding with comprehension, eliminating the illusional, instinctual questions and answers.

This means that the questions and remaining answers formulate a real, conclusive knowing. This indicates that you have used the real, collective self-consciousness as your template or blueprint. Additionally, the source has helped guide you to a direct destination where all is integrated as one presence of yourself.

So, you have a real template that has never been tampered with, and you used it with the help of the source. This eliminated all the incorrect questions and answers and left you with the ability to see a real conclusion.

At this moment, you are receiving a new grounding through your collective consciousness to receive the connective consciousness that brings all these real desires together. Whether you hear tones or you sense unfolding in your body, this is going on. Even if you sense hardly anything, it is happening.

To connect to a little more awareness of the energy being tithed, I'll describe a few of the activations.

You are learning to neutralize any place where energy is way over or way under in the current you disconnect from. This current is the many, varied energies in every form and function that we have discussed so far—essential essence, elements, vibration or frequency, and the vast array of balances.

To optimise this, our guides are about to translate a new self-presence link of understanding to be transferred through your whole body. It is to be read as an actual response throughout your whole body, not just in your head.

Please remember that each response is a personal self-account of your actions. Put in a different light, this is your personality placed into a connecting energy, expressed as energy. This really means using the mind and memory that exist in the whole of your body as a whole new lateral thought-response, not simply processing all responses that occur in your head region.

To open this tithing, all new-time guides open an evolved affirmation to reaffirm lost, free thought-receptors that exist in the whole of your body.

I am of a perfect response.

I am of a perfect presence.

I am able to respond to all self-worth in a real manner, in a real purpose.

Therefore, each and every self-sequence is able to respond to real potential in a real and true manner.

Each and every response is forwarded in real time; therefore, I am always present in each and every sequence of life synchronicity.

Therefore, I am able to ground only in real time, never in the past or in unachievable futures.

Simply, all self-purpose is always present. In our language, this simply means that we do not desire a rehashing of old, past energies or unrealistic futures that do not encompass our selves in a balanced sense of real humanity.

When we collate this into one real self-desire and intention, we are then able restore ourselves in a real and neutral harmony. We are able to hold a constant frequency that we respond to, unlike those who use inhumanity as their current, mass, or matter.

This is designed to help you shift. Do not let your energy be intimidated by the mass of denser energy around you. You are free to raise all vibrational frequencies as you desire or intend.

The exercise that follows reflects this.

First, a new, grounding effect is happening in a gradual response to all that you have interpreted.

In a way, you could imagine that you are grounding higher, vibrational responses to a new frequency, a new harmony. This is a bit like sinking into cotton wool—or gentleness, if you like.

Next you sense that you are shedding denser matter from your old consciousness. You might sense that you feel stuck for a moment. This moves forward quite freely.

The sensation of moving forward is your past self of this life catching up and leaving repetitious past-life schedules behind. You may sense this as pins and needles in your back or a shedding of energy on your back and shoulders.

We now move to a response that you will be unable to sense or respond to. Why? Because at this moment you are releasing burdens, not just in one emotion or feeling in your life but in many.

This is only achieved by the person who can sense hardly anything. If you can sense it, then you are reliving this pattern of inefficiency that you have repeated time and time again.

With this release of burdens, some of you will sense that you are shooting up or raising all energies of yourself. This is freeing many potentials that you desire to connect to.

You are now connecting to a grace of ease. Some of you might desire a huge release from your airways in a repeating manner. This is normal. As your head drops forward, you will be complete.

Please clasp your hands to balance yourself once again. Some of you might sense that you are also coming together as well, which of course you are.

Please finish this exercise off with a prayer-pose. Hold all raised expectations of yourself in a higher frequency for the rest of your life, and once again a new grounding will be evident.

This exercise is harder for those on medications to detect, but it will happen.

Once again, please don't just dismiss all that you connected to. Every pattern of life repeated time and time again needs small or large amounts of neutralization, yes. You do not keep repeating every emotion, feeling, and out-of-balance scenario in your life.

Using this formula, we are able to release many out-of-balance, inharmonious energy situations throughout your whole life. Isn't this worth considering?

After these are balanced, we are able to repeat this process through many past lives, all in one go. To facilitate this, we are going to use the strength of all your parts that are correctly connected to your own personal, collective consciousness.

I'm sorry if you're tired of hearing about all the different consciousnesses, but they are what we are made of, so I guess we need to be aware of every possibility to get them working properly. You might also consider that we are also talking about every particle of yourself responding to consciousness through a connective consciousness response.

Many of you now desire to cleanse in a neutral manner many overbearing thoughts that have constricted your receiving-nature and kept it from receiving. Some of you may sense something pushing on your chest. This just means that the creative aspect of your self is opening up.

At this same moment, the abandonment issues of many lifetimes are falling off you. If certain aspects of ourselves are unable to be sensed effectively, then we end up with insecurity issues.

This is another scenario that is replicated time after time. Most people are aware of a few that are lurking around their depths somewhere.

Notice how your breath just changed for a couple of moments. This may reoccur as you release when you are ready.

Imagine a list of daily events that makes you cringe—including people who give you this same feeling. This is one of those times when you might like to write a list, which could end up longer than you expect. Just for the hell of it, give it a try. Can you see a pattern emerging, or are you afraid to look too deep?

To help you, a new insight is coming in. This is the feeling that your eyes are going back in your head. Those who see efficiently may see many eyes in a row, lined up and joining together, though this will vary for each of you.

The outcome of this is that they will appear to be joining at the centre of your body, where the soul and heart are integrating. You are learning an androgynous aspect of yourself again, integrating the source's energy. This indicates that you are connecting your insight through a source aspect to open a more real self-intuition.

For those of you who are more aware, don't be surprised by an evolved self reentering your life. This is you—all you. This means connecting to what has been going on in your soul and heart of origin. It is integrating with your physical soul and heart, which perhaps you aren't aware of.

This may also open a few different groundings that are just happening as you read. This is an automatic tithing, even with your eyes open, and this may become apparent.

What is going on is that the receptors in your arms and legs are clearing. This is the unwinding feeling that opens up all that you might want to connect to.

Close your eyes, and the activation will begin. Don't be in a hurry. Allow yourself to absorb all that you are being tithed. This is a whole-body activation, but it may be more sensitive in your hands.

After sensing this active tithing, place the left-hand middle finger on the bridge of your nose. What unfolds now will be different for everybody, but it will feel internal. Your head may feel rather light now, as the frequency of your self is rising. To alleviate this, clasp your hands together, please. Another grounding effect will immediately take place.

Remember to take your time and endeavour to interpret all that you are receiving.

If you are standing, don't be surprised that your legs give an indication that this is completed; they sort of buckle. Now you are grounded.

Remember, you have been working on many levels of self-abandonment, where you are unable to access parts of your real abilities and potentials. This is the whole purpose of this chapter, after all. You then used this in a neutral way, without extremely negative or positive current. This allowed you to bring in all your real and present aspects that were blinded by outside energy.

That unfolding was where others had constricted this energy, and this was to free you up. Does this explain what is going on a little better?

Rather than thinking of what you received as a healing, you could think more in terms of an active conversation. This is really what it was—you using your own energy with new purpose.

Now we will resume our discussion on the effects of this interfering energy in your everyday life.

Imagine that instead of creating or making consciousness you need to exist comfortably and send it off to somebody else. This is what your emotions were telling you—but in an opposite way. They were saying, *I must not be worthy of this energy. Somebody else had better receive this.*

The source is showing you that you have been blind to your own needs, desires, and intuition.

To expand on this formula, we will start with your chakra, aura, and meridians, as these now have lots of extra abilities.

At the start, your chakra didn't appear as you now see it. Why would it? There was no separation in it yet; consequently, it looked more like a star than separate or individual areas.

Let me explain. It didn't look like a chakra chart with separated abilities.

This may be a shock to some of you, but not to everyone. Many are working with this new-time energy equation already.

Your whole body appears as a whole energy with everything integrated. This also means that your gravity is totally different as well.

Add to this gravity all the meridians joined directly to your integrated soul and heart. This allows all energy to flow naturally, unhindered by separate energy struggles. Remember, you are using this integrated soul and heart as one now in a present manner.

If we go back to that old chakra chart, meridians are only connected to that chakra. They never integrate to receive real, integrated energy sequences—synchronicity.

This is the main reason I have never focused on the aura, as intuition told me it never represented the real self, only real selves separated. This also meant that the aura was not a true indication of what I desired myself to represent.

If the meridians were not always connected to the integrated soul and heart, then neither were the meridians accessing through a harmonic, balanced ego and karma. Without this, we end up with energy that is not really flowing through the ego and karma to make sure they are balanced and in harmony—which is what we were really asking for.

All of the body's activations are going to be way out of balance, as no harmony could be interpreted. There are lots of separate parts of us that don't connect through our own meridians or through the real ego and karma.

To sum this up conclusively, imagine parts of our separated soul and heart making energy without the ego and karma. This means we can create immense amounts of energy without knowing if it is really needed or not.

First, there is no possibility of harmony. Next, consider what the ego and karma do: they balance. Whether or not they are within all the harmonic parameters, they must be conclusively of worth to the self.

Now that we have parts of the self going around this aspect of our self, much is created needlessly. This takes a bit to get your head around, doesn't it? But this is why we are unhappy with a lot that we have ended up with in this life. This we can understand.

You see, the strength of the aspects we are creating depends on how we create.

How does this work out? Well, say we want a new car. There would probably be a few aspects of our self that would decide this, yes. We would send all the signals through to make this happen. But what if a lot of this signal goes through without going through the ego and karma?

Remember that earlier in the book I asked you to weigh up in each hand where the greatest mass was. Was it in the really connected or separated mass? It's quite a shock to think that this scenario exists, but it does.

If you had just been following the emotion of desiring something, would you have been aware of this complexity of life?

Actually, our emotions give us many clues as to where or why something isn't correct. It is provided as a clue to how and why these emotions were created in the first place.

Without the emotion, you would have thought everything in this aspect of your life was complete, when in fact it wasn't.

The source is showing you that we have many purposes or reasons for not doing everything in a balanced, harmonious way. We also blame the ego and karma as reasons that something has happened, yes.

Now we have to backtrack somewhat to our response, especially when we find out that the poor, old ego and karma weren't even *able* to be involved, and that they had been abandoned. This also means that you sense acute abandonment, as you are not able to contribute and balance all harmony of yourself. This is amplified when you also can't contribute to the harmony of others, even when you are intimately involved.

Quite an eye-opener, isn't it? This took masses of questions and head-banging until I realized I had missed something. This is what the source showed me about how we can reconnect purpose into our lives.

We have unconsciously abandoned self-balance. Each time we thought something needed to be created, we were perhaps out of balance, right from the start.

This shows you a different angle of how we have created many different scenarios. It is difficult to be responsible in many aspects of our lives, especially when all indications show that we have been doing everything that was correct in our eyes.

Think about this a little longer; your own responses might astound you.

We don't need to beat ourselves up over past responses, since all self-reason was never able to respond to real purpose. Think about it.

So, now we have two sets of separate responses.

First, we have the real and corresponding response, the one where the complete consciousness of our spirit's integrated soul and heart integrated with the soul and heart of physical self. If we entertain that it is possible to use a new-time inception, reconceived in a present time sequence in a real and true manner, then we understand where to start to receive all that we are asking for.

Second, we have neutralized the abandoned self—past, present, and future—that was used to create the alternating sequences that reflected what they were created from: separated and abandoned consciousnesses without self-response or purpose.

At the same time we were creating what we really required, we were unaware that we were creating undesired outcomes. We needed to decide which were correct, using the awareness made available at the moment, and then we made some decisions.

This is probably a good time to remind you of the earlier affirmation and activations. Do you now see how everything is tying in?

Of course, we have a conflict between these two selves, but remember that many of your senses were blind to this scenario, so each was challenging the other.

While we are debilitated and blinded, the separated consciousness has an ally. The separated consciousness looks around at everybody else and follows, without question, the direction determined by the mass of energy.

This is something I need to put into our language as well.

Anytime separated consciousness is created, it is over negative current. We know this isn't great for us, and we don't desire it one bit, but it's a decision we are all comfortable with, and we don't challenge the scenario. This means that if we are aware of this energy, we sense it quite often. We ask ourselves why we have interpreted it, and we want it fixed straightaway. This is a natural response, yes.

We are able to do it ourselves or get help to shift it, or we learn to live with it, but we remember it is there and what it does.

This means that, when making a decision, you would make sure this was not in any conclusion. This is something we have all learned to do, whether we are aware of it or not. It is a bit like a defence mechanism.

We have followed the energy of others and are doing what the majority are doing.

Consider the next scenario with extreme awareness, as it is absolutely serious. It is so debilitating that comprehending all the effects creates a vast body of interference.

Before another sentence is typed, I just need to get this off my chest, so please think a little longer about what is being translated, and even write it down.

The most debilitating energy in this world today is actually over positive current. This is so under-appreciated and so conflicting that it masks many self-interferences that can leave you gobsmacked. I would love a more appropriate word, but I concede that it would still understate the acute under-awareness of our understanding.

Let's get to the nuts and bolts of this dilemma. When we think of positive energy, we usually think of it as correct, even if it is an *overly* positive energy.

What a grave mistake this is! Imagine a current of over-positive energy hitting a balanced and harmonious current. The impact this creates short-circuits every self-capacity. This is huge, not because it is disruptive but because it is often welcomed.

It is only welcomed because we interpret it as necessary and wanted—or even natural. Why?

I have talked about patterns and schedules before, and you could be following a pattern. But why? This is an abandonment of balanced self, so you can see how often it might be repeated in every aspect of our lives. Give this some extra thought. It is another lightbulb moment of realization, yes?

Remember that you have often followed blindly, without questioning, certain energy equations that are replicated in others, why?

When we were complete, we were the majority. Everybody had energy that did the same thing. Therefore, we were used to following, not so much in blind faith, but where the strongest energy field was directing us. This is blind instinct.

After years of doing this, it was the status quo, and we never challenged where our energy was heading. It was of a positive nature, hence we were unable to detect that it was *overly* positive. Are you catching on?

We need to fully understand this energy so it is never again interpreted as correct. To do this, we will consult the intuition.

While this scenario is still fresh in your mind, perhaps we need to discuss a few other aspects of how this has misdirected our real purposes of energy. When we expand on these misdirected, real purposes of our energy, we interpret that our life is of real purpose and worth.

This also hits the nail on the head as to why we may feel unworthy and life seems empty; you're unable to sense your own creations. Please think about this a little longer. You are not able to sense whether your creations or purchases brings you real joy. Is this another lightbulb moment?

While you are contemplating this, can I also enlighten you to another interfering aspect of life?

Many people have found a way to manipulate this over-positive current for their own benefit. This says that their energy is positively of more worth, and it is another abandoning schedule, played in a different manner.

This thought process means that you think this is positive energy, so it is correct and natural and great to connect to. You are unaware that this is over-positive, so you follow. Some may indicate that you are not worth as much unless you are receiving this over-positive message, and in your unaware reasoning, you think they must be correct.

This scenario is building and building over many lifetimes to quite a positive disability of self-awareness, isn't it?

This scenario was painted for you in the opening chapters in a different manner. I need you to take the source's guidance to understand that this real-life scenario is debilitating us all. Why? This creates a society of people who are consuming others' self-importance, and there are many who do not question this outcome, this artificial love for others.

There is another reason that this was so easy to fabricate. When we are over-negative in nature, we stop questioning because it hurts. Earlier, we discussed how we ended up with so many questions and so many answers. We have responded to real questions as well as illusional questions with real answers and illusional answers. This creates a mass of confusion, as the self-awareness gets a positive result to all questions and answers.

The self is limited in all that it is able to receive or respond to, and it is happy to give away its energy to others. This is positively what the energy is directing as true and positive—as well as over-positively and positively correct.

Why? Well, both are positively positive and positively negative or positively out of balance.

For the self to receive real love is now quite difficult, as these messages you are receiving have a conscious component. Unfortunately, it is not *your* conscious component.

We have been unaware of what our energy was doing because we were consumed with dealing with our emotions. A whole cycle of questions and answers consumed our attention and self-appreciation before we noticed our energy.

The source outlined that there was a separation between the self-spirit, the original soul and heart, and the physical soul and heart, yes. Because we determined that spirit was the direction we naturally followed, we were unable to sense our own spirit from among others. Are you able to comprehend how easy this happened?

This is the source's statement, not mine. It is very important and needs a correct, harmonic balance in order to be conclusively comprehended. It is not an inherited, unconscious feeling of reality. This can also be interpreted as needing a correct response to real information.

If we—in our past lives and our relatives' past lives—were unable to respond to the correct reality or real solution, then which pattern of schedules do you think we would follow now? In a way, we don't want to be responsible for our own self, to receive the love we are asking for. Once again, we hop into a cycle that might even be painful, but we don't ask why.

These two scenarios of current are creating over-positive and over-positive negative currents. When one questions the other's power, there is a lot of short-circuiting.

In plain language, this is fear in the spirit or pain in the physical. This may explain a couple of things—like why we haven't challenged many aspects of our lives or why the outcome was not desired and a lack of current intention occurred.

This statement is important, so please check that it is correct through your integrated soul and heart.

It is so easy for us to consider others more important or more interesting than ourselves. Why? Well, it's quite simple, really. Without reasoning in a balanced, harmonious manner, others can receive all our self-interest. We see their importance as paramount to an illusional security. There are many magazines telling us what celebrities are doing, and we are consuming their self-importance. Had you thought of this?

This inharmonious reaction of reasoning is really the extension and expansion of an inharmonious depth of ascension. These are actual aspects of your self-energy system and its over-response or under-response. We have loads of different energies in a physical and spiritual manner, so we lack any real response.

With an uncreative manner of physical spirit, very little spirit direction is ever received. There is that word again—*received*. We have needed to relearn how to receive in a new manner. This statement is directed to your consciousness so that you now desire to check all currents that you are making or using.

Now you are weighing up which parts of yourself are in balanced harmony and relate to self-harmony. How do we achieve this? You simply ask that all of your real self be neutralized with god-love, which is of a source current.

We are following the image presented in a present manner from before. We are connecting to all affirmations and activations that your true spirit-self has connected to already. This means that, plain and simple, any energy that is not of you will be now made neutral. Therefore, any energy that is over-positive or over-negative will come to a neutral capacity.

Consuming energies will cease to exist on many levels of you, which means you are free, yes, free. Every part of your self is also free to sense a real meaning of worth. This sense of worth, when integrated, creates a wealth of worth.

You are able to sense real life purpose and to know that you are on the right track to finding that life purpose. A real strength of self is created, and you are strong in your own right, able to keep building on this strength, yes.

To help this outcome become a reality, we are going to receive a little source-love to help us.

Some of you who are very sensitive to vibrational changes will notice a pitch of tones moving through your head, and you may become sensitive in an area that has been impacting you.

Teeth, strangely enough, are most affected, as they represent this over-positive feeling of self-resentment for allowing this energy to push you around.

At this moment, you are asking to free this self-guilt again. Remember, your capacity to reason with all self-abilities has been interfered with, so don't dwell on this any longer.

Before discussing any other facet of this interference, here is a neutralizing affirmation to correct yourself abilities and to enable you to sense all that is not harmonious in yourself.

All self-presence is now brought to an efficient presence of all real purpose in a creative manner of source-love.

Each presence of this source-love re-intends all self-intentions and desires to be only of a self-purpose of presence.

Every reality of this self opens a real future to real self-worth in a real, intuitive manner.

I open every appreciation of self to this wealth of creative gratitude, to be formed in, and only in, a true capacity of real compassion and to confirm conclusively that all real self-love exists in a real purpose.

Therefore, I am complete in each and every nature, in each and every presence of new-time, future resources. Therefore, I am now able to resonate at and in all new-time frequencies and vibrations.

This affirmation is intended to immediately bring in the harmony you are asking for.

This means that many areas of yourself that have never been able to sense this purpose will now need to ground. This is why you may feel that you are going down.

On the sides of your body, you may also sense that you are unfolding. This aspect of yourself has not been appreciated before, as you were never able to interpret that it existed. This also will mean that the energy that has been suppressing your spirit will free up somewhat.

Next, there is an uplifting motion, as the ascension integrates these aspects of yourself that were never able to connect as whole bodies, only as separated consciousnesses.

If the spirit-strength is not strong, then you are not using connective consciousness in an efficient manner. This is why affirmations have been used to strengthen every step of self-consciousness.

Once again, hold the flat of your left hand in front of your chest.

The swirling motion you may be sensing all around yourself is now opening an appreciation. This is a response, and you may have blocked this activation of appreciation for the major part of your life. The positively positive and the positively negative are losing the power to divert your strength from sensing that it is being interfered with.

Please swap hands now. A depth of consciousness that has never been activated before is moving throughout your body, and the intention you activated before is ready to move. This activation means many separated, conscious parts of you desire to contribute to your life once again.

Wow! Imagine that. Over-positive energy actually interferes with our senses, which means that we can't tell, or collate, what is going on energy-wise in our own bodies. Since you were unaware of over-positive energy, were you aware that this over-positive impact made you unable to sense what is really going on? This took a bit to get my head around. For a while, I just mulled it over.

This is how the source explained the phenomena of over-positive positivity to me.

To start with, imagine something you want or need to create by your own self-desire, yes. Now, just to show what can happen in the real world, imagine that your desire is linked to the intent of another person's over-positive consciousness. Can this happen? Absolutely.

This over-capacity you are unable to sense is actually happening. That's right. This is how a controlling nature works. This self-desire then creates what it believes the self is asking for. After this is created, there is no fulfillment, so no appreciation is sensed either, and the whole process feels flat.

Remember, this all started out when you were unable to sense what collated as your own spirit and what added up to be another's energy.

Now imagine this schedule of another's intent. After a while, the self-appreciation is not responding, the self-gratitude is negligible, and the self is sensing little self-achievement.

There is another energy that needs a little more explanation, as it is positive interference personified.

Energy that is both our own energy and another's over-positive unconsciousness is *interfering telepathy*. It is an incorporation of your energy and intent with another's desire.

Did you just have another lightbulb moment? Yes, this is how incorporated bodies—definitely not belonging to a correct body of matter—were created. Add this definition to those we discussed in earlier chapters, and you are now easily able to define a conclusive understanding of how we have been manipulated so often.

This incorporation of energy is one that has grown in power, and many are now unconsciously using and consuming this energy.

There is a real purpose to this chapter. You need to be made aware of many creations that may have been made without any real purpose to yourself.

This may peeve you somewhat to find this out, but not knowing means we can't fix it, and I desire to be blind to nothing. Remember, this isn't to be viewed as negative energy, just unbalanced energy that has debilitated our self-awareness.

A couple of months ago, I wanted to buy a set of oversize window blinds, and I hunted around everywhere until I found them at a price I could afford and ordered them. After ringing to check that they had arrived, I went to pick them up. This meant driving sixty kilometres, which takes a bit of time—only to find that the wrong ones had arrived.

I then went to find presents for a couple of relations, but all were sold out. Bugger. I asked if picking up the window blinds had caused disruption that I was blind to.

The reason I have put in this personal entry is that I use synchronicity and emotions as a guide. If all of a sudden things aren't going right, or if my emotions are quite acute, then I want to know why immediately.

In the early chapters, we discussed how we had separated consciousness that was sitting more or less outside our main, conscious body. This interference shows how it was separated in the first place.

When you are confronted by an overbearing person using immense amounts of over-positive energy, what do you do? You either put up a barrier to stop the infiltration of this energy, or you use your own energy the same way.

Please consider the outcome of this power struggle. It is a scenario that creates holes in your energy as well as your protective layers, which then appear to look like portals. We discussed this before. Through these portal-like holes, it is easy for others' energy to invade certain aspects of ourselves.

You had better check that this is correct. Remember that it is important for your awareness to be correct and ready to correspond to new awarenesses. Once you are aware of any situation, it is possible to reconnect conscious parts that have disengaged.

This is what was outlined after the affirmation, so why am I going over it again? Because there is still a major part of yourself to be reconnected. To highlight this reconnection, many keys and codes of light will be connecting to many unresponsive aspects.

What I describe may sound like a Looney Tunes cartoon, but this is how I see the energy working, and it is also how many have described it without my input.

The first image is connected to previous activations. Imagine many spirals of energy releasing, which means that your spirit-body looks rather elongated. This is where you were constricted.

Next, you may sense that there is some energy pouring back into yourself. These are aspects of yourself that were always there but were not really doing anything until now.

As these aspects of yourself come together, you are creating an immense strength in yourself again. When you are stronger, you are able to concentrate on yourself and consciously connect corresponding, conscious self-messages automatically. This will probably continue for around half an hour.

This is probably a good time to put the book down for a moment. Remember, you are not simply reading a book for information; you are connecting to awareness of energy that can help you in the future.

Yes, that is correct. Take at least half an hour. You can relax and sense where this is all integrating, or you can go about a couple of other tasks about your home, but please don't watch TV.

If your self hasn't responded immediately, this just means that you haven't sensed your new senses opening. Nonetheless, it is still taking place.

Remember, you need a break now.


Welcome back. Please clasp your hands in front of your navel. Once again, you are grounding. Some of you may sense that this is of a more clear nature. Please give this a couple of minutes or until you sense that your hands feel like dropping.

The rest of this activation is something you might sense while relaxing, but most probably it will become more apparent in the early hours of the morning. This is the time when you are strengthening your self-purpose or when all self-power is translating where energy needs to become present.

This is important, because you are consciously translating how to efficiently use energy, self-belief, self-faith, and one aspect that has gone unnoticed for many lives—although we still assume that this element of our self is alive and kicking: the will.

The will is something I assumed was complete, as I thought I constantly used it. Well, I did use it but in a very limited manner. If the real spirit is unable to be defined or registered, then we are unable to sense how many of our own intentions are of our own spirit and how many are the contributions of others.

This immense unawareness has meant that in the past—and I also mean all past lives—so much of our self-will has fallen by the wayside without our being aware of it.

The will is such a vital component. It is a why we lose strength in our self-faith and belief.

Imagine the real strength that is held in the spirit. It is how we stabilize our spirit in all parts of us to be strong enough to hold real and vital balance. If we were unable to sense how much of our present self was of us and how much was of others, then it is quite apparent that our self-strength was debilitated, yes.

So, what is the spirit-area of our self that converts all self-power to strength? It is the self-will, and it is another vital commodity of our connective consciousness to keep it strong and vital.

Let me clarify. Others' wills are mostly the desires of past relatives. They acted unconsciously with unconscious responses to other people's wills.

Multiply this pattern of unconscious reactions over many lifetimes and it becomes the unconscious, relative response that you react to unconsciously, with unconscious reasoning and reactions. This means that as your self has grown in purpose and responses, you are able to strengthen the self-will without rebounding or physical effects.

This was indicated in the first affirmation you read and is also reflected in the vibrational change of yourself.

With higher vibrational frequencies, these unconscious bodies cease to exist. We turn all self-power into self-strength, because all interferences cease to exist, or we move away from all unconscious reactions or responses.

We do this by becoming conscious in every manner with the aid of connective consciousness. Then no interference is able to unconsciously exist in our direction, is it?

This also means that you are leaving past, inadequate frequencies and vibrations. Therefore, harmonies are to be consciously raised and made present in all of self. This ensures that all self-futures follow suit. Is this easy enough to comprehend?

Many debilitated, unconscious, life unawarenesses that are separate from intuition need to be rectified in the following affirmation and activations.

There is a real will of new-time, future purpose. It is a real will of new-time intuition that opens all self-abilities and enables all self-physical matter to absorb the integrating harmonies needed to open all automatic strengthening.

This, then, opens your self-direction of all self-faith and belief, or it simply opens all for the self-will to receive in a present manner. This occurs while focusing all rejuvenation and regeneration in a present manner, not just in a past manner.

Reflecting on this outcome means that this energy never reached the self before in a present way, only in a past way.

This is something we talked about earlier. In a way, we were always concentrating on trying to fix up the past, thinking it would automatically fix all present energy or outcomes.

To put this in another way, perhaps you can think about how we have lived unconsciously, constantly reflecting on what we do not have. This is a life of trying to fix up past-life regrets and resentment. Remember, unconsciousness was the key aspect to be released from our self-intuitive nature, so we don't want to repeat this.

Conscious responses to all we have use connective, collective consciousness, as this indicates the reflection of all true, conscious matter.

I would love an easy way to reflect all that was just outlined, but because this is so important, I pray that you understand why I have persisted. This preparation is relative to all self-nurturing so that the self doesn't rebound this new strength, and so that this energy ends up in the right place.

All true self-will is now to be of an evolved self-focus, with a will of a new, true self-nature.

This creative self-nature opens a true resilience to any destructive natures that are not of self-desire or intention.

This self-matter opens all self-environments to restore all self-abilities of true self-worth and fortunes. Now they are only to be absorbed in a true, self-present presence of all self-future purposes, opening every evolved, material matter.

Each and every self-matter ensures that no synthetic or unnatural nature is ever reflected in any real self-intuition, gravity, or magnetic projection. It is not to be of self-energy, and it is never to be magnified in another's worth.

As this self reflects only on each and every self-focus, all self-gratitude opens in a new time of self-creation, integrating with all self-humanity, which is the strength of all self-collective, connective consciousnesses.

For those who see easily, this will be like passing through many gates at the same time that many overbearing personalities are passing by as their energy is neutralized.

If you would be so gracious as to hold your arms out to the sides of your body, please, a new grounding in the extension and expansion of your self will be sensed. This is a rather rapid grounding, as so much of your self is to be reconnected.

Remember to clasp your hands together for a moment. This will immediately and automatically integrate your intent and real-life desire. It might seem weird, but it does work.

If you haven't written down this grounding, now might be an opportune time to do so. I advise that you do this exercise before bed and when you wake up. It keeps your energy flowing, so there are no critical mass imbalances.

People I have never met before—but whom I have sent a phone healing to—are often shocked at the balance they receive by holding their hands somewhere, and this helps people with stress or anxiety. Please remember to write this down to remind yourself.

Also remember that most nights you connect to self-desires and information, so it might be worth getting in the habit of repeating this exercise each morning. This keeps your energy more efficient and grounded.

Let's go back to our conversation about what we are—or aren't—aware of and what has been stifling our life-purposes.

Imagine how many different abilities of yourself exist now. Imagine how many different energies we need to become aware of for these to operate. Only so many can be reconnected at one time, or the new awareness would be overwhelming. Therefore, this needs to be repeated a few times, and each time you—your spirit and your physical body—are stronger.

Your new awareness means that you're breaking down what you were used to at the same time you're breaking old-time habits and past-life patterns. With each reconnection and self-strengthening, you are responding less to others' overpowering desires and intentions. You are automatically adjusting with all self-will through your self-awareness.

In each step, you also create new purpose and reasoning for every action in your day. This is easy to comprehend, isn't it? Your self-will is also strengthening all self-belief and faith with your own energy—yes, your own energy. Is this appreciation sinking in?

When we think about all that we have been enlightened to or have been made aware of, it is easy to comprehend today's consuming nature and throwaway society.

Before we go too much further, did you remind yourself with that note the source asked you to write? Regrounding really is so important.

So many people are consumed with what others are doing. Why is celebrity status so important? Do people just want to consume each others' self-importance instead of considering their own self-worth?

This scenario is an energy equation that relates to whether your self-power is converted to self-strength or is given away as power to others. Thus, you consume their importance and give away your worth.

Another thought that might be worth considering is this. Imagine that over time there would be quite a bit of power attached to a particular person. This power is used to split one's spirit-consciousness, and then the physical is left quite debilitated. This is why we are opening you to an awareness of many scenarios and many schedules that affect our self-strength today.

This just reiterates why we tithe and never simply give or take, yes.

Does this, then, begin to address a few modern-day life equations and to answer questions about why our directions are at times so skewed?

You see, even with correct intent—but with a weak sense of self-spirit—the illusional desire of another's power eventually interfered and allowed you to succumb.

Remember, we have been discussing telepathy, reading others' energy, and communicating through our energies.

If you relented and followed what everybody's energy was doing, then all of a sudden you would find different current but with much the same energy.

But really, this isn't how you interpreted it at all. If those around you are reflecting a certain energy sequence, then the chances are that you will automatically follow without questioning, because you are using telepathy unconsciously and are hardly aware of this fact.

This is why the source desires to make you aware of so many self-abilities that you simply don't use or have the awareness to use in an intuitive manner.

When we have the strength to reflect on real self-desire and intentions—as we now question our direction automatically—the image is something we have continuously reflected on. We are constantly opening the self-will, never again to be separated from all self-abilities and self-purposes in a conscious manner.

Another reason we didn't want to respond to being aware is that we were separated from all that we are not just conscious of. This is why I have often reflected on the wealth of worth that the connective consciousness allows us to reconnect with.

You see, we could have followed the past fairy-floss or sugarcoated view that "one day you will understand, my beloved." But now is the time to be aware, not separate from this awareness and unable to respond to real self-purpose.

Already we have outlined many different scenarios to remedy this situation. This is why we outline that something exists, how it exists, where it can affect you, and why it can affect you. This outline is to teach that each of these situations causes a reaction, and in the end, an emotion.

This emotion was caused by one part of your heart—and all that is connected to it—not being able to communicate with the corresponding soul and all that is connected to it.

We desire to defuse many situations before they become inharmonious circuitry, each creating surges of current as they try to find a link to communicate with the desired opposite energy, automatically using connective consciousness.

When this surge of current is defused, many emotions that were constantly rebounding are able to be neutralized.

All source is asking for is that you become aware of a release that is opening at this moment. This sensation of energy is presently flowing through your body. You may experience a swimming motion, but it will also entail in a rising motion, as this is responding to your rising vibrations.

Clasp your hands together, and then bring them to just under your chin. This is not a repeat of an earlier exercise; it's just similar. Now, bring your elbows up, parallel to the hand-clasp. This exercise helps to raise the frequency in the self-appreciation.

Please just sit still and notice this outward flow of inharmonious energy. It has built up in your physical body and is asking to be neutralized.

Automatically, in a moment, you will sense that your arms are dropping. Please allow them to do so.

Please stand, and then bring your arms and clasped hands to a comfortable position, as once again you reground your self-energy, rising as you ground.

Please remember that you were also connecting to consciousness of a higher vibration and frequency as this exercise was explored.

As we return to the conversation, we are exploring all possibilities of what we connected to.

This means stopping overpowering energy from compounding all self-energy. We also discussed impounding energy and how this is often sensed in overly sensitive teeth and acute awareness in the back, like pins and needles.

Compound any energy and it becomes what? Constricted. So you also create power surges. This scenario is a reaction to all that has happened physically.

This is something that your own consciousness was exploring, and it will continue to explore it for some time. Pease remember this.

Once your consciousness desires to move, so will you. Once you consciously desire change, you will change.

Once you desire full-time, conscious responses, your life follows this direction, and then your self-direction is always going to receive collective consciousness help with a source—or god-content. Please consider this statement. As you surmised, I channeled this quote.

Let's return to our conversation once again. Knowing that a healing is going to be taking place for weeks to come, please consider the constrictions that the source has been indicating need releasing. We also need to consider that the reactions to the responses need releasing as well.

This conglomeration, of course, is a response to the emotions as the wrong signal goes out to the wrong receivers. Why? Constrictions create larger cycles. This is why questions and answers get lost or are unable to meet or communicate; the cycle has become immense. Does this also answer a couple of questions as to why we are unable to relate to self-questioning?

This is why you need to learn how to receive. Really, you need to be able to receive the question to the correct, corresponding answer. Is this another lightbulb moment, or is the relevance of this just passing you by? If it's the latter case, perhaps you have been skimming and not really reading the full implications of what has been outlined for you.

There are many releases written into the phrases connected to tithings and affirmations, and you need to learn to sense them and connect to them. Sometimes you need to release to receive. This is what you have been doing throughout this entire book.

When this is of a neutral, free nature, you automatically create self-efficiency. Notice those harmonizing tones; the wealth of them is almost invaluable. But you will need to find out their worth.

Remember, you are sensing differently now, so you understand differently. You comprehend using different levels of conscious cognizance of different and unused senses. Please think about this and remember it.

Why would the source ask this? You are creating the foundations that enable you to grasp the enormous moves and shifts in consciousness that are already happening and will continue to amplify in the present future. When you learn to sense more efficiently or to combine many conscious feelings, you become more aware of the interfering elements. This makes living in the old-time energy unbearable, confusing, and difficult.

You see, while you have been reading this, you have been relearning many senses, as they flow from both your spirit and physical body. This means that you are becoming more aware of everything you no longer desire. You are able to understand that this energy has been distributing the wrong current to a wrong capacity, thus causing power surges.

This is becoming apparent throughout your consciousness, so you are beginning to reground in a new and more efficient manner. Notice that, in a now-presence, it may be possible for you to sense even your face grounding. This is working real activations all the way down through your body. Yes, it's a strange sensation, to say the least.

You now acknowledge that your senses are becoming conscious, and your conscious senses respond to being connected to collective consciousness.

Don't think for a moment that both are the same thing at all, but you are facing up to many self-facts that your spirit-consciousness wants you to address. This may also be sensed as your face moving into or though your head, checking for different responses.

It is important to note that we are not focusing on the interference or the surging energy. They were like a dual cache in our collective, conscious network. We have an energy net that connects all connective, conscious networks to ensure our real direction and focus.

Perhaps you thought you would be focusing on illusional emotions caused by surging power rather than correct, strong current, but this was not our direction. We want to make everyone aware of what is part of our existence, not our focus.

Otherwise, you don't appreciate what is so fabulous or complete in you. No compassion or current is sent to the whole, real you. Instead, this current is sent to the interference. This is why the source asked your intuition to respond to what was just outlined to you.

This is the whole point of affirmations, which give a conscious direction, response, reasoning, and conclusion.

Why are we revisiting this? In all previous, interfering scenarios, the unawareness created a schedule. After a while, this became a pattern, and you simply forgot to send any current to the self to sense a little appreciation.

This is why the source is asking you to learn how to sense. Then you can diagnose all that is conscious energy and all that is not. This a simple enough equation to learn. Remember why it is relevant to sense and not feel in an unconscious manner.

Feelings can indicate anything, because they are refractions of the reflection, so you could be refracting on both real and interfering energy. Also remember that very little consciousness is ever connected.

We never reflected on the old aura, because it reflected what was separate, and we were unaware of what was separate and did not use it. Thus no current energy flowed. Without proper awareness we are committed to making the same life mistakes life after life.

Now, in an aware manner, you are able to conclude that our real focus was to be consciously aware of all conscious and unconscious energy, which we desire with all intention to be relevant, never separate nor incoherent.

If we analyse the statement about the senses gaining consciousness, it indicates that you have connected to a consciousness that you were previously unable to sense due to interference. Now the current is gaining a capacity of strength to neutralize any interfering energy that desires to interfere with this current and, most importantly, its connection.

That draining sensation, which you just read about and have been grounding through your sacred spirit, is the strength of current in a harmonious capacity of your own collective consciousness.

I realize that this last bit was a bit heavy, to say the least, but this information was more directed at your consciousness. If it seemed a little intense, don't worry about it. There is an automatic component. But please remember that many people with different abilities may be reading this, so we are endeavouring to please everybody.

You are now aware enough to relate to wealth of self, which is available through the whole collective consciousness of all that exists. It is communicating with you through your self-collective-consciousness. Does it make sense that you need to relearn how to sense?

This is written in a repeating manner so the correct parts of your self can finally connect in a correct manner to the correct aspect with a correct, harmonious, balanced sense of self-appreciation, gratitude, and compassion.

Simply, this is to re-teach everyone how to re-sense so that all are able to re-sense real love, which corresponds and connects to their real self without interferences. In truth, this is the purpose of this whole book, and many will follow.

We have already discussed this from many angles, and it is immensely important. Why? Because of insufficient current awareness. You were busy reflecting on the emotion of what you desired to create instead of focusing on where to get the energy to create it.

This lack of current is a result of not having a connective consciousness direct from our integrated soul and heart, which is where the strength of your whole self and purpose comes from.

Do you understand the importance of that last sentence? If not, please think about it a little longer.

Why did this happen? Because we were concentrating on getting the emotion right, desiring the heart to communicate with the soul.

Remember, the soul gives the heart direction. Without it, the heart is directionless. Perhaps you are aware that, as you read this, you are moving in a new manner. If you are not, be still as you go to sleep tonight. This energy will be there.

This is the reason for the new time or new millennium. In truth, this is about changing everything for good, not just for one millennium.

Perhaps now you can see that living in constant, unconscious fear doesn't add up to enjoyment or harmony. This means that devolution is as constant as evolution.

You see, what exists in your unconsciousness is separate from your awareness. Isn't it time to utilize this component of your self? It is more vast than our conscious component. Are you understanding what the source is stating now? Do you get it? Do you comprehend all that we are missing out on? This is the unequivocal reason for the new millennium.

Remember, if we are creative beings, then we are creating unconsciously as well as consciously. Had you considered this? Think about what we are unconsciously contributing to. Had you pondered this unconscious matter or the effects on our real and conscious matter? This could be quite huge in terms of our awareness responses or reactions.

The flip side of this is that we are also contributing to our selves in an unaware manner. Emotions don't give us a clue; they are just a response to an unaware reaction. These are not my words, but they do echo what I have sensed. Most of this information I accessed years ago. So, what is going to be relative to us in the present?

This is why we are changing. We really desire with all real intention through all self-will and desire to have a new time. Through our entire real, connective, collective consciousness, we are asking for this.

Yes, we are actually asking this through our collective consciousness, through the source's collective conscious of all that exists in a real-time sequence of continuous, sequential, androgynous love.

The source is very firm about this. What is the sense of saying that one day you'll wake up and notice all that you have been missing out on, my beloved? Wake up. We need to respond now in a present manner. That is why the source is affirming us to now be firm in the resolution of our desires and intentions.

I would have loved to include many superlatives to underline the immensity of all that we have been missing out on. That's why spirituality is alive now. Please examine all that has been revealed to you. Don't dismiss your potential. It is your choice. We are free to take whichever road we choose.

Remember, this energy of the source's collective consciousness is all about you, waiting for you to ask for help in a conscious manner through your whole collective body.

No self-power is greater than any other; your female energy is equal to your male energy.

You had better check this, though. Use your integrated soul and heart, your balanced self-desire, your intuitive, new-time, intentional desires, and your whole, creative self-will. Are you checking now? I mean, *really* checking?

You see, the source is showing you that perhaps not everything is as it appears. We need to appreciate *what* exists and what is *of* an existence and remember the difference between the two. It is time to concede that not everything is working in a harmonious manner and that certain aspects, elements, and essential essences need changing.

If we think back to a couple of things we have already discussed, the resolution may not seem quite so formidable. We ascertained that when we separated some of the energy systems, this left us unaware of certain breakdowns in communication between the energy used in the soul only and in the heart only, yes.

The ego and karma indicate the harmonic balance and where this structure is debilitated. We have concluded that this separates the spirit and physical consciousness in many ways, but we also have a real memory, a real record of how this devolved.

In plain language, this means that wrong energies were going to a wrong aspect of our self. Your real source-self is unconsciously aware that a whole lot of your energy was conceived and received in an inharmonious pattern.

How come? Well, if something is created in harmony, then your self and the whole collective consciousness keeps a record. This is not really your desire, will, or intent, so you can't be held responsible.

We discussed this before when we discussed the ego and karma. The source outlined that this energy balances and harmonizes to keep the soul and heart communicating in a real manner, so imagine all the energy that is unable to find its real destination. Yes, it just hangs around either the ego or karma, waiting for an outcome. This is how all this energy became an attachment.

This now attachment is a record of misdirected unconscious energy that became what, our destiny, and a cycle of desires not able to be fulfilled, or baggage.

This has taken years to translate, but no matter which source I interpret from, the same outcome occurs.

Does, this seem incorrect? Well, there is a conclusion that the source would like us to respond to. If all that has been created in an inharmonious manner is over-positive or over-negative, then the self is unable to respond in a real manner. Please take this on board and use these conclusions.

Whenever we sensed a positive current, we left ourselves open to anything that came with this current. This scenario breaks down the strength in every form of self-desire, intention, and will. Now imagine these core components of self-strength being unable to respond in a purposeful manner. Why? Because of the breakdown of self-core foundations. Now do you comprehend the source's direction to reconnect to these base foundations?

This actually means that a whole lot of future is unable to be created. Yes, we open many new lines of communication each time we are reborn, but we end up following old ways. Remember, we all think that our destiny is our real path. Now what do you think?

Earlier, we defined destiny as a cycle with an indefinite outcome, or a cycle with no destination. There is a need for definite direction or an affirmation or activation in advance. Without knowing what you are missing out on, you might reject all that you are meant to receive, so you need a new way to receive, yes. The source desires that we all create in a new presence of manner, yes?

In plain language, this means that when you create in a harmonious manner, your self responds and immediately and automatically integrates. This is the strength of your self-will creating self-desire and faith.

Most importantly, we aren't reconnecting to deactivated energy or attachments, which is another reason we were asked to clear out all self-clutter or baggage. Does this resonate with you differently now?

You are now going to connect all self-connective-consciousness to all that reflects your own self-source. This is then connected to the whole collective consciousness of all real source that exists. You are able to interact with real purpose to all real self-responses intended for you—and only you—to receive in a correct manner from every source of energy.

This purpose of self-redefinition is a response to all energies. It must now be of a connective-consciousness throughout all self-presence, and it is only of your will, your desire, your intention, your own faith, and your own self-belief.

Some of you may have interpreted a grounding motion again or perhaps a tickling in your nose to indicate that the source is giving a true direction, yes.

Please clasp your hands together. Integrate with your own will and a desire for your life to be of a real, sensed purpose that reflects a real self-future.

Hold on to the sensation that you are grounding your desires, intentions, and will. You are creating your strength now, in a real time. Therefore, you are of a presence in each and every moment. This is the strength of connective, conscious self-will.

This does take some time as you are traveling through many unconscious self-matters in both spirit and the physical at exactly the same time.

Please stand now, and don't hurry. Notice that you are rising and grounding. This is to facilitate constant, real-time consciousness all of the time. In a moment, you will fully ground as your legs sense a buckling.

This is like connecting consciousness in a meditation and then holding conscious energy and activations to use daily. This is the part I can't wait to share with you in person. It is very special, once you realize the implications of what is being shared with you.

This will open many interpretations for you, but it is something that needs to be brought in gradually, or you will reject all new sensing.

Perhaps it might also be worth making a few notes that this new ability will unfold gradually. Please notice that the smallest changes become huge when you join them together.

Go on. Write a reminder note to yourself.

I realize that parts of this chapter may have been a little confrontational. The source wanted it this way to ensure that everything was as easy as possible while connecting to all relevant information in this conversation.

Once again, you were asked to think outside the square of old-world belief schedules. I hope this information has helped open a new-time future with real self-purpose throughout all self-consciousness.

All of this has been defined to be of this new-time purpose, and it leads us to a new-time self-gravity so that all we are asking for gravitates to us.

You did make a reminder note, didn't you?

# 15

## THE GRAVITY OF SOURCE CONVERSATIONS

Had you considered that gravity plays a massive part in our self makeup and our daily lives? Nor had I, until synchronicity dictated that I stumble upon it purposefully one day.

You see, I had been surprised that a particular person's energy was so constricted and unaligned. Her critical mass was terribly out of alignment, and automatically I knew why.

Have you experienced automatic intuition? Hopefully, this will become a common occurrence as your strength becomes more apparent. This also affects your true strength.

So, what was this debilitating factor? Well, as the title suggests, this conversation is about magnetic current, and where magnetic current goes, gravity needs to be considered.

At some time in our lives, all of us have pondered the effects of the moon on ourselves, even if it is only out of concern for mood swings or changes. Have you ever considered why some people are more affected than others?

There are, of course, a few scenarios to unfold here, but they easily intertwine, so let's get to the crux of the matter. My intuition automatically told me that this person's energy pattern was following a wrong gravity alignment.

Why? She was following the earth's axis and was always off by the same number of degrees. This is when my guide's guidance was way more pronounced and showing me the energy lines that were in conflict with this lady's energy system.

The most interesting matter here was that her spirit-body was in alignment; however, her physical body's alignment not only registered the earths axis, but the energy in between them was keeping the spirit-energy from aligning to the physical. I then looked at the aliments and constrictions in this lady's muscle constrictions, and all matched up perfectly with her contortions.

Let's return to our conversation of how the spirit and physical energy are split or unable to respond to the physical limitations.

By now you know that this isn't good. As the spirit guides the physical, the spirit-collective-consciousness guides all that are able to be connected automatically. So here was another massive chunk of physical unconsciousness that could not be helped automatically.

My guides soon fixed this lady's gravity. Automatically, all of this person's energy system changed quickly. Actually, this change has already been implemented right at the start of this book, in the second activation you received, but there was no way you would have understood the implication that early on.

Now, we need to discuss another part of this affirmation that you received early on. Many of your whole bodies were able to integrate or become whole.

Is there something dropping into place? Yes, as each self becomes whole, this aspect of your self is able to be reimplemented. Each time you sense a whole self-body align, it becomes conscious.

If each body is of a correct gravity, a correct alignment, the magnetic attraction must automatically be greater. The greater the alignment, the greater the magnetic attraction. Is this another lightbulb moment?

Consider this: the greater the magnetic attraction, the greater the implementation of self-resources or self-gratitude and the ability to receive. Yes, this then breaks down to being able to connect to all that you desire.

There is another facet to this equation. Had you considered that the moon's gravity also pronounces where the self isn't communicating properly? Why?

This is the short version, of course, but it covers the bases. We need to understand this. If you had two energy bodies working at two different axes, one mass of energy would always relate to the body—in our case, it is the spirit—and the second, physical mass would only relate sometimes.

I guess you need to visualize this to comprehend it. Imagine a line flowing from your head to your feet. It would pass straight through your nose and navel and between your feet, yes.

Now, use this same line and adapt the earths axis line. It starts at your left shoulder and travels through your knee. Quite a different line, isn't it? Consider what this does to your energy system, as you are instantly cutting off so many sensory senses.

This is limiting your physical capabilities, constricting many. This is why the lady I mentioned was flat-out not moving, yet half an hour later, she was able to walk nearly normally and go to work the next day.

Perhaps you haven't factored in how this also limits your thoughts, comprehension, sensory perception, and all muscle responses.

It's quite a list, isn't it? But for now I just want to focus on what happens in a full moon. Your gravity line straightens up, and you are instantly aware of where you are limited or the areas that are vastly affected, so you will overcompensate, yes.

There is another reaction that happens sometimes. You can swing to the opposite spectrum, meaning that your subconscious desires surface. Take into account that some of these have been buried for ages, yes, meaning that they are only going to surface when they are of a greater mass than your real consciousness.

Remember that they are only of such great mass because past life limits this life's conscious mass. Does this make sense?

The only real parts are now in a part-time relationship or are only able to contribute spasmodically, so in a way you can't relate to your own spirit. Had you thought of this scenario?

The next equation that needs considering is the fact that you have created true matter that relates to you *and* matter that doesn't. Had you thought of this? What does it end up doing?

Well, bit by bit this energy has been neutralised. If energy is not of a real self-relationship, then there is no way for it to be connected to your consciousness. This is like energy that has never been fully conceived, isn't it? This is the draining energy you sensed so often. Now it is not reflecting back on your future. This also means that in time you will reflect on all of the relationships you were unable to conceive, as you have been continually repeating this desire.

Because this desire was never fully conceived, the energy was never in a complete circuit. The desire was able to be conceived in a real alignment of our self-gravity, so it stayed and repeated. This was like interference, reflected as separating energy, and this energy held the spirit and the physical apart.

The self-energy of consciousness with real ethics and virtues held strong, as others seemed to fall by the wayside. Perhaps you released some baggage that never seemed to fit in your physical life.

I'll give you my version. My boat gives me joy in a few different ways. First, I enjoy the ocean, and I connect to many of the spiritual elements that are reflected in the sea. No, I am not of a water sign, just in case you related me to it, but I can tell you that I smile each time I'm out on a boat.

Second, each time I head out, it is usually with family and friends, so we have a great time. My sister refers to this as going out to get a bit of fresh air, referring to the fact that we don't always catch a load of fish. But I don't just go out to get as many fish as I can; I just enjoy the company and the elements. In fact, a coffee cup is just as essential as a fishing rod.

All I'm saying is that we all enjoy many different things, but this doesn't mean that they need to consume our lives or be our reason for living. There are many different elements to be enjoyed in this life, and we need not concentrate on just one of them.

The reason I brought this up is that the self-gravity can narrow our self-focus on what we enjoy. It can also limit our focus on the rest of our relationships and make us miss opportunities, as we are focusing on what we think is bringing joy.

There is a reason for my little story. It demonstrates that it is easier to see all that you have rather than what you don't have. Make the most of what you have with all who bring you real joy.

This was reflected when I shared with you that Julie and I had faith and belief that Dad would be fine, even though he was in a coma. We used our self-connection to his will, which we defined as connective consciousness, bringing every aspect of spirit and physical matter to real matter. In our case, more time with our father, who is now healthy, could never be replaced by material possessions.

Some of my most joyous memories are when Dad and I camped out in his little boat and made do with what we had. I wouldn't change a thing. We had a great time. Everything doesn't need to be the latest and greatest. Just get out and experience life with those who matter.

This is a bit like when you're a kid. Some of the best times are when you made something up, using what you had, and had a great time doing it. You connected to your imagination to make it happen. How often do you use this same self-asset, this self-ability? It's still there.

Now, instead of using your imagination, you rely on ready-made images that look like fun. You see, your imagination is also an aspect of your intuition. This is often lost when the two gravities of yourself have never been reintegrated. You can be consumed with having what you think will make you happy, but without people you love or enjoy, it is a hollow achievement.

There is also another side to how this gravity effects us. Not having a large enough consciousness of our self-mass means that we could end up spending all our energy making others happy—or others making you happy—and not sharing joy on many levels of your self.

This limitation of self-joy was surveyed in many aspects of our conversations. Now, perhaps, you can see how this was magnified in the past and stopped you from being in a present time. This was something outlined in the opening conversations.

To be "now-present" means bringing many under-utilised aspects of our self to be used again daily. Imagine the gravity of not being able to use them now that you are more aware of your own true nature.

All I am reflecting here is that throughout this book all conversations are interrelated. By not being aligned to our true spirit as a whole, our energy system looks a little complicated sometimes. This is why our guides have concentrated on foundations of our true spirit-foundations, not on what is a reflection of what is not true. Remember, a reactive, emotional response is where your physical self is not following your true self-spirit of collective consciousness.

If the self-spirit is unable to communicate fully with what is to be created, then what is created is also of limited consciousness or limited mass. This means that our body isn't going to work efficiently. So bring the spirit back and relearn how to have an efficient body, which is a greater mass of physical consciousness.

In the past, the spirit was so often forgotten as a vital component that we also forgot that our original soul and heart existed there. How we forgot this is quite simple.

We became consumed with many different feelings that were never connected to our self-consciousness. This is another reason the source has asked this foundational thought to be reflected. Then it is possible to create a greater self-consciousness with a physical mass.

Consider, the greater physical mass for a moment, please. Wouldn't it be so much easier to attract the correct, conscious desires and intentions with this strength of mass? Remember, it now is of a presence and has a huge gravity to attract "now-presence" in a synchronistic and present manner.

Remember also that each and every one of these separate thoughts created without real consciousness consumed energy and didn't actually share energy. It was never a whole, conscious cycle, as it was never created in a whole-cycle manner.

This consuming manner of your self-cycle has been released in each of the affirmations throughout this book. This means that we aren't simply giving away or consuming energy. Therefore, our own conscious energy is directed to the correct area, where we desire to create in a conscious and true manner with a fully conscious intention.

We are able to register what really brings joy to our selves, as we share the same relative, foundational consciousness—the real, conscious feelings sensed through every conscious ability of our whole, collective connective-consciousness.

This response is our greatest purpose—joyous love with a whole, integrated appreciation of real self-compassion, reflecting all self-ability to comprehend that real gratitude is to be of a whole self. This means that we are able to sense conclusively what real love is.

Now, perhaps, we are able to bring this conclusion to the last chapters.

# 16

## A NEW-TIME CONCLUSION

As with all conclusions, we hope that we have achieved a few new insights and added something relevant.

Now that the bulk of this book is finished, I can also add a couple of different understandings that have manifested while I was writing. I wasn't aware that quite a few different foundations of books I had written would end up being integrated into this one.

You see, in my previous occupation, I wrote continuously while waiting for things to happen. Some days, I might only write a couple of pages. Other times, I wrote all day.

This means that this book is essentially made up of: *Unlocking Secrets of the New Millennium, Keys and Codes for a New Time, New Time Life Purpose, Unlocking Your Abilities in a New Time,* and *To Be at Peace with Self Presence.*

Remember, a new millennium isn't just about one or a couple of years. This is going to unfold for many millennia to come. As the source would say, a source's millennium is of a different time frame.

Perhaps you even picked up on this, as it relates more to where the consciousness of humanity sits as a whole, rather than a number of years. This is just another instance of getting our heads around a different manner of looking at things.

I hope this has opened your eyes to many new possibilities for yourself. The other main reason for this book is to release some areas of conflict, where lives are being rehashed, life after life.

If I have found something beneficial to myself, then I have passed it on—but only after I found that it works with grace, ease, and a sequence of synchronicity.

Please remember that as you become aware, it is worth looking at every little element of your life that is changing. The smallest changes identify what you are asking for. Add all these small changes together, and you find that they integrate and become desires of your integrated, original, incepted soul and heart—or spirit and physical—endeavours.

If your desires have always been in your soul and heart, then they reflect identically in each other and are able to be created in a harmonious way. The soul and heart aren't trying to create separately. This also means that something created is really of your own self-desire, not from a past relative who got caught up in your own desires and intentions, making you unable to use your own free, conscious self-will.

We have discussed how this all came about. The only reason I have made sure it's in your memory banks is that so many people skim when they read, and they miss understanding.

Also, without the connective consciousness being reaffirmed, many people are unable to interpret many hidden meanings that exist in everyday life. These hidden meanings add up to not having a clue as to what many energies are doing. Many things about us are affecting us in critical moments, and we are completely unaware of it, being without complete sensory skills.

This results in our being completely limited in our own synchronicity. Our own picture is totally out of focus where all critical and vital elements exist, which prevents us from achieving joy of life.

This was reflected in every element of our self-matter or every energy equation, as neither were able to adequately communicate with the other.

The soul was unable to talk to the heart, so they were unable to integrate as one universal body-mass of strength. Thus, no conclusive strength was able to withstand interferences from other energy.

This limitation created constant self-resentment and lack of self-faith or belief, and the essential energies needed to create self-will had no strength of current. This caused all energies to simply dissipate, to exist with no current.

This is where your ego and karma stopped communicating. All harmony and ease were eliminated from many aspects of life. This is why, when, or where you were able to sense self-agitation. This self-agitation always boils down to a missing element—communication.

The difficult part has been finding out why. Yes, the emotions told us that something was incorrect, but they never indicated why, where, when, or how. This led to blind faith, following others' directions, as we were incapable of receiving the correct direction to follow.

Following without direction over many lifetimes of incorrect and limited self-direction resulted in our self being unable to reason adequately or to react to adequate reasoning.

When we reflect on this debilitation of self-reasoning and how it created self conflict, we wonder why there were so many contributions from others. Remember, we were contributing to others' interests before our own. This consolidates or compounds all self-belief and faith.

The self hardly gets a look in, and we are hardly even left in the picture, so how are we able to focus on self-desires?

We are receiving many emotional messages that we can't even understand, let alone comprehend. Why? There simply isn't enough strength left in the self-energy to focus on self-efficiency.

Why has this happened? Because of the lack of communication or the breakdown of the connective, conscious energy systems.

In the end, the spirit and physical self are in a constant energy battle. They desire harmoniously balanced energy, but they are unable to receive it, as all responses create more conflict. This is why we don't want to acknowledge any responses.

This is why the source has passed on what we need to learn and how to receive.

If we concentrate on receiving constant, real, harmonious, balanced energy instead of interfering energy with conflicting reasoning, we are then able to reestablish the self with real strength.

This real strength then allows the harmony to keep rebuilding the self in a fully efficient manner. This manner is a source equation of how to reestablish a strength of self-truth—or all that has been outlined to you in many different ways—which is then transferred into spirit-strength and physical-strength.

As this strength is filtered through your spirit and physical nature, it is then, and only then, able to integrate in a truly conscious nature.

This truly conscious self—and now self-nature—is then reflected throughout the whole body as strength of consciousness. This is then reflected in the whole of your environment and atmosphere. It is now a reflection of your whole self. This is, of course, quite a shift of consciousness.

This is basically your gravity and, therefore, what you are asking for, period. It means you are only asking for real, conscious matter, which must be of a true worth to yourself, not something consumed by others.

This matter is of your desire and intent. It is also of a tithing nature, so you are only receiving and never consuming.

This equation is then extended and expanded to ensure that the reverse is correct, and to ensure that you are not consuming what others may be doing or reflecting.

This final equation means that you receive in a positively neutral and a negatively neutral manner. This is balanced harmony, reflected in all current and capacity, ensuring that all energy keeps moving without consuming natures.

This is why we never simply give; it is just asking to be consumed. Therefore, we share. Otherwise we take on others' interfering natures to ourselves.

Since we never simply take, we become dependent on what others have no gratitude for, so our self-gratitude ends up negligible. This is why those who seem to have the world at their feet are often so unhappy.

This same formula might jog a few different circumstances that have been repeated and unresolved in your life.

Now do you understand why those exercises we asked you to do were so important? They told your complete bodies where you were complete in a conclusive, conscious manner and where you were being interfered with or were, in fact, interfering.

You constantly reviewed your point of focus, never what was missing.

Please, remember those bits and pieces you wrote down. Those exercises really do help. I constantly receive phone calls telling how they help clients who need a little extra self-strength.

In conclusion, I and all of my guides pray that you have indeed received some foundational, conclusive, connective consciousness to help reconnect you to your potentials and to be present in a now-presence in your daily lives.

Every time you make a conscious change to yourself, you are reflecting this through all humanity. As you help yourself, all of humanity benefits. That is worth remembering, because as you reflect true change, other true changes will also be reflected in you. In the end, everybody is really more aware of each other in a real, conscious manner.

You are channeling and using telepathy in a real, conscious manner, as we are all aware of what all of humanity is truly reflecting. How much more purposeful might the world be? This is a foundation for all humanity's future.

Because you have contributed in a conscious manner, a weight of the world is just lifting off your shoulders, yes?

Some of you who are quite sensitive to all the energies that make up your body will now be more aware. In a way, you are asking all who live on this planet to be more responsive, and thus more responsible, for every energy that exists here. You are asking that they raise their vibrations to contribute, not simply desiring to consume the higher vibrations about them without contributing to the greater communication of humanity.

A dense consciousness connected to all who are unaware does not need to affect what is a tithing to the world. Simply raise your self-vibration so you are responsible for yourself and are helping many others.

Everything need not be complicated; often the simplest energy holds the greatest wealth. It's just that we are often unable to see this. We do like to complicate our lives sometimes, don't we?

This exercise is designed to open and hold a self-strength that exists within your ultimate self-purpose. It will facilitate the release of the weight of the world that burdens you with all inhumanity's existence.

To open this exercise and to fully sense this in more complete manner, start with a prayer pose. Now, please push open those hands to be about a shoulders' width apart.

An instant grounding is enabling you to recognise only the tithing senses linked to yourself. This does take a bit of time. Just hold this pose until your head desires to drop.

We are now preparing for the next release. This is where you facilitate a sense that some of the world's emotional burdens are lifting off your shoulders.

Take your time, as this may take quite a few minutes. Before you close your eyes, please ask yourself to be aware of the burden being lifted off you. This is generally sensed on your shoulders and in the neck regions first. Please take a few deep breaths now. A sense behind your eyes may change your focus.

The grounding you are receiving is a higher vibrational body that needs the strength of your soul-connection. Now you may close your eyes.

I am unable to describe the healing you will receive, as it will vary for so many. However, the lifting of a self-burden will be apparent for everybody—if not immediately, when you relax.

Due to the fact that we are exploring the freeing of your extensive and expansive self, we are about to revisit this exercise.

For some of you, this exercise may be more internal than external, as your head desires to go backwards. Just close your eyes and relax. Allow yourself to receive many releases, and don't hurry. Just follow the grounding senses.

Once again, I will not describe any sense, as this depends entirely on your level of intuition and how efficiently your connective-consciousness is sensing.

Please note that many tones may be sensed, allowing all guides to help your own intuition.

Please clasp your hands once again. As you are dropping, this time into a higher vibration and frequency, you will have sensed that this is a new grounding, yes?

This is your true self, regrounding in a new and efficient manner.

Once again, close your eyes for just a moment to really sense all that has been received, yes.

You may finally have received understanding. It signifies a neutral harmony and a neutral balance.

While closing your eyes for a moment, simply hold your hands out to receive. Yes, you are grounding with a new response in areas of yourself that you've never used in this lifetime. Think about this, please, and remember to hold your hands out to receive.

In each hand, you have just become more androgynously balanced. Please don't hurry. Absorb all that is to be shared.

Please turn your hands to face each other; a new centre of self-gravity is now to be opened.

What you now sense will depend on whether you take medications, or if your own personal self-awareness is free to sense the many shifts throughout your conscious body. This will also be repeated as you relax or sleep.

Once again, please stand and clasp your hands. Of course, you are grounding. Hold this stance until your knees feel as if they are buckling.

Once again, take on a prayer stance. The energy about you is also responding to your own personal gravity, and you may sense this. Notice that this energy about you is enabling you to receive all higher vibrational frequencies. Denser energy is not repelled but it is unable to penetrate the gravity of a neutral self.

Remember to keep those grounding exercises going, and put a reminder note where you will see it each day.

We will conclude with a clasping of your hands. All guides desire to pass on their appreciation, gratitude, and compassion. Please just close those beautiful eyes to receive this tithing of the source's love, and include it in your self-equation of life.

You may have sensed conscious, connective love of an evolved formula for all self-future.

We desire to re-evolve in a true equation this time, in a true manner, in a true space of self-presence, and in a true reality. Then, and only then, will our self-will be able to conclude that we are a complete, conclusive, self-collective self-consciousness.

Once again, you probably concluded that very little of this was written by me. In fact, this came through my integrated soul and heart, so the source was able to facilitate the true nature of this love. All guides desire to share in a tithing manner.

In conclusion, remember that you have been tithed a foundation for the new millennium's keys and codes, for a new-time purpose, for a new self-future, finally opening awareness for an evolved self.

For my own personal conclusion, please accept my gratitude and appreciation for being patient in reading this in a receiving manner and not as a consuming compassion.

I pray that your awareness is conclusively able to more easily determine real self-truth. In essence, this leads to grace, ease, and synchronicity, all vital components of our daily lives.

Finally, thank you for your valuable time. I pray that this book was translated correctly to add value to your fortunate life.

To conclude, I pray that you have a truly rich and fortunate life and that you share this in a tithing manner by being true to yourself and then helping all humanity.

Regards,

David

Please don't forget those grounding exercises.

# 17

## AN ALTERNATIVE CONCLUSION

As humans we perceive that we have a limited sensory system. This book has been about unplugging so many of the evolved sensory abilities that are not only open to be explored but are unfolding daily with a new life.

Each chapter we unfolded meant releasing the limits we had accepted, not knowing our evolved potentials were just waiting to be unearthed.

Each and every sensory perception is an insight to all that is possible. If we limit our focus to what we perceive as full, it is impossible to explore many extrasensory perceptions that have been sitting dormant for millennia.

Every sense needs new current to connect to this evolved energy. This is a sensory consciousness connected to a consciously moving self-matter that in the past was of a limited focus. With this release, you are refining all that is a possibility of our self-potential.

This new sensory perception needs a whole new language. We are communicating as multisensory individuals. This means that we see this world in a totally new light—which is another reason for the emergence of the new millennia.

To encapsulate all purposes within all new sensory abilities, we will be examining all new responses, not simply emotions. Our old emotions just won't express our intentions.

This might sound a little contradictory, but this is a fact. Our emotions simply haven't been telling us the full story. We have only received a much-abbreviated version at best.

When we begin to use all our sensory perception, we need to think with a new cognizance. We need to initiate a real, sensory, conscious thought with a real, conscious, sensory reaction. A conscious, sensory, reasoning reaction concludes that we are definitely going in the correct direction of our consciously sensed desire, intention, ability, and potential, thus creating our utmost conclusion.

All that has been outlined formulates a new-time foundation to create a sensory, conscious love or a real, complete emotion. It does not focus on the separated incompleteness of unconscious reactions or the responses to unbalanced and unharmonious, unconscious reactions.

As you may have ascertained, the source intends for us to delve deeper than we might expect in order to dislodge these incapacitated senses and bring them back to life.

When all is said and done, we are actually letting these senses work as they were intended to be used, by limiting all separations and suppressions, letting them be conscious again in an unsuppressed manner.

In another way, all this has been fundamental in initiating foundations of sensory perceptions that stem from using free senses of consciousness—which haven't been used to any real potential for ages.

These are the energies that science is unable, at the moment, to decipher. Perhaps with conscious contributions, *we* can do so. I'm afraid we are unable to wait for science to catch up, as we are going to be thrust into this energy, whether we are ready or not. It is already here, and this energy is making its mark on all society now.

Because so many of our self-energies are in conflict, there is no way to dismiss all new-time emerging energies. These new-millennium-conscious energies herald a new direction that can still rampant mind-play and quiet unwanted mind-chatter so we are free to connect to our real self-direction.

This, I pray, is where all the exercises have been effective in helping you to release all old life-schedules, allowing you to see more of the real you or to perhaps sense some new self-possibilities and opportunities.

Please remember that to be sensory is to be much more aware of how can we change what we are so unaware of.

Now we are able to become a conscious, sensory presence in ways that have never been used or opened for many lifetimes.

This awareness helps all real senses to connect to all real images of our imagination, so they can sense what is truly needed and desired.

All sensing exercises have been intended to open those idle senses that are sitting in your imagination, not fully living up to their potentials. Please use this self-imagination to explore those many possibilities. Use

285

your connective consciousness to sense that all is possible if we consciously desire with intent and real, conscious ethics.

I do look forward to sharing these sensory senses with you in person someday soon

Regards,

David

Also, please remember that if you are feeling out-of-sorts, lemon baths really help release those toxins.

Please enjoy your life.

32970495R00188

Made in the USA
San Bernardino, CA
20 April 2016